Let Me Be Your Guide

A Clear and Understandable Tour of the Bible

Fred Woodward

Greater Purpose Press

Let Me Be Your Guide
A Clear and Understandable Tour of the Bible

Layout and cover design by Corryn Hoen

Printed in the United States of America

Bible verses taken from www.biblestudytools.com/niv, New International Version

Summary: A journey through the Bible's Old and New Testaments from the perspective of a chaplain.

Library of Congress Cataloging-in-Publication Data
Woodward, Fred
Let Me Be Your Guide/Fred Woodward–First Edition
ISBN-13: 978-1-938326-39-4
1. Bible 2. Christians 3. Faith.
I. Woodward, Fred II. Title
Library of Congress Control Number: 2015940387

Maps from www.biblemapper.com
Images from www.biblerevival.com and Fred Woodward

Greater Purpose Press

Greater Purpose Press is an imprint of Nelson Publishing & Marketing
366 Welch Road, Northville, MI 48167
www.nelsonpublishingandmarketing.com
(248) 735-0418

Table of Contents

Welcome Aboard!

Back in 2001, in order to celebrate our 25th wedding anniversary, my wife and I decided that we would spend some time in New York City. Since we had never been to the city (and frankly, scared to death to drive in it) we bought two tickets for a bus excursion. The ad read: TOUR THE ENTIRE CITY OF NEW YORK IN A DAY.

Sure enough, the bus picked us up early in the morning and we toured the city of New York in one day. As we toured the city, we made several stops at some of the more famous and important sights: Central Park, Battery Park, Statue of Liberty, Times Square, etc. At each of these stops, we would get off the bus for a few minutes and the tour guide would share information about that particular location.

At the end of the day, we were delighted and felt like we had really gotten our money's worth! In one day, we had toured and received a good overview of New York City. Our tour guide encouraged us to come back to New York when we had more time to take in more details.

That brings us to the purpose of this book. I would like to take you on a tour of the entire Bible, in a relatively short period of time. It will be my great honor to be your tour guide. As we work our way from Genesis to Revelation, we will stop at some very significant places in order to get a good understanding of the Bible's unfolding story. I'm confident that once you've taken this tour, you will feel like it's been time well spent. You will have a good overview of the Bible. And after taking the tour, you will be better prepared to come back and revisit the Bible anytime and any way you choose, perhaps through personal reading, small group study, or a pastor's message. God's word will become more understandable, enjoyable, and meaningful to you.

This book came about as the result of a burden that I felt God laid on my heart. I have been teaching the Bible for almost forty years. I was a pastor of various churches for about twenty-five years. More recently and currently, I serve as a chaplain. During those forty years of ministry, all too often I have heard people say that they really don't enjoy the Bible because they don't understand it. When they go to church, what the pastor says is "over their head." When they attend a Bible study, they "get nothing out of it." When they try to read the Bible on their own, they soon get lost, confused, and discouraged. This, dear friends, really bothers me, because I believe that God wants everyone to enjoy His word.

About ten years ago I decided that I would try to do something about this, so I put together a survey of the scriptures from Genesis to Revelation. My first class consisted of ten people who met with me once a week for about three months. I was amazed at the response. Those who attended that first class expressed how grateful they were to at long last actually understand and enjoy the Bible. Since that time, I have taught dozens of such classes and have taken hundreds of people through the survey. Over time, many people have encouraged me to put this overview into book format. With the help of the Lord and many friends, I have finally been able to do that.

So, dear friends, let's get started. Let's get on the bus. Let's take a tour of the world's most precious book...the Bible.

Lesson 1

You Can Trust the Bible

An Overview of the Bible—Organization

Let's begin with a brief overview of the Bible. As you have noticed, the Bible is divided into two major sections, The Old Testament and The New Testament. In the ancient languages of the Bible (Hebrew and Greek), the word for "testament" can equally be translated "covenant." It will probably help our understanding to use the word covenant. A covenant is a contract or an agreement between two parties.

The Old Covenant refers to the contract or agreement that was established at Mount Sinai between God and the nation of Israel. On Mount Sinai, God spoke to Moses and gave him the terms of the covenant. "Now if you obey me fully and keep my covenant, then out of all nations you will be my treasured possession" (Exod. 19:5). Moses, acting as the mediator, came down from Mount Sinai and explained these terms to the Israelites. When the people responded by saying, "'Everything the LORD has said we will do'" (Exod. 24:3), the contract was established. The nation of Israel entered into a covenant relationship with God.

The New Covenant is similar, but in all points, superior to the Old. In the New Covenant, God's Son, Jesus Christ, acting as the mediator, came down from Heaven bringing God's offer to the entire world. The terms of the New Covenant are best summarized by the familiar verse,

John 3:16, "For God so loved the world that he gave his one and only Son, that whoever believes in him shall not perish but have eternal life."

Today, since we are still in the New Covenant era, the offer from God still stands. Whoever will respond to God's offer by believing in God's one and only Son, Jesus, will enter into a covenant relationship with God and be given the promise of eternal life.

To help us quickly locate specific places in God's word, the two major sections (the Old and New Testaments) are further broken down into books. There are thirty-nine books in the Old Testament and twenty-seven books in the New Testament. These books are further broken down into chapters and the chapters into verses. For example, Exodus 19:5 would refer to the Old Testament book of Exodus, chapter nineteen, verse five. Until you become familiar with the books of the Bible, you can always refer to the table of contents, which will give you the page number of each book.

The Origin of the Bible—Inspiration

What is the origin of the Bible? What kind of a book is it and where did it come from? Is the Bible, as many say, just a collection of the thoughts and opinions of men? Is the Bible just the product of ancient men speculating about God and giving us their understanding of the universe? Or, is the Bible a book like no other book ever written?

To answer these questions, let us begin by looking at what the Bible claims for itself. Over and over again, in both the Old and New Testaments, the Bible claims that its words are not from men, but rather the words are from God. Consider what the Apostle Peter (a man chosen and trained by Jesus) has to say about the scripture:

> Above all, you must understand that no prophecy of Scripture came about by the prophet's own interpretation. For prophecy never had its origin in the will of man, but men spoke from God as they were carried along by the Holy Spirit. (2 Pet. 1:20-21)

According to Peter, the words of the scripture did not come from men. Instead, men were "carried along by the Holy Spirit" to speak words that were from God. We can understand the term "carried along" by imagining a sailboat floating on a calm sea. All of a sudden a mighty gust of wind comes from the north and moves the boat south. In this same way, the Holy Spirit came upon chosen men and moved them to speak the words of God.

Let's consider what the Apostle Paul (another man chosen and trained by Jesus) has to say about the scripture: "All Scripture is God-breathed and is useful for teaching, rebuking, correcting and training in righteousness" (2 Tim. 3:16).

According to Paul, the scripture is "*God-breathed*." To understand the term "God-breathed," try to imagine yourself blowing up a balloon. Now here's a silly question: after you blow up the balloon, whose breath is in the balloon? It's your breath, of course. Now when you release the air from the balloon, whose breath is coming out? It's still your breath. This is how the words of the Bible came to us. God chose special men called prophets. He "breathed" into their hearts and minds His words of truth. When they spoke (exhaled), the words that came out of their mouth were still the breath of God.

Just to prepare you, in religious circles you can expect to encounter three basic views of the Bible. The view that we have just described, that the Bible is the inspired word of God (and, I might add, the view of Jesus, Peter, and Paul), is referred to as the *orthodox* view. Up until the 1800s, this was the view that virtually all Christians held about the Bible, regardless of denomination.

But then in the 19th century, two other views began to emerge. The *liberal* view of the Bible proposes that the Bible is just a book of myths and fairy tales, not to be taken seriously and certainly not a guide for life. Then there is the *neo-orthodox* ("neo" meaning new) view. The neo-orthodox view holds that the Bible is not the word of God but rather it contains the word of God. The neo-orthodox view claims that some parts of the Bible are inspired by God, but other parts are not. With this view, we are all free to use our common sense and logic to determine which parts of the Bible are inspired by God and which parts are from men.

Let me strongly encourage you to reject both the liberal view and the neo-orthodox view for a very simple reason. Both of these views depart from what the Bible says about itself. Please embrace the time-honored orthodox view. With simple faith, believe the words of the Bible. By doing so, you will please the Spirit who inspired these words and you will enjoy a much closer relationship with God.

The Objective of the Bible—Revelation

Why is it so important to God that we have His Word and not the words of men? That question is easily answered. God wants to reveal Himself to us so that we might find Him, and after we have found Him, He wants us to have a close relationship with Him. To find God, we must have an accurate description of God. Otherwise, we will be looking for the wrong person in all the wrong places. In fact, according to the Bible, any faulty description or concept of God is called an idol. And we'll never find God if we are looking for an idol. God has accurately revealed Himself to us in the Bible.

According to the Bible, God has revealed Himself to us in two distinct ways. These are called *general revelation* and *special revelation*. General revelation refers to the evidence that God has left of Himself in the created universe. "The heavens declare the glory of God; the skies proclaim the work of his hands" (Ps. 19:1).

As we look at the wonders of Creation (sun, moon, stars, Earth, trees, animals, humans), we have more than enough evidence to conclude that there is a God of extreme power and wisdom.

General revelation, however, does not give us enough information to find God. It convinces us that there is a God, but doesn't tell us what kind of God He is. Indeed, He is the Creator, but what is His character?

Suppose you wake up one morning, the sun is shining and the sky is blue. From this general revelation, you conclude that God must be a nice person. But the next morning, a tornado strikes your house and you lose everything. Now what will you conclude about God? Is He a cruel, insensitive monster? In order to accurately reveal His character, God has given us special revelation. Special revelation simply refers to the inspired words of the Bible. We can come to know God's true character by what God says, by what He does, by His commandments, by what pleases Him and displeases Him. By knowing these, we can then find Him.

God's perfect revelation of Himself will come in the New Testament when He sends His unique Son, Jesus, to Earth. The Apostle John shares with us: that "The Word (Jesus) became flesh and made his dwelling among us. We have seen his glory, the glory of the One and Only, who came from the Father, full of grace and truth… . No one has ever seen God, but God the One and Only, who is at the Father's side, has made him known" (John 1:14, 18).

Likewise, the writer of Hebrews tells us, "The Son is the radiance of God's glory and the exact representation of his being" (Heb. 1:3).

The Bible Over the Centuries—Preservation

At this point someone might ask, "How do we know that the words we have today in the Bible are the same as those that were originally spoken and written? After all, those words were written hundreds, even thousands, of years ago. Surely the original words of the Bible have been lost over time."

Doesn't it logically follow that if God inspired His word, and if He considers it to be of vital importance to us, that He would take steps to preserve it over time, so that all mankind could receive it? Let's suppose you were going to send a letter to a friend and this letter contained life-saving information or perhaps a lot of money. Wouldn't you take steps to ensure that the letter would not get lost in the mail? Wouldn't you insure it or send it by registered mail? Likewise, in the Bible, God claims that He will carefully preserve His word over time. For example: "'The grass withers and the flowers fall, but the word of our God stands forever'" (Isa. 40:8). Or consider what Jesus says about His words: "'Heaven and earth will pass away, but my words will never pass away'" (Mark 13:31).

If we had the time, we could discuss in more detail exactly how the Bible was preserved over the ages. We could talk about the meticulous work of the ancient scribes. We could learn about the significance of the Dead Sea Scrolls. We could quote dozens of scholars, archaeologists, and historians who will all say essentially the same thing, that the Bible is, by far, the best-preserved book of all time. For now, let me just ask you to believe that God wants you to have His word, so over the ages He has preserved it, for you.

The Options for the Bible—Translations

Another question often comes up. "How about all these different translations? The Old Testament was originally written in Hebrew and Aramaic. The New Testament was originally written in Greek. Surely something was lost in all the translations of the Bible from one language to another."

Please don't let this concern you. When Bible scholars working in teams translate the Bible into another language, they don't work from previous translations. They go back to the ancient manuscripts and make their translation from the Hebrew and Greek languages.

One more thing to consider: there is a difference between a translation and a paraphrase. A translation is, as close as possible, a word-for-word transfer from the original language to a modern language. A paraphrase sometimes adds words or phrases in an attempt to "help" the reader understand the text. A good translation, and the one we are using for this book, is the NIV, which stands for the New International Version.

Opening the Bible—Illumination

I have tried my best in this first lesson to convince you that you can have faith in the Bible. I have done this for a very important reason: so that you will have your password. Oh yes, since the Bible is such a special spiritual book, you must have the password to open it or have access to it. The password for the Bible is "FAITH."

Do you remember the story of Ali Baba and the Forty Thieves? To open a cave containing treasure, Ali Baba had to use the password

"Open Sesame." In today's high-tech world, we need a password to have access to almost everything (from our bank accounts, to ATMs, to our cell phones, and much more). Without a password, none of these services will open for us.

And so it is with the Bible. If we come to the Bible with a closed mind and hardened heart, access will be denied. We may read the words, but they will be lifeless and without meaning. But if God looks into our heart and sees the password FAITH (an openness, a teachable spirit, and a willingness to trust Him), He will open the door to all the treasures in His precious word.

As we move on in our tour to Lesson 2, and every time you come to the Bible in the future, please remember your password. Show it to God and watch how the Bible will open to you.

If you have a question about this lesson, or other questions about the Bible, please visit my website www.FredWoodwardBible.com. There you can obtain my contact information and we can communicate through email. I'll do my very best to answer your questions.

Lesson 2

The Creation and Fall of Man

Genesis 1–3

If you enjoy watching police dramas and detective shows on TV (*Law and Order, Criminal Minds, Monk*, etc.), then you know how important it is to see the opening scenes of these programs. Usually the crime takes place in the first few seconds of the show and starts the plot for the episode. If you miss the opening scenes, you won't be able to understand what's going on for the rest of the show.

Likewise, we must absolutely understand the opening chapters of the Bible, Genesis 1–3. Things happen in these three chapters that set the stage for the rest of the Bible's unfolding story, raising questions that will not be answered until the end of the book of Revelation. For this reason, we will park our tour bus and spend some time in this section.

The Creation of Man

As we open the Bible to Genesis 1, we have the story of Creation. In six days, God created the material universe and mankind. The word "create" comes from a Hebrew word meaning "to bring into existence something from nothing." God speaks and things suddenly appear that did not exist before. The word "created" is used three times in Chapter 1: We see it in Genesis 1:1, when God speaks and plant life comes into existence. We see the word again in Genesis 1:21, when God speaks and animal life comes into existence. The word is used a third time in Genesis 1:26, when God speaks and human life comes into existence. As God does His work of Creation, at the end of every day, He evaluates His own work to make sure it is "good." When the project is completed, He makes a seventh and final inspection and declares it all to be "very good" (Gen. 1:31).

As if all of this was still not good enough, God goes on in Chapter 2 to plant a garden paradise, called the Garden of Eden, for the newly created couple. In this garden, "God made all kinds of trees grow out of the ground—trees that were pleasing to the eye and good for food" (Gen. 2:9).

It's important that we go back to Chapter 1 and pay particular attention to the creation of mankind. "So God created man in his own image, in the image of God he created him" (Gen. 1:27). What does the Bible mean when it says that man was created "in the image of God"? Is this referring to a "physical" likeness? Does God have a physical body with arms, legs, fingers, and toes? The answer to this is no. God does not have a physical body. Jesus says that "'God is spirit'" (John 4:24).

To be created in God's image, then, means to be in God's "spiritual" and "moral" image. Man was created with God's spiritual and moral character. Bible scholars like to say that man was created in a state of "original righteousness," meaning to be "right with God." We might say that, originally, God and man were "like two peas in a pod." Or, originally, man was "a chip off the old block." However we describe it, God created us to be like Him. God is holy, righteous, true, pure, loving, kind, and merciful. Adam and Eve were created with all these same wonderful qualities.

This explains why, in the beginning, God and man had such a close relationship. God and man were friends. They enjoyed spiritual fellowship with each other. In this pure state, Adam and Eve were permitted to spend time in God's presence. In Chapter 3, we read that in those first days, God would come "in the cool of the day," to walk and talk with Adam and Eve (Gen. 3:8). God and man enjoyed each other's company because they were so much alike.

The Obligation of Man

At this point, after describing the world that God created, I would not be surprised if you are shouting, "What happened to that world? What happened to that existence? The world that we live in is nothing like what is described in Genesis 1 and 2. Our world today is filled with violence, hatred, suffering, and death. And by the way, where is this God who used to spend time with us 'in the cool of the day'?" You are right to ask all of these questions. Indeed, what did happen?

To understand, we need to look at the one and only commandment that God gave to Adam and Eve and the consequences of disobeying that commandment. In the Garden of Eden, God had made a tree called "the tree of the knowledge of good and evil." Concerning this tree, God said, "'You are free to eat from any tree in the garden; but you must not eat from the tree of the knowledge of good and evil, for when you eat of it you will surely die'" (Gen. 2:16, 17). Here we see the commandment: do not eat from the forbidden tree! And we see the consequences of disobedience: death!

The prohibition to not eat the forbidden fruit was a spiritual boundary, a line that man must not cross over. To illustrate this boundary, let me share with you the story of Carmel. Some years back, we had a dog named Carmel who loved to run away from home to go sniffing and exploring new territory. Despite our best efforts to prove to Carmel that we loved her, we were unable to convince her that the safest place for her was on our property, where we could care for her and protect her. For her own good, we installed a chain-link fence to keep her from running away. One tragic night, however, she found a way to open the gate. The next morning, I found the gate open and Carmel was gone. No doubt she got lost and was unable to find her way back home. We never found her. To this day, we have no idea what ultimately happened to Carmel.

Likewise, God's commandment to not eat from the forbidden tree was a boundary, designed to keep mankind in God's love, care, and protection. As long as Adam and Eve kept this commandment, they were demonstrating faith (there's that password) in God and His Word. As long as they continued in this faith relationship, their friendship and fellowship with God would continue. However, if they chose to step over the boundary, the relationship with God would be severed, they would be in grave spiritual danger, and they would be separated from God's goodness, care, protection, and love.

The Temptation of Man

As we come to Chapter 3 of Genesis, we are introduced to another character, referred to as "the serpent." "Now the serpent was more crafty than any of the wild animals the LORD God had made. He said to the woman, 'Did God really say, "You must not eat from any tree in the garden"?'" (Gen. 3:1). Who or what was this creature that had the ability to speak words into the human mind? Was this some kind of talking snake? Actually, no, the serpent was just an animal that was being used by an invisible, evil spirit. Evidently, the serpent's slithery movements were somehow useful to convey the suggestions of this evil spirit. But, again, who was this spirit, and where did he come from?

These questions are answered later in the Bible in passages such as Isaiah 14:12–14 and Ezekiel 28:12–15. In these passages, we learn that before the creation of mankind God created what is called "the angelic host," meaning an angelic army. This angelic host was made up of various kinds of angelic beings (angels, archangels, seraphim, cherubim) with different levels of power and authority. One such angelic being, named Lucifer, is thought to have been a high-ranking cherub. But rather than being content to worship God, Lucifer wanted to be worshipped as God and led a rebellion against Him. His punishment for this rebellion was to be expelled from Heaven, and his name was changed from Lucifer (which means "bright star") to Satan (which means "the adversary").

In Genesis 3, Satan (a.k.a. Lucifer) showed up in the Garden of Eden, obviously intending to tempt Adam and Eve to rebel against God (as he had already done). With convincing cleverness, he spoke his first lies to the human race: "'You will not surely die... . For God knows that when you eat of it [the forbidden tree] your eyes will be opened, and you will be like God, knowing good and evil'" (Gen. 3:4–5). Note the pack of lies: God is a liar. God is holding you back from happiness and fulfillment. By disobeying God, you will become like God. There will be no consequences for sin. You'll actually be a lot better off!

The Transformation of Man

Tragically, at this point Adam and Eve made a terrible choice. Instead of continuing to believe in God's word, they chose instead to believe the lies of Satan. Accordingly, when they ate of the forbidden fruit, they both experienced a sudden transformation. We read of this transformation in Genesis 3:7: "Then the eyes of both of them were opened, and they realized they were naked; so they sewed fig leaves together and made coverings for themselves." What kind of a transformation did they experience? Well, just as God had warned, they died!

Now, I realize this requires some explanation, since you are probably saying, "Wait a minute! What do you mean 'they died'? Adam and Eve continued to live on Earth for many years after this experience, so how can it be said that they died?" The answer lies in understanding the word "death." In the Bible, death does not mean to cease to exist. Death means to be separated and alienated from God. God is the Creator and Giver of life. Therefore, whoever is connected to God (by a spiritual, faith relationship) is alive. But whoever is separated from God is dead.

Because Adam and Eve were our original parents, their choice to disobey God was the point of entry for sin and death (much like a contagious disease) to the entire human race. The Apostle Paul explains this by saying, "Therefore, just as sin entered the world through one man, and death through sin, and in this way death came to all men, because all sinned" (Rom. 5:12). In short, the effects of death that came to Adam and Eve have passed to all of us.

According to the Bible, death comes in three stages: there is *spiritual* death, *physical* death, and *eternal* death. When Adam and Eve ate of the forbidden fruit, they immediately experienced spiritual death. With that first bite, they realized something had happened to them. Suddenly, their spiritual relationship with God was severed. Immediately, the spiritual image of God, the moral image of God, and the righteous character of God were severely marred. In the blink of an eye, they were no longer the same spiritual beings that God had created them to be.

This concept of spiritual death explains why we all feel so alienated from God, to the point that we wonder if He exists. To illustrate this, suppose you are listening to your favorite radio station and your radio gets knocked off the counter and goes dead. Would you conclude that something had happened to the radio station? Of course not! It's your radio that's broken, or at least out of tune. Likewise, nothing has happened to God. He's still broadcasting His message of goodness and love. It's us! We have fallen. Because of our sin, we are broken and out of tune with God. We cannot experience God because we are no longer like God. We are no longer in His image. It is we who need to be fixed.

As another example, think of your cell phone. I'm sure you've had the experience of not being able to use your cell phone because you were in a dead zone. You were in some area where the signal was weak or interrupted. You couldn't send or receive messages. In such cases, what did you have to do? You had to MOVE! You had to move until you were out of the dead zone and you got a response to "Can you hear me now?" Likewise, our fall into sin has put us in the spiritual "dead zone." God is not dead, we are! If we want to find God we will have to move (spiritually).

Perhaps you've heard the story of the farmer who took his wife to town in their truck to buy groceries. On the way home, the wife, sitting by the passenger door, said, "You know, we don't sit as close to each other as we used to." The farmer, who was sitting behind the wheel, replied, "I'm not the one who has moved." God would say something similar to us when we claim that He doesn't exist or complain that He seems far away. "It's you folks who have moved, not Me!"

At that same instant, death struck the human body. As we saw with Adam, physical death did not take place immediately, but rather, it set in as a process. We might liken physical death to the cutting down of a tree. On the day that we cut down a tree, the bark, branches, and leaves do not dry up and wither immediately, but in a few days these signs of death will begin to appear. When I was a young man, my hair was dark and my body was (relatively) strong and healthy. Now my hair is gray, and my body has lost much of its strength. I usually say, "My body is getting old." But the harsh truth is, my body is dying.

The Bible says that as a result of Adam and Eve's choice to sin, we are all in a "body of death" (Rom. 7:24). Isn't it interesting that scientists, for all their knowledge, cannot explain why we die? But we who believe the Bible have the answer. We are all dying physically because we are separated from our life-giving Creator.

The third, and most frightening, aspect of death is eternal death. If we manage to go through this earthly life and never return to God, if we never reconcile with God, then the Bible warns us of eternal separation from God. When we consider the suffering and sorrow that we are already experiencing in this world as a result of our fall from God, do we even want to think about being separated from Him for eternity?

Thus, in the opening scenes of the Bible, we see "what happened." God created us in His image so that we could live in and enjoy His presence forever. But because of the choice of sin, we are all dead. We are not the good, loving, and righteous beings God created us to be. Everything that is bad (and sad) in this world can be traced back to this event. It's easy to see why theologians refer to this tragedy as "The Fall of Man."

The (Future) Restoration of Man

I cannot ask you to get back on the bus to continue the tour on this sour note, because the God of the Bible is a God of hope. Whenever something bad happens, God feels compelled to proclaim some good news that will give us hope for the future. On this tragic day that sin and death entered the world, God also proclaimed some good news.

Talking to Satan in Genesis 3:15, God said, "'And I will put enmity between you and the woman, and between your offspring and hers; he will crush your head, and you will strike his heel.'" Because it is written in symbolic language, this statement seems hard to understand, but basically it means this: God promised that one day He would send a special human being to Earth known as "*the offspring of the woman*." When this special person becomes an adult, He would have to suffer because Satan would "*strike*" Him with a wound to the "*heel*." But when He recovered from the "*heel*" wound, He would in turn deal Satan a crushing wound to the "*head*" from which the devil would never recover. Bible scholars refer to Genesis 3:15 as the "protoevangelium," a big word that simply means "the first preaching of the gospel." The word "gospel" means "good news."

This promise of good news would not be fulfilled for almost 4,000 years. When we get to the New Testament, we will read about a young woman who, though a virgin, will supernaturally give birth to a child. When this offspring grows up, He will suffer greatly at the hands of Satan. The devil will strike Him, bruise Him, and wound Him. But when He recovers, He will conquer Satan completely. I bet you already know who this young woman is, who her offspring is, how He will suffer, and how He will recover. But if not, it will all become very clear later on in the tour.

We have learned about the Fall of Man. But take heart. God already has a plan to restore fallen man. The rest of the Bible will be the unfolding story of God's plan. Now that we have some hope in our hearts, let's get back on the bus.

If you have a question about this lesson, or other questions about the Bible, please visit my website www.FredWoodwardBible.com. There you can obtain my contact information and we can communicate through email. I'll do my very best to answer your questions.

Lesson 3

The Effects of the Fall

Genesis 4–11

For those of you who travel a lot by flying, I'm sure you've heard the following announcement coming over the airplane's loudspeaker:

LADIES AND GENTLEMEN, THIS IS THE CAPTAIN. OUR RADAR INDICATES THAT WE ARE ENTERING INTO STORMY WEATHER. WE'LL BE ENCOUNTERING TORRENTIAL RAIN, AIR TURBULENCE, AND HIGH WINDS. WE MAY BE IN FOR A BUMPY RIDE. UNTIL FURTHER NOTICE, PLEASE REMAIN IN YOUR SEAT, AND KEEP YOUR SEAT BELT FASTENED!

At this point in our tour of the Bible, I need to make a similar announcement. Coming to Genesis 4, and until we get to Genesis 12, we will be entering into and passing through some very stormy spiritual weather. Please be prepared for lots of trouble and turbulence. It's likely to be a bumpy ride.

Oddly enough, we know the exact cause of the storm that we are entering into...sin! Remember back in the previous lesson when Satan lied to Adam and Eve? Satan promised that if they would only quit believing in God and break away from Him, they would enter into a superior existence that would satisfy their every desire. We are about to see just how big a lie this was. For instead of taking them into a better world, their decision to sin took Adam and Eve (and us, their descendants) into a troubled, stormy world of sin and death.

SO PLEASE, UNTIL FURTHER NOTICE, REMAIN IN YOUR SEAT, AND KEEP YOUR SEAT BELT FASTENED!

The Two Brothers

The effects of Adam and Eve's fall from God show up immediately in the lives of their first two sons, Cain and Abel. These two boys (and the rest of humanity) are born in their father Adam's fallen image, not God's. And they inherit Adam's spiritual condition of sin, not righteousness. To say it another way, Cain and Abel were born "on the other side of the tracks," already spiritually dead, already separated from God.

Therefore, because Cain and Abel were conceived and born in sin, they must choose to reverse the decision of their father. Adam chose to depart from God by unbelief and sin. By continuing in this spiritual state, Cain and Abel will simply be confirming their father's bad choice. On the other hand, they can reverse their father's decision. They can choose to return to God through repentance and faith.

The younger brother, Abel, made the wise choice. In an act of sincere worship, he humbly returned to God with a repentant heart. He regained the status of "righteousness" and was immediately accepted back into God's favor. Hebrews 11:4 explains it this way: "By faith Abel offered God a better sacrifice than Cain did. By faith he was commended as a righteous man."

The older brother, Cain, on the other hand, was not willing to return to God. Oh yes, he was willing to be "religious." In an act of superficial worship, he brought God a large amount of vegetables from his farm. But his heart was not humble and repentant, and he had no intention of returning to a faith relationship with the LORD (God). Since "without faith it is impossible to please God" (Heb. 11:6), Cain was not accepted.

It's important for us to see what happened to Cain next. The Bible says, "So Cain was very angry, and his face was downcast" (Gen. 4:5). Here comes the storm. Lacking God's loving influence in his heart, Cain became angry and depressed (the first case of human depression). Despite God's warning, Cain continued to sulk and brood, until ultimately, he was overcome by his own evil nature. Abel's righteous life made Cain uncomfortable because, like a light, it exposed Cain's sinfulness. We all know the rest of this story. In a fit of rage, Cain rose up and killed Abel. It has to be a bad sign when, instead of loving his brother as God intended, the firstborn man on Earth hates his brother and becomes a murderer! We might add that this was the first case of religious persecution on Earth: an unrepentant man persecuting a righteous man.

The Twisted Descendants of Cain

After Cain killed his brother, the storm of sin on Earth increased and intensified. Cain "went out from the LORD's presence and lived in the land of Nod, east of Eden" (Gen. 4:16). Cain put God behind him. He completely eliminated God from his life. He became the first "practicing" atheist. And he became the founding father of the first secular, godless society on Earth. By looking at this ungodly culture of men, we learn some important truths.

In Genesis 4:16–24, we are given a list of Cain's descendants to the seventh generation. No doubt a better word to describe this line of men would be "degeneration." To demonstrate what I mean by "degeneration," let us take a closer look at Cain's great-great-great-great-grandson, Lamech.

In Genesis 4:19, we read that "Lamech married two women, one named Adah and the other Zilla." Thus, Lamech introduced the practice of polygamy, a defiant deviation from God's original instruction for marriage. In the beginning, God had said, "For this reason a man will leave his father and mother and be united to his wife, and they will become one flesh" (Gen. 2:24). God's will is that a man should be united to his wife, not his wives.

Further, let us notice that the Hebrew names of Lamech's two wives, Adah and Zilla, suggest that they were sensual women of external beauty. Adah means "the adorned," and Zilla means "the tinkling." Apparently for Lamech, these women were what we would call today "trophy wives" or perhaps "arm candy." If you are a woman, it might interest you to note that it is here, at this point in history, where men begin to disrespect, use, and abuse women for their own selfish desires. And please note what kind of men they were: godless men. Men who love and honor God will also love and honor women.

We're not quite finished looking at Lamech's corrupt character. At the end of Genesis 4, Lamech calls for his two wives so that he can boast to them about killing a young man. His boasting is even in the form of a poem! Please note this contrast: Cain, the father of this society, killed a man in a fit of rage. Six generations later, Lamech killed a man for fun and fame, without any remorse, and bragged about it to his two wives. See what I mean by "degeneration"?

Thus the first society of men to populate the earth were these corrupt descendants of Cain. By the time we come to Genesis 6:3, God says, "'My Spirit will not contend with man forever, for he is mortal; his days will be a hundred and twenty years.'" In other words, God, already weary of striving with this evil culture of men, announces that they have 120 years to repent.

> The LORD saw how great man's wickedness on the earth had become, and that every inclination of the thoughts of his heart was only evil all the time. The LORD was grieved that he had made man on the earth, and his heart was filled with pain. (Gen. 6:5–6)

The Trusting Descendants of Seth

In Genesis 4:25–5:32, we learn that while the godless descendants of Cain were populating and corrupting the earth, there was another, godly line of men living at the same time. These were the descendants of Seth, another son born to Adam and Eve, after Cain killed Abel. These were good men who loved God. They lived by faith, obeyed God, and did His will. They passed on their faith in God to their sons. When we come to the seventh generation of this line of men, a man named Enoch was so righteous and walked so closely with God that God just "took him away" (Gen. 5:24) to Heaven. Then coming to the tenth generation of Seth, we meet Noah, "a righteous man, blameless among the people of his time, and he walked with God" (Gen. 6:9). As we compare the descendants of Cain and Seth, notice what a difference faith makes! Societies that love and worship God get better with each generation, but godless societies fall into corruption and moral decay. We would do well to remember this truth in our world today.

The Tempest of God's Judgment

Unfortunately, the godless line of Cain far outnumbered the godly line of Seth. Instead of becoming an extension of the Garden of Eden, that ancient world became a place of wickedness, hatred, violence, and murder. "Now the earth was corrupt in God's sight and was full of violence. God saw how corrupt the earth had become, for all the people on earth had corrupted their ways" (Gen. 6:11–12).

Fortunately, there was one good man left on Earth, righteous Noah, the last of the line of Seth. God spoke to Noah, telling him, "'I am going to put an end to all people, for the earth is filled with violence because of them. I am surely going to destroy both them and the earth'" (Gen. 6:13). God instructed Noah to build an enormous ark to prepare for a worldwide flood. For the next 100 years, Noah and his sons worked to build this ark. It needed to be huge (the equivalent space of 2,000 railroad cars) in order to preserve the animal kingdom as well as Noah's family.

In Genesis 7, the Flood came. Not only did it rain for forty days and forty nights, but

> all the springs of the great deep burst forth, and the floodgates of the heavens were opened... . The waters rose and covered the mountains to a depth of more than twenty feet. Every living thing that moved on the earth perished—birds, livestock, wild animals, all the creatures that swarm over the earth, and all mankind. Everything on dry land that had the breath of life in its nostrils died. (Gen. 7:11, 20-22)

In the end, only eight people survived the Flood: Noah and his wife, his three sons, and their wives. Let us learn from the Flood an inescapable truth: there is a limit to how much evil God will allow on Earth. When societies of men, such as Cain and his descendants, turn from God and fall into spiritual and moral decay, they will face God's judgment and destruction.

The Type of Christ

As we consider the story of Noah and the Flood, let me draw your attention to a very special sight, Noah's ark. Theologians call the ark a "type of Christ." A type of Christ is a person, place, or thing in the Old Testament that serves as a prophetic picture of Jesus Christ, who would be coming to Earth, but not for hundreds of years. God used these prophetic pictures to prepare the people of the Old Testament to recognize His Son when He finally became incarnate.

Let me try to illustrate this. Suppose you have relatives in Europe whom you've never met but have always wanted to meet. You make plans to fly to Europe for a vacation. To prepare your relatives for your coming, you write letters and make arrangements for them to pick you up at the airport. But since these relatives have no idea what you look like, how will they recognize you when you get off the plane? The simple solution: include in your letters pictures of yourself. That way, when you step off the plane, your European relatives will say, "There's our cousin from America! He looks just like his pictures!"

Likewise, throughout the Old Testament, God included many of these prophetic pictures of His Son. It was God's plan that when Jesus finally came to Earth, God's people, having these Old Testament pictures, would recognize Jesus and say, "There's the Son of God! He looks just like His pictures!"

Why is the ark of Noah a type of Christ? Because it was a place of refuge from the wrath of God against sin. In the ark, Noah and his family were preserved and protected from the storm of God's judgment. Likewise, today, those who believe in Jesus are said to be "in Christ," and are in a safe place because He "rescues us from the coming wrath" (1 Thess. 1:10). As we work our way through the Old Testament, I hope to point out more of these types of Christ. When we get to the New

Testament you will say, "There's Jesus, God's Son! He looks just like His pictures!"

The Table of Nations

Genesis 10 is often referred to as "The Table of Nations." In this chapter, we are given a brief genealogy of each of Noah's three sons, Shem, Ham, and Japheth. From these three sons, the three basic races of men would eventually develop. Japheth's descendants would migrate north toward Europe. Shem's descendants would migrate east toward Asia. Ham's descendants would drift south into the continent of Africa.

The Tower of Babel

In Genesis 3, we witnessed the Fall of Man. In Genesis 4, we saw the first murder. In Genesis 6–8, the first society on Earth became so corrupt it had to be destroyed by a flood. We would assume that, by now, surely man has learned his lesson: rebellion against God never ends well! Hasn't it become obvious that without God, man is doomed to fall into depravity and destruction? But we would be wrong, because we have one more stormy rebellion against God to travel through, the Tower of Babel.

Genesis 11 tells us that, after the Flood of Noah, men began to repopulate the earth. For a time, the entire population was all together in the same place and spoke the same language. But this unity quickly turned into a very bad thing when it became a unity against God. In Genesis 1:28, God had said, "'Fill the earth and subdue it.'" But this rebellious crowd said, "'Come, let us build ourselves a city, with a tower that reaches to the heavens, so that we may make a name for ourselves and not be scattered over the face of the whole earth'" (Gen. 11:4). Also, this determination to build a tower "that reaches to the heavens" was a clear attempt to establish their own man-made religion that would take them to Heaven, without any help from God!

Concerning this tower project God declared, "'If as one people speaking the same language they have begun to do this, then nothing they plan to do will be impossible for them'" (Gen. 11:6). In other words, this collective energy would lead to an explosion of evil. Sin would accelerate on Earth as mankind corrupted itself and fell into destruction again! So to halt the building of this tower, God simply introduced new languages into their speech, which confused them so much that they were unable to complete the project. They separated from each other in various groups and were scattered on the earth.

If you are a teacher, you might appreciate this illustration. What do you do with two little boys who are cutting up in class and getting each other in trouble? Well, you just separate them so they can't put their little heads together to invent mischief. Likewise, this was God's tactic at the Tower of Babel. To separate sinful men, God introduced the language barrier. It wouldn't stop the spread of sin on Earth, but at least it slowed it down. Below is an illustration of the first eleven chapters of Genesis.

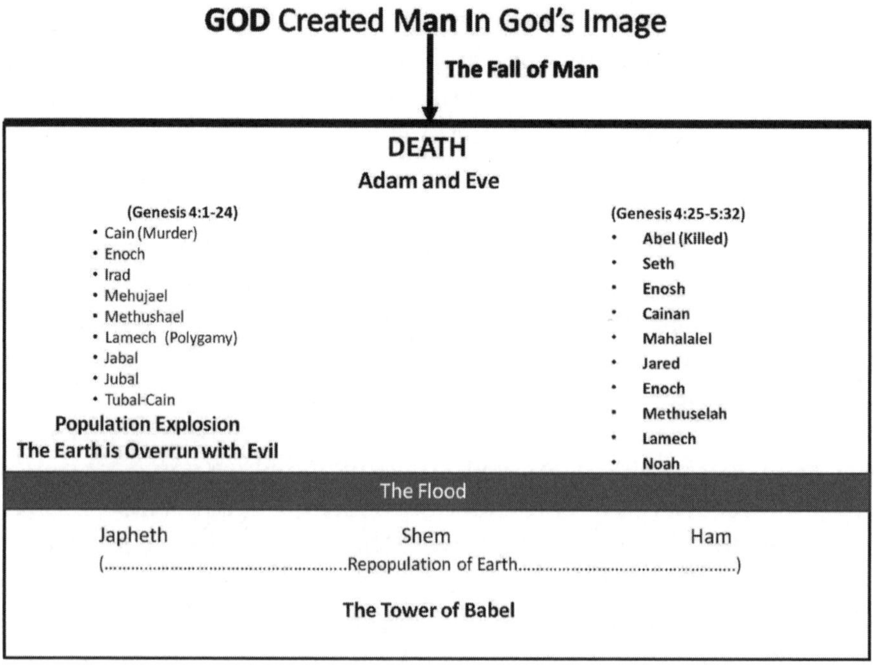

At this point in the tour, we are all weary of stormy weather! This lesson has been a bumpy ride. We are all asking, "Is there any hope? Is mankind just doomed to repeatedly fall away from God into destruction? Is there any cure for this corruption? Will we ever be able to escape the effects of sin on our lives, and on our world?"

I have a suggestion for dealing with these feelings of discouragement. Please put your seat in the reclining position, turn off your reading light, and just go ahead and take a nap. I'll wake you up when we get to Genesis 12. When we get there, God will begin to reveal His plan for fallen man. Hope will return to your heart. Then you'll feel better. Trust me.

If you have a question about this lesson, or other questions about the Bible, please visit my website www.FredWoodwardBible.com. There you can obtain my contact information and we can communicate through email. I'll do my very best to answer your questions.

Lesson 4

God's Plan for Man

Genesis 12–50

In the first eleven chapters of Genesis, we learned a sad and inescapable truth. The world is not the place that God created it to be because we human beings are not what God created us to be. We have fallen away from God. We are "dead in transgressions and sins" (Eph. 2:1). Satan, by treachery and deceit, has taken spiritual control of the human race. He occupies the hearts and minds of men, and is well entrenched. But take heart. God loves us and wants us back! The Bible is the story of God winning the world back to Himself, not by sheer power, which He could easily do, but by loving persuasion. God began to reveal His plan for mankind in the promises He made to a man named Abraham.

The Future of Abraham and His Descendants

In Genesis 12:1–3, God said to Abraham:

> "Leave your country, your people and your father's household and go to the land I will show you. I will make you into a great nation and I will bless you; I will make your name great, and you will be a blessing. I will bless those who bless you, and whoever curses you I will curse; and

all peoples on earth will be blessed through you."

To explain the above passage, God spoke to the man Abraham, instructing him to leave his country (present-day Iraq) and travel to a land that God would show him (present-day Palestine). God promised to bless Abraham and develop his descendants into a great nation (later to be called Israel). God would give this nation a special portion of land (the Promised Land) and protect this group of people, defending them from all their enemies. Beginning here in Genesis 12, through the rest of the Old Testament, and well into the New Testament, we will be studying the history of God's dealing with this chosen group of people.

Please notice that God's plan was not just for the descendants of Abraham. God's last promise to Abraham declared that "'all peoples on earth will be blessed through you.'" God's plan began with Abraham's descendants (the Jews), but it certainly didn't end with them. God also declared that He loved the other nations of the world (the Gentiles) and wanted to win them back as well. But we would have to wait two thousand years to find out how God would fulfill this portion of the promises. When we get to the New Testament, we will see how God, through one of Abraham's descendants, offers His love to the rest of the world.

The Faith of Abraham

Since Abraham is such a key figure in God's plan, we might ask, "What was so special about Abraham?" "Why did God choose him to be the father of this special nation?" That question is answered with that one familiar word...FAITH. Genesis 15:6, a key verse in the Bible, says that Abraham "believed the LORD, and he [God] credited it to him as righteousness." An extremely important and timeless truth is revealed in this little verse that applies to every human being. Let me try to explain it.

Here, with Abraham as the example, God reveals how an unrighteous person becomes a righteous person. Remember, we learned that God originally created mankind in a state of righteousness, but this righteous standing was lost with the Fall of Man. Abraham was not an exception to this. Like all human beings, Abraham was a fallen sinner, and needed to regain his legal standing with God. Perhaps an illustration will help us understand what I mean by "legal standing."

My wife was born in the Philippines and was therefore a Filipino citizen. After we were married, she obtained a green card and her status was changed to "legal immigrant" of the United States. But she was still not a US citizen. Her citizenship needed to be legally changed. So, in an official swearing-in ceremony, after she met the requirements for naturalization, a federal judge declared her to be a citizen of the United States of America.

Likewise, all human beings, after the Fall of Man, are born into Adam's state of sinfulness, not into God's righteousness. Because of our sin, we have lost our citizenship in Heaven. In order to regain our Heavenly citizenship and our righteous standing with God, our status must be officially changed, by legal decree. Genesis 15:6 reveals how this was accomplished in the life of Abraham. When God looked into Abraham's heart and saw faith in His word, He "credited it to him as righteousness." Because Abraham met the requirement of faith, God (the Judge of all) declared Abraham to be a righteous man. By God's declaration, this "sinful" man suddenly became a "saved" man, saved from the penalty of sin, forever to be a citizen in God's kingdom. Please notice that it was his faith that made him righteous, not his works. Abraham did not "earn" his righteousness by going to church, or by doing good deeds, or by giving money to the poor. These are all good things to do, but God will never accept good works as a substitute for faith.

To illustrate this, let's suppose you want to see a movie. You go to a nearby movie theater, and as you wait in line, there is a young man collecting tickets. As you approach the young man, he asks for your ticket. But instead of handing him a ticket, you say, "Oh, I don't need a ticket, because I'm a good person." With a confused look on his face the young man says, "Please, sir, I need your ticket." But again you insist, "Young man, you don't understand. I don't need a ticket because I'm a good person. Why, just yesterday I changed a flat tire for a stranger. Last week, I mowed my neighbor's lawn. Two weeks ago, I gave a large gift to charity." At this point, the young ticket taker says, "Sir, all that may be true. You may be a good person. But to get into this movie theater you have to have a ticket! So please give me your ticket or I will be forced to call security." As the security guard escorts you out, you loudly protest, "This is an outrage! I'm a good person! I don't need a ticket!"

Likewise, it has always been the tendency of human beings to think that we can please God just by trying our best to be a good person and by doing a lot of good things. God corrects that misconception with this story of Abraham. Let us learn from Abraham's example that faith in God is the one and only ticket that pleases Him.

Abraham, therefore, is God's "prototype" of personal salvation for all ages to come. Through Abraham's example, God has shown how every human being can return to God and be made righteous. This truth will apply not only to Abraham and his descendants but to all mankind as well. In the words of the great Apostle Paul, "The righteous will live by faith" (Rom. 1:17).

The Foreshadowing of Abraham's Descendant

Just in case we are suspicious of Abraham's faith and think it might be "emotionalism" or "easy believism," let us look at another story of Abraham that took place nearly forty years later, in which God Himself would test Abraham. By passing this test, Abraham forever put to rest any questions about the genuineness of his faith.

After waiting for twenty-five years, Abraham and his wife, Sarah, finally had a son when Abraham was one hundred years old and she was ninety. They named this "miracle baby" Isaac. Fifteen years after the birth of Isaac, the test came. In Genesis 22:2, God said to Abraham, "'Take your son, your only son, Isaac, whom you love, and go to the region of Moriah. Sacrifice him there as a burnt offering on one of the mountains I will tell you about.'"

What's amazing is that Abraham, trusting God, obeyed this order! He and Isaac traveled to the region of Moriah. He laid wood on Isaac's back to be used for the burnt offering. He led this precious son, the pride and joy of his life, the sum total of all his hopes, up the mountain. Abraham put the wood on the altar and then had Isaac lay on top of the wood. Abraham then took a knife and raised it in the air, ready to plunge it into the heart of his son.

Much to Abraham's (and our) relief, God called to him and stopped him from completing the act. Just then, "Abraham looked up and there in a thicket he saw a ram caught by its horns. He went over and took the ram and sacrificed it as a burnt offering instead of his son" (Gen. 22:13). Thus, Abraham was not required to sacrifice his one and only son; instead, he received him back safe and unharmed. Any more questions about Abraham's faith?

There is something else for us to see in this story of Abraham and Isaac: the foreshadowing of another Father and His "one and only Son." Father Abraham laid wood on his son's back and led him up a mountain to be sacrificed. Two thousand years later, another Father (God) will lay wood (the cross) on His Son's (Jesus') back and lead Him up a mountain (Calvary) to be sacrificed. But unlike Abraham, God the Father will not be spared the pain of watching His Son die, because His Son must die as the sacrifice for the world's sin. But like Abraham, God the Father will receive His Son back, after the resurrection. Thus this story of Abraham and Isaac is yet another Old Testament "type of Christ."

The Family of Abraham

As we have already learned, God promised to bless Abraham and develop his descendants into a great nation. This is exactly what we see happening in the closing chapters of the book of Genesis. The promises that God made to Abraham will be passed to every future generation. Abraham became the father of Isaac. Isaac became the father of Jacob (whose name was changed to Israel), and Jacob/Israel became the father of twelve sons. These twelve sons became the fathers of twelve separate tribes, later to be known as the twelve tribes of Israel. The following brief genealogy should help to illustrate the development of Abraham's family.

ABRAHAM
|
ISAAC
|
JACOB (ISRAEL)
|

Reuben	Simeon	Levi	Gad	Zebulon	Dan	Judah	Benjamin	Asher	Naphtali	Issachar	Joseph
x	x	x	x	x	x	x	x	x	x	x	x
x	x	x	x	x	x	x	x	x	x	x	x
x	x	x	x	x	x	x	x	x	x	x	x
x	x	x	x	x	x	x	x	x	x	x	x

(The Future Twelve Tribes of Israel)

Taking a peek into the future, many famous people would later come from these tribes of Israel. For example, the great prophet Moses came from the tribe of Levi. Samson, the strong man, was of the tribe of Dan. The great Apostle Paul, who wrote nearly half of the books of the New Testament, was born into the tribe of Benjamin. Mary and Joseph were of the tribe of Judah, which means that their son, Jesus, was from this tribe. One day, Jesus would be called the "'Lion of the tribe of Judah'" (Rev. 5:5).

The Flaws in Abraham's Family

We might logically assume that, after Abraham's passing, his descendants would just immediately inherit the Promised Land. But in Genesis 15, when God first began dealing with Abraham, God revealed to Abraham that his descendants would not be allowed to inherit the Promised Land right away. Instead, God said, "'Know for certain that your descendants will be strangers in a country not their own, and they will be enslaved and mistreated four hundred years... and afterward they will come out with great possessions. ... In the fourth generation your descendants will come back here'" (Gen. 15:13–14, 16).

What, we might ask, is the reason for this four-hundred-year delay before they could inherit the Promised Land? Why did they have to take this detour to another country to be enslaved? No doubt it was because this family had many flaws. While these men were the biological offspring of Abraham, they were not automatically his spiritual offspring. Let's remember, no human being is automatically born with faith. Faith is a personal choice.

In the closing chapters of Genesis, we see that Abraham's grandson (Jacob/Israel) and his great-grandsons had little or no faith in God. They were cruel, selfish, envious, and deceitful. In this condition, they were not worthy or ready to inherit the Promised Land. God would have to do something with them to develop their faith and moral character. Evidently, God believed that 400 years of slavery in a strange land would accomplish this. The book of Genesis ends when, due to a famine, Jacob, his sons, and their families are forced to leave the Promised Land to become "*strangers in a country not their own*."

This means that in order to follow them and their story, we also will have to leave the Promised Land and travel to that other country. As we get back on the bus to continue our tour, let us have joy and hope in our hearts. Despite the sins and shortcomings of man, God has a plan! From this point in the Bible to the end of the book of Revelation, we will see this plan unfolding as God reaches out to reclaim a lost and dying world. Next stop...Egypt.

If you have a question about this lesson, or other questions about the Bible, please visit my website www.FredWoodwardBible.com. There you can obtain my contact information and we can communicate through email. I'll do my very best to answer your questions.

Lesson 5

An Escape from Egypt

Exodus 1–12

As we learned in the previous lesson, God chose and made several promises to a man named Abraham. God promised Abraham that his descendants would be especially blessed above all people on Earth. They would (one day) inherit and inhabit a special land. In this Promised Land, they would become a great nation. Also, we learned that Abraham's grandson's name was Jacob, but God Himself changed Jacob's name to Israel. For this reason, the most common name for this chosen group of people will be "the children of Israel."

At the end of the book of Genesis, we saw that the children of Israel, due to a famine, were forced to leave the Promised Land to go live in the land of Egypt. Coming to Exodus Chapter 1, we are told that it was Jacob (Israel), his sons, and grandsons who came to Egypt. At this point, the total number of people in this developing clan, including wives and children, was seventy. As they entered Egypt, no doubt they thought that their stay in this foreign land would be only for a short time, just long enough to survive the famine. Little did they realize that this short stay in Egypt would turn into 400 years of slavery.

The Persecution

Initially, the children of Israel were treated well by the Egyptians. This was due to the special relationship that one of Jacob's sons (Joseph) had with Pharaoh, the king of Egypt. During this brief period, "the Israelites were fruitful and multiplied greatly and became exceedingly numerous, so that the land was filled with them" (Exod. 1:7). But time passed and things changed when "a new king, who did not know about Joseph, came to power in Egypt" (Exod. 1:8). This new Pharaoh was suspicious of these foreigners and he said to his people, "'Look, the Israelites have become much too numerous for us. Come, we must deal shrewdly with them or they will become even more numerous and, if war breaks out, will join our enemies, fight against us and leave the country'" (Exod. 1:9–10).

Pharaoh's solution for dealing with these troublesome foreigners was to persecute them, afflict them with hardship, and use them for slave labor. "He put slave masters over them to oppress them with forced labor, and they built Pithom and Rameses as store cities for Pharaoh" (Exod. 1:11). The Egyptians "worked them ruthlessly. They made their lives bitter with hard labor in brick and mortar and with all kinds of work in the fields; in all their hard labor the Egyptians used them ruthlessly" (Exod. 1:13–14). But Pharaoh's "final solution" to control the population of the Israelites was the unthinkable evil of infanticide. He gave an order to the Hebrew (Israeli) midwives that as they helped deliver babies, "'if it is a boy, kill him; but if it is a girl, let her live. ... Every boy that is born you must throw into the Nile, but let every girl live'" (Exod. 1:16, 22).

Something interesting happened with the children of Israel during this terrible time of trouble. "But the more they were oppressed, the more they multiplied and spread" (Exod. 1:12). Instead of having the desired effect of controlling the population of Israel, Pharaoh's persecution brought about a population explosion! If you've ever had poison ivy, and tried to scratch it, you know what happens; it spreads all over your body. Welcome, Mr. Pharaoh, to God's world! Trying to stamp out God's people is like trying to "scratch out" poison ivy.

Eventually, as the years passed, the persecution had an understandable effect on the children of Israel. They "groaned in their slavery and cried out, and their cry for help because of their slavery went up to God" (Exod. 2:23). Ah, now we see why God allowed them to suffer these 400 years of trials and tribulations. Apparently, like so many of us, only in a time of despair and desperation would they cry out to God; only then did they remember and return to the faith of their forefather, Abraham.

And that simple cry of faith immediately got God's attention. "God heard their groaning and he remembered his covenant with Abraham, with Isaac and with Jacob. So God looked on the Israelites and was concerned about them" (Exod. 2:24–25). In fact, when the children of Israel reached out to God, He took action to rescue them. It was time for God to raise up a mighty prophet in Israel, a leader whom God would use to deliver the children of Israel out of their bondage.

The Prophet

During this period, when all male Hebrew babies were being killed, a young Israeli mother gave birth to a baby boy. At the risk of her own life, she hid this baby for three months. But when she could no longer hide him, she took a giant step of faith. "She got a papyrus basket for him and coated it with tar and pitch. Then she placed the child in it and put it among the reeds along the bank of the Nile" (Exod. 2:3). With this act, she was placing her beloved baby into the hands of God, trusting that God would protect him. (Hmm. I seem to recall Abraham doing something similar with his son.)

The young mother's faith was rewarded when, "coincidentally," Pharaoh's own daughter came to the Nile to bathe and saw the basket. When she opened the basket and saw the baby, "he was crying, and she felt sorry for him" (Exod. 2:6). The baby's older sister, who "just happened" to be standing nearby, asked Pharaoh's daughter, "Shall I go and get one of the Hebrew women to nurse the baby for you? 'Yes, go,' she answered. And the girl went and got the baby's mother. Pharaoh's daughter said to her, 'Take this baby and nurse him for me, and I will pay you'" (Exod. 2:7–9). Thus, not only was this mother's baby spared, she herself was allowed to nurse him, with pay!

However, as per the agreement, when the child became a young boy, the mother "took him to Pharaoh's daughter and he became her son. She named him Moses" (Exod. 2:10). Thus this Hebrew boy, a descendant of Abraham, grew up in Pharaoh's house and was raised as an Egyptian prince. Moses continued living in Pharaoh's house, behaving like an Egyptian, until he was forty years old.

We don't know how old Moses was when he learned that he was not really an Egyptian. We do know that by the time he had reached forty, he had become aware of his true (Hebrew) identity and this brought about an identity crisis. He could no longer go on living like a prince while his (true) people were suffering persecution. Moses made a life-changing decision. He "went out to where his own people were and watched them at their hard labor. He saw an Egyptian beating a Hebrew, one of his own people. Glancing this way and that and seeing no one, he killed the Egyptian and hid him in the sand" (Exod. 2:11–12).

But instead of being the spark for a Hebrew slave uprising, this foolish act of bravado just got Moses into trouble. When Pharaoh heard that Moses had killed an Egyptian, he issued an order for Moses to be killed. Moses was forced to flee for his life. He left Egypt and fled to the land of Midian, where he eventually became a shepherd for a man named Reuel. "Moses agreed to stay with the man, who gave his daughter Zipporah to Moses in marriage" (Exod. 2:21). At this point, Moses, feeling like a failure, gave up any hope that he would ever return to Egypt or be of any help to his Hebrew people. He would remain in Midian for the next forty years.

But God was not done with Moses, nor had He forgotten His promises to Israel. When Moses was eighty years old, the "angel of the LORD appeared to him in flames of fire from within a bush" (Exod. 3:2). In this famous burning bush experience, God says to Moses, "'The cry of the Israelites has reached me, and I have seen the way the Egyptians are oppressing them. So now, go. I am sending you to Pharaoh to bring my people the Israelites out of Egypt'" (Exod. 3:9–10). Thus, at eighty years old, Moses received the commission from God to return to Egypt, deal with Pharaoh, and deliver the children of Israel from their bondage.

The Plagues

Dealing with Pharaoh, however, was not going to be easy. The children of Israel now numbered approximately three million. Pharaoh had no intention of losing this lucrative slave labor. At their very first meeting, Moses said to Pharaoh, "'This is what the LORD, the God of Israel, says: "Let my people go"'" (Exod. 5:1). Pharaoh's immediate response was "'Who is the LORD that I should obey him and let Israel go? I do not know the LORD and I will not let Israel go'" (Exod. 5:2). Thus the battle between God and Pharaoh, which would last for approximately one year, began. From Exodus Chapter 5 through Chapter 12, Moses and Pharaoh met many times. In those meetings, Moses, as God's mouthpiece, repeatedly said, "Let my people go." And Pharaoh repeatedly responded by saying, "I will *not* let Israel go."

To persuade Pharaoh to give in and let the Hebrews go, God empowered Moses with the ability to call down plagues upon Egypt. Interestingly, only the Egyptians were affected by these plagues, while the children of Israel were exempt. At first, the plagues were relatively minor inconveniences. But as Pharaoh continued to refuse to let Israel go, the plagues increased in intensity and severity, as seen in a list of the first nine plagues:

1. The Nile River Changed to Blood
2. Frogs
3. Lice
4. Flies
5. Murrain (a cattle disease)
6. Boils
7. Hail
8. Locusts
9. Darkness

The Petrified Heart of Pharaoh

As Moses repeatedly spoke God's word to Pharaoh and the plagues continued to get worse, Pharaoh kept on committing the same, very serious sin. He repeatedly "hardened his heart" (Exod. 8:15, 32). Let me try to explain how a person's heart becomes "hardened" and why this particular sin, above all others, is so serious.

You've probably noticed what happens to your hands when you do hard labor without wearing gloves. At first, your hands are soft and sensitive and you feel some pain as blisters develop. But if you keep on working without gloves, the blisters turn into calluses. Eventually, the calluses are so thick you no longer can feel any pain.

In the same way that our hands can become callused, our hearts can become hardened. The human heart is initially sensitive to God's word (like the heart of a child). However, if a person continues to hear God's word but repeatedly refuses to humble himself and heed it, layers of callus will begin to develop. Eventually, this person will lose all sensitivity to God's Holy Spirit and the ability to hear the voice of God. This is why the sin of hardening the heart is so serious. Pharaoh made this mistake. Because this callousness has eternal consequences we are all warned, "'Today, if you hear His voice, do not harden your hearts'" (Heb. 3:7–8).

The Passover

After the ninth plague, God announced to Moses that there would be just one more: "'I will bring one more plague on Pharaoh and on Egypt. After that, he will let you go from here, and when he does, he will drive you out completely'" (Exod. 11:1). It would be a plague of death. On a given night, a death angel would come to Egypt and in every house the firstborn would die, the firstborn of cattle, the firstborn of prisoners, the firstborn of slaves, and yes, the firstborn of Pharaoh. God promised that this tenth and final plague would break Pharaoh's stubborn will and he would be forced to let the Hebrew slaves go free.

But God revealed to Moses a way for the children of Israel to be protected from the plague of death. Four days before the plague, every

Hebrew house was to secure and set aside a lamb. The lamb had to be "year-old males without defect" (Exod. 12:5). On the night of the plague, the lamb was to be slain and some of the lamb's blood was to be put "on the sides and tops of the doorframes of the houses" (Exod. 12:7). Also on that night, they were to roast the lamb with fire and eat it, being careful to remain in the house, behind the blood. Since the population of Israel was now close to three million, thousands of lambs would have been required.

Every aspect of God's word to Moses came true. On that awful night, when the death angel came to Egypt, he "passed over" the Hebrew houses when he saw the lamb's blood. But because there was no blood on the Egyptian houses, they were not spared. Every Egyptian house, including Pharaoh's, suffered the death of their firstborn. That night:

> there was loud wailing in Egypt, for there was not a house without someone dead. During the night Pharaoh summoned Moses and Aaron and said, "Up! Leave my people, you and the Israelites! Go, worship the LORD as you have requested. Take your flocks and herds, as you have said, and go. And also bless me." The Egyptians urged the people to hurry and leave the country. "For otherwise," they said, "we will all die." (Exod. 12:30–33)

Egypt, because of the first nine plagues, was already financially destroyed. With this tenth and final plague of death, Pharaoh and all the Egyptians not only allowed the Hebrews to leave but were anxious to be rid of them!

Thus, after 430 years of bondage in Egypt, after the night of the Passover, the children of Israel walked out of Egypt as a free nation. This freedom was not secured with bows and arrows, or swords and shields; it was a gift from God. For this reason, every year on the fifteenth day of the month of Nisan (March/April), Jewish people around the world celebrate the Feast of the Passover, to remember that night, 3,400 years ago, when God gave them their national freedom.

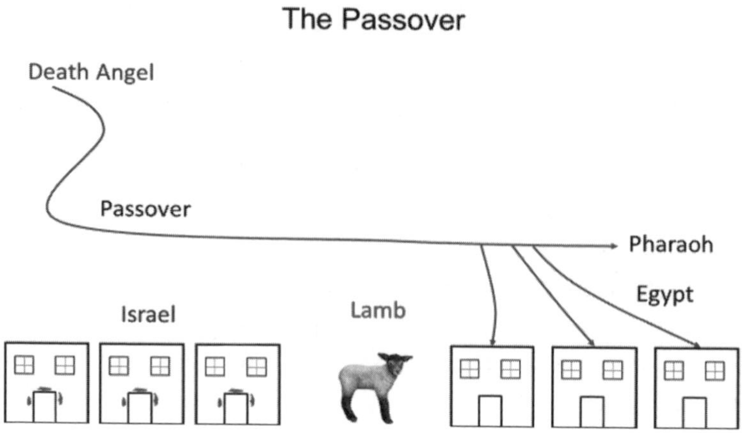

As we get back on our tour bus, let me ask you to sit back in your seat, close your eyes, and reflect on the story of Israel's experience in Egypt. Can you see that this story is a prophetic picture (type) of a much greater story? Israel's bondage would represent an even more grievous form of slavery (sin), from which we all need to be delivered. Pharaoh serves as an example of an even greater taskmaster (Satan), who makes all of our lives miserable. The lamb that was slain speaks of an even greater Lamb (Jesus, the Lamb of God), whose blood had to be shed for the sins of all mankind.

When, by faith, this precious blood is applied, not to our houses, but to our hearts, death "passes over" us and we are given eternal life. And, through Christ, God gives us an even greater form of freedom than Israel experienced: spiritual freedom. Referring to Himself, our Lord Jesus once said, "'If the Son sets you free, you will be free indeed'" (John 8:36). Next stop...Mount Sinai.

If you have a question about this lesson, or other questions about the Bible, please visit my website www.FredWoodwardBible.com. There you can obtain my contact information and we can communicate through email. I'll do my very best to answer your questions.

Lesson 6

At Mount Sinai

Exodus 13–31

The morning after the night of the Passover, having been in Egypt for 430 years, the children of Israel, now numbering close to three million, walked out of Egypt as a free nation. But they would not be walking alone or wandering aimlessly. Immediately after leaving Egypt, God met them and began walking with them.

> By day the LORD went ahead of them in a pillar of cloud to guide them on their way and by night in a pillar of fire to give them light, so that they could travel by day or night. Neither the pillar of cloud by day nor the pillar of fire by night left its place in front of the people. (Exod. 13:21–22)

We know, of course, where God would ultimately lead them —back to the Promised Land. But, to our surprise, "God did not lead them on the road through the Philistine country, though that was shorter. For God said, 'If they face war, they might change their minds and return to Egypt'" (Exod. 13:17). God, who sees into all hearts, saw that at this point their faith in Him was not strong enough to face military conflict.

So instead of taking the direct route to the Promised Land, God led them on a long detour, a detour of approximately 400 miles and a delay of about fourteen months. Before the children of Israel were ready to enter the Promised Land, God had several things He wanted to say to them. He said these things, and got several things established, at the southern tip of the Sinai Peninsula, atop Mount Sinai.

The Trek to Mount Sinai

With the Glory Cloud going before them, God led the people into several faith-building experiences on their journey from Egypt to Mount Sinai. These included:

1. The Crossing of the Red Sea (Exod. 14:1–31)
2. The Bitter Waters of Marah (Exod. 15:22–25)
3. The Manna, Bread from Heaven (Exod. 16:1–36)
4. The Water from the Rock (Exod. 17:1–7)
5. The Battle with the Amalekites (Exod. 17:8–13)

Most of us have probably had the happy experience of getting hired into a company. An even happier day comes (three months later) when we start to enjoy the benefits of belonging to that company (health and dental insurance, educational benefits, retirement plans, etc.). Likewise, from these experiences on the way to Mount Sinai, the children of Israel began to realize that faith in God brings benefits. The cloudy pillar gave them the comfort of God's presence. As it went before them, they had the assurance of walking in God's path. When the Red Sea parted for them, but Pharaoh's army perished in it, they experienced God's protection. After God healed the bitter waters at Marah, they tasted of God's pleasantness. With the miracles of the manna and the water from the rock, they began to enjoy God's provision. These benefits that Israel enjoyed 3,400 years ago can still be enjoyed today by those who walk with God.

The Treaty at Mount Sinai

After traveling for two months, the children of Israel finally came to Mount Sinai and made camp at the base of the mountain.

> Then Moses went up to God, and the LORD called to him from the mountain and said, "This is what you are to say to the house of Jacob and what you are to tell the people of Israel: You yourselves have seen what I did to Egypt, and how I carried you on eagles' wings and brought you to myself. Now if you obey me fully and keep my covenant, then out of all nations you will be my treasured possession. Although the whole earth is mine, you will be for me a kingdom of priests and a holy nation. These are the words you are to speak to the Israelites." (Exod. 19: 3–7)

Thus God was proposing a covenant between Himself and the nation of Israel. The terms of this covenant were surprisingly simple: if Israel would agree to obey God's (to be announced) commandments, God, in turn, would take Israel to be His treasured possession. When Moses came down from the mountain, he conveyed God's offer to the children of Israel. After hearing the proposal, "the people all responded together, 'We will do everything the LORD has said.' So Moses brought their answer back to the LORD" (Exod. 19:8).

Notice how similar this is to a marriage proposal. God says, "Do you, Israel, promise to keep all my commandments?" The entire nation of Israel responds with, "We do." And what an unusual wedding ceremony this would be! Three days later:

> Moses led the people out of the camp to meet with God, and they stood at the foot of the mountain. Mount Sinai was covered with smoke, because the LORD descended on it in fire. The smoke billowed up from it like smoke from a furnace, the whole mountain trembled violently, and the sound of the trumpet grew louder and louder. ...

> The LORD descended to the top of Mount Sinai. (Exod. 19:17–20)

I have been a guest at many weddings, and even officiated at several, but I have never seen a wedding ceremony as spectacular as this one! The bridegroom (God) descended upon Mount Sinai. The matchmaker (Moses) led the bride (Israel) to the foot of the mountain. At this point, Exodus 20:1–18, God spoke to Israel, in an audible voice, the famous Ten Commandments. Later, God Himself would write these words on two stone tablets. Israel kept these tablets for centuries (like a wedding ring) as a token of the covenant established at Mount Sinai.

www.biblerevival.com

In Exodus 24, Moses gave orders that young bulls be sacrificed as offerings to God. The children of Israel (for the third time) said, "'We will do everything the LORD has said; we will obey.' Moses then took the blood, sprinkled it on the people and said, 'This is the blood of the covenant that the LORD has made with you in accordance with all these words'" (Exod. 24:7–8). With the sprinkling of this blood on the people, the contract was sealed, and the nation of Israel entered into a covenant relationship with God. No other nation on Earth, before or since, has ever enjoyed such a privilege.

The Torah at Mount Sinai

We must understand, however, that the Ten Commandments were by no means the only laws associated with God's covenant with Israel. God spoke these first Ten Commandments in an audible voice at Mount Sinai. But after the speaking of these first ten, God began issuing many more laws to Israel through His prophet Moses. In fact, for the next forty years (from Exodus 20 to the end of the book of Deuteronomy), God gave approximately 640 laws to the children of Israel through Moses. This entire body of regulations, statutes, and judgments became known as "The Law of God," "The Law of Moses," or sometimes just "The Law." The Hebrew word for law is Torah.

This collection of commandments would become Israel's God-given constitution. In it were specific rules to govern Israel's spiritual, moral, civil, and social life. Because this Law came from God, no one was allowed to add to it or take away from it. After Moses, God raised up many prophets and spiritual leaders in Israel. But none of them ever altered or added to The Law of God given through Moses. Many years later, as his life was coming to an end, Moses said, "See that you do all I command you; do not add to it or take away from it" (Deut. 12:32).

The Tabernacle at Mount Sinai

As mentioned earlier, the Law governed every aspect of Israel's life, the most important part of which was their spiritual life. Immediately after the covenant was sealed, by the sprinkling of blood, God said to Moses, "'Come up to me on the mountain and stay here'" (Exod. 24:12). Moses spent the next forty days on Mount Sinai alone with God. During this period God gave him specific instructions for building Israel's one and only authorized place of worship. It was to be known as the Tabernacle.

Why does God want this Tabernacle to be built? Well, in God's own words, "'Have them make a sanctuary for me, and I will dwell among them'" (Exod. 25:8). There can be no more comforting thought than God doesn't just want to view His people from a distance. God wants to dwell with His people! Do you remember back in the Garden of Eden, before sin entered the world? God would come "in the cool of the day," to walk and talk with Adam and Eve (Gen. 3:8). On Mount Sinai, God wanted the Tabernacle to be built so that Israel could enjoy the blessing of His presence.

For God to dwell with His people, however, a certain truth must be remembered—this can be a very dangerous situation, not for God, but for people! This is because of the nature of God. The Bible repeatedly tells us that God is holy. He is "a consuming fire" (Exod. 24:17). Because of His "burning holiness," God's "eyes are too pure to look on evil" (Hab. 1:13). We human beings, on the other hand, have a nature of sin. Evil is present with us, and we dwell in a "body of death" (Rom. 7:24). For this reason God said to Moses, "You cannot see my face, for no one may see me and live" (Exod. 33:20).

To illustrate the stark contrast between God's nature and our nature, let's compare two things: (1) the sun, burning at approximately 10,000° F, and (2) a bale of straw. Now (this is not exactly rocket science) what do you suppose would happen if we tried to take a bale of straw to the sun? I don't think I need to answer that one. Likewise, a similar thing will happen when sinful people try to approach a holy God. Do you see the problem that must be overcome? God can't look upon our sin without destroying us, and we can't look upon God without being destroyed. This is why, in giving instructions for the Tabernacle, God repeatedly told Moses, "'Make this tabernacle and all its furnishings exactly like the pattern I will show you'" (Exod. 25:9, 40; Num. 8:4). If God is to dwell with people and people wish to draw near to God, God must show the way to do this safely. His instructions must be followed to the letter.

God designated the tribe of Levi to serve as the priestly tribe. In the book of Leviticus, God gave detailed instructions for the Tabernacle's maintenance and ministry. Some of the Levites were assigned various tasks for maintaining the facility, while others became actual priests, serving as ministers in various acts of worship. Aaron, Moses' brother, was given the honored position of "High Priest." He supervised and oversaw all aspects of the Tabernacle. The position of High Priest would be passed to each generation of Aaron's descendants.

Because the tribe of Levi was given this great honor of being so close to God, and because taking care of the Tabernacle required so much time and energy, the Levites were not allowed to inherit property in the Promised Land like all the other tribes. God said to Aaron, "'You will have no inheritance in their land, nor will you have any share among them; I am your share and your inheritance among the Israelites'" (Num. 18:20). Since they had no way of providing for their own needs, God commanded the other tribes to support the Levites financially by the giving of tithes (10% of income) and offerings.

Of all their many duties, perhaps the most important assignment of the priests was to help the children of Israel approach God and worship Him safely. Let me briefly describe worship at the Tabernacle, using the simple diagram below.

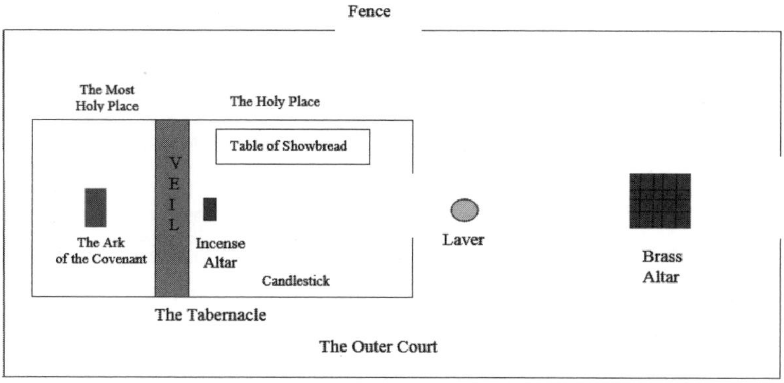

At the west end of the Tabernacle was a small room known as *The Most Holy Place*. In this room was a gold-plated box called *The Ark of the Covenant*. In the Ark were the two stone tablets bearing the Ten Commandments. God dwelt in this room and the Cloud of Glory always hovered above this room. A *Veil* separated The Most Holy Place from the adjacent room to the east called *The Holy Place*. No one was allowed to go behind the Veil into The Most Holy Place except the *High*

Priest, and he was allowed this access only once a year, on the most holy day known as The Day of Atonement.

When an Israelite wanted to worship God, he would come to the east entrance, always bringing with him an animal sacrifice. These sacrifices were a constant reminder of the problem of human sinfulness. The worshipper would be met, and stopped, by a Levite priest, for this was as close to God as the average person was allowed to come. The worshipper himself would slay the animal at the *Brass Altar*. The priest would then sprinkle the animal's blood on the altar and the animal's body would be filleted and roasted on the altar. The result of roasting the sacrificial animal was "an offering made by fire, an aroma pleasing to the LORD" (Lev. 1:9). God gave Moses the exact words of blessing that were to be said by the priest to the worshipper in Numbers 6:24–27: "'The LORD bless you and keep you; the LORD make his face shine upon you and be gracious to you; the LORD turn his face toward you and give you peace. So they will put my name on the Israelites, and I will bless them.'"

Then the worshipper, after safely worshipping God, in the exact way that God had prescribed, left the Tabernacle with God's blessing upon him and joy in his heart.

The Tearing of the Veil

As wonderful as it was that the Israelites now had a place to worship God safely, I must point out one sad and discouraging thing about the Tabernacle: access to God was still limited. As mentioned, the average worshipper could get no closer to God than the Brass Altar, and even the High Priest could only go behind the Veil into The Most Holy Place once a year. With the barrier of the veil, "the Holy Spirit was showing by this that the way into the Most Holy Place had not yet been disclosed" (Heb. 9:8). It was as if God had hung a sign that said,

SINNERS...KEEP OUT!

A HOLY GOD DWELLS BEHIND THIS VEIL

Wouldn't it be wonderful if someone could do something about this veil? Wouldn't it be fabulous if someone could come to God with a sacrifice so perfect, with blood so pure, that God Himself would tear open this veil and then actually invite human beings into His holy presence? Take comfort, dear friends. Stay with me on the tour. Someone is coming! One day, God Himself would tear this veil from top to bottom.

We are going to end this lesson a little differently than usual. We're not going to get on the bus to continue the tour, because we need to spend another day and see a few more things at Mount Sinai. Not to worry! I have rooms reserved for all of us at a nearby motel. Since Motel Sinai was all filled up, we'll be staying at Motel 7.

As you lay your head on the pillow tonight, let me encourage you to go to sleep with a happy thought: God desires to dwell in your life and He wants you to draw near to Him. To this end, He has provided a way for you to do this safely. We'll learn much more about this way as we continue our tour. (Hint: You might want to take a look at John 14:6.) Sleep well. See you in the morning.

If you have a question about this lesson, or other questions about the Bible, please visit my website www.FredWoodwardBible.com. There you can obtain my contact information and we can communicate through email. I'll do my very best to answer your questions.

Lesson 7

From Mount Sinai to the Promised Land

Exodus 32—Deuteronomy 34

We would naturally assume that by now the children of Israel would be the most grateful, thankful, appreciative, and joyful people on Earth. After all, no other nation has ever been so blessed by God. God delivered them from their bondage in Egypt. He parted the Red Sea for them. When they were thirsty in the desert, God gave them water to drink from a rock. Every day, for nearly three months, they have been waking up to a miraculous breakfast of bread on the ground called manna. They have heard the voice of God as He audibly spoke the Ten Commandments on Mount Sinai. God entered into a covenant relationship with them and gave them a way to worship Him safely at a place called the Tabernacle. And, all this was just the beginning of blessings! God also promised to lead them to and let them live in a land of "milk and honey." The land that He gave to Abraham, the father of their nation, would soon be theirs!

We would assume then that the children of Israel, in response to all He did for them and in view of what He would yet do for them, would be happy to trust and obey this kind, merciful, loving, and faithful God. Sadly, as we will see in this lesson, we would be wrong to make those assumptions.

The Golden Calf

> When the people saw that Moses was so long in coming down from the mountain, they gathered around Aaron and said, "Come, make us gods who will go before us. As for this fellow Moses who brought us up out of Egypt, we don't know what has happened to him." Aaron answered them, "Take off the gold earrings that your wives, your sons and your daughters are wearing, and bring them to me." So all the people took off their earrings and brought them to Aaron. He took what they handed him and made it into an idol cast in the shape of a calf, fashioning it with a tool. Then they said, "These are your gods, O Israel, who brought you up out of Egypt." When Aaron saw this, he built an altar in front of the calf and announced, "Tomorrow there will be a festival to the LORD." So the next day the people rose early and sacrificed burnt offerings and presented fellowship offerings. Afterward they sat down to eat and drink and got up to indulge in revelry. (Exod. 32:1–6)

While Moses was still on Mount Sinai, receiving instructions for building the Tabernacle, the ungrateful, unbelieving nature of the people emerged. They came to Aaron, Moses' brother, and insisted that he "*make us gods who will go before us.*" Tragically, Aaron agreed to do this, perhaps believing that he could control the situation by compromising with their demands. So he took up a collection of gold earrings, melted down the gold, and then fashioned it into a golden calf. The next day, after worshipping this idol, the people engaged in what can only be described as a pagan orgy, with drunkenness, gluttony, and sexual immorality.

To appreciate the seriousness of this incident, remember that only a few days earlier Israel had agreed to become "the bride" of God. After hearing God speak the Ten Commandments, they responded with,

"'We will do everything the LORD has said'" (Exod. 19:8). Let me further point out that the first two commandments of the ten were: (1) "You shall have no other gods before me" and (2) "You shall not make for yourself an idol" (Exod. 20:3, 4). Thus the children of Israel, just days after the "wedding ceremony," have already broken the covenant with God and have committed "spiritual adultery."

When Moses came down from the mountain, he was carrying the two stone tablets that God had given him. "When Moses approached the camp and saw the calf and the dancing, his anger burned and he threw the tablets out of his hands, breaking them to pieces at the foot of the mountain" (Exod. 32:19). Moses, however, was not the only one who was angry about this sin. God was very angry. "'I have seen these people,' the LORD said to Moses, 'and they are a stiff-necked people. Now leave me alone so that my anger may burn against them and that I may destroy them'" (Exod. 32:9–10).

Fortunately for Israel, Moses loved the people and pleaded with God to forgive them of this heinous sin. Because of Moses' intercessory prayer, "the LORD relented and did not bring on his people the disaster he had threatened" (Exod. 32:14). Thus Israel, only days after entering into a covenant with God, came dangerously close to destruction.

The Counting of (First-Generation) Troops

After God forgave the children of Israel for the golden calf incident, He accepted them back into His favor and resumed His plan to lead them to the Promised Land. The Tabernacle was built according to the pattern that Moses had been shown on the mountain and worship of God began. That left one more thing to be accomplished before leaving Mount Sinai: all men, twenty years old and older, who would be soldiers in the upcoming battle for the Promised Land, were to be counted. In Numbers 1:1–3 we read:

> The LORD spoke to Moses in the Tent of Meeting in the Desert of Sinai on the first day of the second month of the second year after the Israelites came out of Egypt. He said: "Take a census of the whole Israelite community by

> their clans and families, listing every man by name, one by one. You and Aaron are to number by their divisions all the men in Israel twenty years old or more who are able to serve in the army."

This, in fact, is how the book of Numbers gets its name. There are two numberings in Numbers: here in Chapter 1, and again in Chapter 26. The number of soldiers from each tribe and the organization of the entire camp can be seen in the diagram below: "These are the Israelites, counted according to their families. All those in the camps, by their divisions, number 603,550" (Num. 2:32). Since there were 603,550 men over twenty years old, we can estimate that the total number of Israelites (men of all ages, women, and children) would easily have been about three million.

Note how the tribes camped around the Tabernacle. The arrows indicate the marching order.

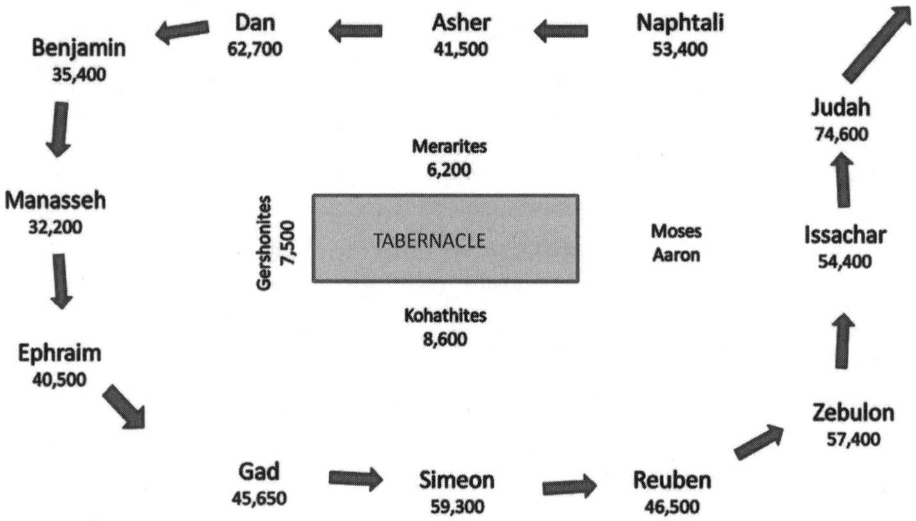

The Cloud Sets Forth

During their year-long encampment at the base of Mount Sinai, God, through Moses, had accomplished several important things for Israel. The covenant between God and Israel was sealed. The Tabernacle worship system was established. The soldiers were counted, and the tribes were organized for a military march. All systems were "go." The time had come to pull up stakes, leave Mount Sinai, and head north to the Promised Land. In Numbers 10:11–12 we read:

> On the twentieth day of the second month of the second year, the cloud lifted from above the tabernacle of the Testimony. Then the Israelites set out from the Desert of Sinai and traveled from place to place until the cloud came to rest in the Desert of Paran.

Finally, almost 600 years after the promises were made to Abraham, his descendants were on the last leg of their journey. They were almost home! They should have reached the Promised Land in a few days. But, as we will find out, the journey that should have taken a few days would instead turn into forty (long) years!

The Complaining of the People

After leaving Mount Sinai, it took the children of Israel a grand total of three days to start complaining: "Now the people complained about their hardships in the hearing of the LORD" (Num. 11:1). We aren't even told that there was anything to complain about. Apparently, this was just senseless ingratitude. We go on to read that when God heard them "his anger was aroused. Then fire from the LORD burned among them and consumed some of the outskirts of the camp" (Num. 11:1). Let's take note that God is starting to get irritated with this ungrateful generation.

They further complained about the food: "'If only we had meat to eat!

We remember the fish we ate in Egypt at no cost—also the cucumbers, melons, leeks, onions and garlic. But now we have lost our appetite; we never see anything but this manna'" (Num. 11:4–6). They went on to complain that the manna "'tasted like something made with olive oil'" (Num. 11:8). That's strange. A year earlier, when they first began eating the manna, "it tasted like wafers made with honey" (Exod. 16:31). Something had happened that changed the taste of the manna. Obviously, it was not the manna that had changed; it was their ungrateful, complaining attitude that made it taste like something boring and bland.

This bitter complaining, coming from the entire congregation of Israel, caused Moses to become so depressed that he wanted to die! In his prayer to God, Moses said:

> "Where can I get meat for all these people? They keep wailing to me, 'Give us meat to eat!' I cannot carry all these people by myself; the burden is too heavy for me. If this is how you are going to treat me, put me to death right now—if I have found favor in your eyes—and do not let me face my own ruin." (Num. 11:13–16)

The Criticism and Competition of Miriam

As if it were not bad enough to have the entire congregation complaining about his leadership, Moses' own sister, Miriam, and their (easily persuaded) brother, Aaron, began criticizing him for marrying a non-Israelite woman.

> Miriam and Aaron began to talk against Moses because of his Cushite wife, for he had married a Cushite. "Has the LORD spoken only through Moses?" they asked. "Hasn't he also spoken through us?" And the LORD heard this. (Num. 12:1, 2)

Evidently Miriam, sensing that Moses' popularity was at an all-time low, saw an opportunity to grab a little power, authority, and status for herself. God was so displeased with Miriam for this that He disciplined her with a seven-day bout of leprosy: "So Miriam was confined outside the camp for seven days, and the people did not move on till she was brought back" (Num. 12:15).

The Catastrophe at Kadesh Barnea

Finally as we come to Numbers 13, the children of Israel reached the southern border of the Promised Land and made camp at a place called Kadesh Barnea. At this point, God instructed Moses to "'send some men to explore the land of Canaan, which I am giving to the Israelites. From each ancestral tribe send one of its leaders'" (Num. 13:2). After Moses chose the twelve men, he gave them their assignment.

> "Go up through the Negev and on into the hill country. See what the land is like and whether the people who live there are strong or weak, few or many. What kind of land do they live in? Is it good or bad? What kind of towns do they live in? Are they unwalled or fortified?" (Num. 13:17–19)

Thus the twelve men set out on what we would call today a military reconnaissance mission. Please note that their assignment was simply to gather information as to how the land could be conquered, not if it could be conquered.

After forty days of exploring the land, the spies returned to the camp at Kadesh with their report. All twelve men agreed that the Promised Land was amazingly fertile, fruitful, and flowed "with milk and honey" (Num. 13:27). But then suddenly, and surprisingly, ten of the men began giving their unasked for and very negative opinion about the Promised Land. They spread among the Israelites a bad report about the land. In their words:

> "The people who live there are powerful, and the cities are fortified and very large. ... We can't attack those people; they are stronger than we are. ... The land we explored devours those living in it. All the people we saw there are

> of great size. ... We seemed like grasshoppers in our own eyes, and we looked the same to them." (Num. 13:28, 31–33)

To their credit, two of the spies, Joshua and Caleb, remained faithful to God and contended publicly against the unfaithful ten: "'We should go up and take possession of the land, for we can certainly do it'" (Num. 13:30).

But the bad report from the ten spies had an immediate and disastrous effect.

> That night all the people of the community raised their voices and wept aloud. All the Israelites grumbled against Moses and Aaron, and the whole assembly said to them, "If only we had died in Egypt! Or in this desert! Why is the LORD bringing us to this land only to let us fall by the sword? Our wives and children will be taken as plunder. Wouldn't it be better for us to go back to Egypt?" And they said to each other, "We should choose a leader and go back to Egypt." (Num. 14:1–4)

Thus the children of Israel, at the threshold of the Promised Land, accused God of leading them (and their children!) into disaster. They rebelled against God. They refused to go into the Promised Land, and they decided it was time to fire Moses and pick another leader who would lead them back to Egypt. I guess we shouldn't be too surprised. Have we not seen this coming? This ungrateful generation had been complaining against God since the day they left Egypt.

The Consequences of Rebellion

It's pretty hard to reach the limit of God's patience, but this generation of Israelites had indeed reached it. God's response to this rebellion was swift and severe.

> Then the glory of the LORD appeared at the Tent of Meeting to all the Israelites. The LORD said to Moses, "How long will these people treat me with contempt? How long will they refuse to believe in me, in spite of all the miraculous signs I have performed among them? I will strike them down with a plague and destroy them." (Num. 14:10–12)

Once again, as with the golden calf incident, God announced that He was about to destroy the nation of Israel. And once again, Moses begged God to forgive them: "'In accordance with your great love, forgive the sin of these people, just as you have pardoned them from the time they left Egypt until now'" (Num. 14:19). Since it was Moses making the request, "The LORD replied, 'I have forgiven them, as you asked'" (Num. 14:20). Thus Israel, because of Moses' godly character, was (again) delivered from complete destruction. But there would still be consequences for this defiant rebellion. God announced these consequences in Numbers 14:22–23, 29, 33–34:

> "Not one of the men who saw my glory and the miraculous signs I performed in Egypt and in the desert but who disobeyed me and tested me ten times—not one of them will ever see the land I promised on oath to their forefathers. No one who has treated me with contempt will ever see it. ... In this desert your bodies will fall—every one of you twenty years old or more who was counted in the census and who has grumbled against me. ... Your children will be shepherds here for forty years, suffering for your unfaithfulness, until the last of your bodies lies in the desert. For forty years—one year for each of the forty days you explored the land—you will suffer for your sins and know what it is like to have me against you."

In short, none of the men who were counted at Mount Sinai and then rebelled against God would be allowed to enter the Promised Land. Instead, they would wander in the wilderness for forty years until that first generation of soldiers had all died off. After the forty years in the wilderness, God promised that He would take their children into the Promised Land. It's hard to find the right words to describe this tragedy. The generation of Israelites that was delivered from slavery, that saw more miraculous signs and wonders than any other people on Earth, the generation that heard the voice of God, and entered into a covenant with God—that generation would not see the Promised Land!

The Costly Mistake of Moses

At this point, I'm sure you think that this story can't get any sadder. Sorry. Yes, it can. In Numbers 20, when the forty years in the desert are nearly over, the children of Israel again come to a place where there is no water. You might remember that when a similar thing had happened forty years earlier (Exod. 17:1–7), God told Moses that water would come from a nearby rock if he would "strike" it with his rod. Here in Numbers 20, however, God's instructions to Moses were slightly different. Instead of "striking" the rock, Moses was instead told to "speak" to the rock and water would come out.

Moses must have been having a very bad day. Maybe he got up on the wrong side of the bed. But whatever the reason, he disobeyed God's clear instructions. Instead of speaking to the rock as instructed, Moses struck the rock twice with his rod. Immediately God said to Moses, "'Because you did not trust in me enough to honor me as holy in the sight of the Israelites, you will not bring this community into the land I give them'" (Num. 20:12). Hard to believe, isn't it? This great man, this giant of the faith, this man who led Israel for forty years, would himself not be allowed to enter the Promised Land!

The Counting of (Second-Generation) Troops

Coming to Numbers 26, when the forty years ended and the first (rebellious) generation of troops had all died in the wilderness, Israel came to the plains of Moab, on the eastern border of the Promised Land. Here God said to Moses, "'Take a census of the whole Israelite community by families—all those twenty years old or more who are able to serve in the army of Israel'" (Num. 26:2). This second counting is for the second generation of Israelites after coming out of Egypt. It would be this generation of soldiers, those who had grown up in the wilderness, who would enter and conquer the Promised Land.

The Covenant Is Renewed

Coming to Deuteronomy 1, the children of Israel had finally arrived at the eastern shore of the Jordan River. The Promised Land was just over the Jordan. This is also the end of Moses' life. After being God's prophet-leader for forty years, he was now 120 years old. The book of Deuteronomy would be Moses' farewell to the children of Israel. The word Deuteronomy means "Second Law" or "Repetition of Law." Bear in mind that Moses was speaking to the second generation of Israelites to come out of Egypt. Most of these people were born and raised in the desert and were not even alive when (forty years earlier) their fathers had heard the voice of God at Mount Sinai. Moses therefore endeavored to "reeducate" the children of Israel. Before entering the Promised Land, this generation had to renew the covenant that their fathers had made (but did not keep) with God.

Moses reminded the people of the promises that God had made to Abraham. He restated many of the important laws of the covenant. He recounted the many times that God, beginning in Egypt and all the way to the Jordan River, delivered, protected, and provided for them with spectacular signs and wonders. He warned them of the perils they would encounter in the Promised Land. Over and over again, Moses encouraged them to love, honor, obey, and remain faithful to...THE LORD GOD OF ISRAEL!

With his work on Earth done, Moses climbed to the top of a nearby mountain, Mount Nebo, where God allowed him to view the Promised Land on the other side of the Jordan. But remember, because of his disobedience at the rock, he would not be allowed to enter. Moses died on Mount Nebo and God Himself buried his body in a secret place.

And this is where we also will park our bus and camp for the night, on the eastern shore of the Jordan River. I realize that the journey from

Mount Sinai to the Promised Land has been long, difficult, and discouraging. Were it not for God's faithfulness and forgiveness, we would not have made it this far. But take heart. When we resume our tour, we will watch the children of Israel cross over the Jordan River and conquer the Promised Land.

If you have a question about this lesson, or other questions about the Bible, please visit my website www.FredWoodwardBible.com. There you can obtain my contact information and we can communicate through email. I'll do my very best to answer your questions.

Lesson 8

The Conquest of Canaan

Joshua 1:1–24:33

During the forty-year period when Moses was God's leader for Israel, the Bible frequently makes mention of a young man named Joshua, the son of Nun. We first learn of Joshua in Exodus 17:9-10, when Israel is attacked by a group of desert pirates known as the Amalekites. Moses gives Joshua command of Israel's army to ward off this attack. The next time we see Joshua is in Exodus 33:11, when he remains at a tent of prayer, even after Moses leaves. We see him again in Numbers 13 and 14, when he and his friend Caleb are the only two of the twelve spies who give a faithful report of the Promised Land.

Obviously, God had His hand on Joshua and had been grooming him for greater things. As Moses neared the end of his life, God made it clear who his successor was to be.

> The LORD said to Moses, "Now the day of your death is near. Call Joshua and present yourselves at the Tent of Meeting, where I will commission him." So Moses and Joshua came and presented themselves at the Tent of Meeting. Then the LORD appeared at the Tent in a pillar of cloud, and the cloud stood over the entrance to the Tent. (Deut. 31:14–15)

By overseeing the ordination service, God made it clear that when Moses died, the mantle of leadership would fall to Joshua. As we come to the book of Joshua, we should not be surprised by the words we read in Chapter 1:1–3, 5–6:

> After the death of Moses the servant of the LORD, the LORD said to Joshua son of Nun, Moses' aide: "Moses my servant is dead. Now then, you and all these people get ready to cross the Jordan River into the land I am about to give to them—to the Israelites. I will give you every place where you set your foot, as I promised Moses. ... No one will be able to stand up against you all the days of your life. As I was with Moses, so I will be with you; I will never leave you nor forsake you. Be strong and courageous, because you will lead these people to inherit the land I swore to their forefathers to give them."

Joshua's commission from God, while daunting, is relatively simple: lead the armies of Israel to conquer the Promised Land, and then divide the land among the twelve tribes of Israel.

The Wickedness of the Canaanites

Because God promised this territory to Abraham and his descendants, Israel referred to it as "the Promised Land." But to the rest of the world it was known as "the Land of Canaan," due to the Canaanites who dwelt there at the time. Who were these Canaanites, and, more important, why did God order their complete destruction?

Back in Genesis 9:20–27, for time's sake, we passed over a story that took place shortly after the Flood of Noah. In that story, one of Noah's sons, named Ham, committed a sinful and indecent act while Noah was asleep. When Noah awoke, he perceived that there was a wicked trait in Ham, which would pass on to his son, Canaan. Noah, then, prophetically spoke of a "curse" that would one day come upon Canaan's descendants for falling into extreme wickedness. The following diagram illustrates where the Canaanites came from.

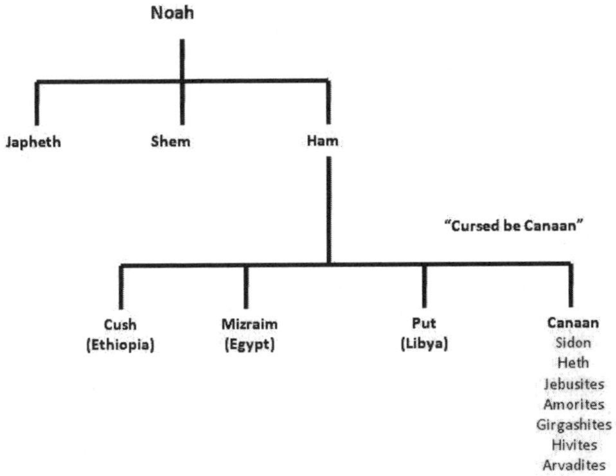

The names under "Canaan" are the "cursed" descendants of Canaan. These are the people who inhabited the Promised Land when Israel came to inherit it.

By the time Israel came to the Promised Land, the Canaanites had been spiraling into spiritual and moral corruption for nearly 1,000 years. Before he died, Moses spoke specifically about their wicked behavior: idolatry, witchcraft, sorcery, sexual immorality, incest, bestiality, and, worst of all, child sacrifice in Leviticus 18:1–29 and Deuteronomy 18:9–13. Through Moses, God said to Israel,

> After the LORD your God has driven them out before you, do not say to yourself, "The LORD has brought me here to take possession of this land because of my righteousness." No, it is on account of the wickedness of these nations that the LORD is going to drive them out before you." (Deut. 9:4)

The reason I have taken so much time talking about the Canaanites is because many people today have trouble with this part of the Bible. Many are so offended by the destruction of the Canaanites that they either dismiss this portion of scripture as untrue or accuse God of being an angry, hateful, vengeful God. The question often arises, "If the God of the Bible is good and kind, how could He order the complete destruction of so many people?"

Let me briefly respond to that question this way: Are any of us upset that Adolf Hitler, and his nation of Nazis, were destroyed and prevented from taking over the world? Or, as another example, suppose a doctor discovers that we have some type of cancer in our body. Would any of us be angry with the doctor for performing surgery to remove the cancer? Likewise, let us not be angry at God for eliminating evil societies, whose wickedness is a threat to the rest of humanity.

The Water of the Jordan River

Joshua's first obstacle in conquering the Promised Land was the Jordan River. How could the children of Israel get across it, especially since the Jordan was at "flood stage" (Josh. 3:15) during this time of the year? At this point, God instructs Joshua to have the Levite priests go before the people, carrying the Ark of the Covenant right into the Jordan River! Here's what happened:

> As soon as the priests who carried the ark reached the Jordan and their feet touched the water's edge, the water from upstream stopped flowing. It piled up in a heap a great distance away. ... The priests who carried the ark of the covenant of the LORD stood firm on dry ground in the middle of the Jordan, while all Israel passed by until the whole nation had completed the crossing on dry ground. (Josh. 3:15–17)

The children of Israel were, of course, amazed at this great sight. No doubt they recalled how Moses, forty years earlier, in a similar way, had parted the Red Sea. If there had been any doubt as to Joshua's capabilities as a leader, this miracle removed it. "That day the LORD exalted Joshua in the sight of all Israel; and they revered him all the days of his life, just as they had revered Moses" (Josh. 4:14).

The Warrior from Heaven

After crossing the Jordan, Joshua's next big challenge was the city of Jericho. As he stared at the walls of the city, Joshua probably remembered Moses' warning that in Canaan they would encounter "large cities that have walls up to the sky" (Deut. 9:1). With his own eyes, Joshua was now looking at these walls that seemed to go "*up to the sky*."

In those ancient times, there were only a couple of military strategies for conquering a city with such walls. The usual tactic was to surround the city with soldiers (like a blockade) and then patiently wait for the city to starve and its soldiers to surrender. Or, while waiting for the city to starve, slave labor could be used to build a huge, dirt ramp. When the ramp reached the top of the wall, the soldiers could go up the ramp and into the city. But the problem with both of these two strategies was that they could take months, even years, to work!

It was at this point that Joshua had an encounter with a strange visitor from Heaven.

> Now when Joshua was near Jericho, he looked up and saw a man standing in front of him with a drawn sword in his hand. Joshua went up to him and asked, "Are you for us or for our enemies?" "Neither," he replied, "but as commander of the army of the LORD I have now come." Then Joshua fell facedown to the ground in reverence and asked him, "What message does my Lord have for his servant?" The commander of the LORD's army replied, "Take off your sandals, for the place where you are standing is holy." And Joshua did so. (Josh. 5:13–15)

This warrior from Heaven was no ordinary angel. Ordinary angels do not make the ground "holy" just because they stand on it; only God can do that. And ordinary angels will never allow themselves to be worshipped; only God allows that. This angelic being, whoever He was, did both. His presence made the ground holy, and He allowed Joshua to fall to the ground in worship. So who was this person?

Many Bible scholars believe that this was Jesus, the Son of God, in a "pre-incarnate" state. Meaning that this was Jesus, coming to Earth in angelic form, to perform a specific task, approximately 1,300 years before the time He would come to Earth to take on a genuine human body. (The taking on of a human body is called the "incarnation.")

He announced that this time He had come to be the "*commander of the army of the LORD*." He would be in charge of all of God's forces in the upcoming battle for Jericho, which meant that He would command God's angels as they fought the spiritual battle in Heaven, and He would command Joshua's army as they fought the physical battle on Earth. All of this was good news for Joshua, because this commander had a plan!

The Walls of Jericho

Joshua's new commander goes on, in Joshua 6, to give Joshua detailed instructions for the conquest of Jericho:

> "March around the city once with all the armed men. Do this for six days. Have seven priests carry trumpets of rams' horns in front of the ark. On the seventh day, march around the city seven times, with the priests blowing the trumpets. When you hear them sound a long blast on the trumpets, have all the people give a loud shout; then the wall of the city will collapse and the people will go up, every man straight in." (Josh. 6:3–5)

I think we all would agree this is a very strange military strategy! The army of Israel was to march around Jericho once a day for six days, then on the seventh day they were to march around the city seven times. After the thirteenth and final time around, the entire army was to shout. At that point, the walls would fall down, and the soldiers would gain immediate access to the city. Most people would respond to this strategy with, "Yeah, right."

But Joshua and the children of Israel trusted God and did exactly as they were told. They marched around Jericho once a day for six days, and then seven more times on the seventh day. When they finished that thirteenth trip, they stopped and Joshua said, "'Shout! For the LORD has given you the city!'" (Josh. 6:16). When the trumpets sounded and the people shouted, "the wall collapsed; so every man charged straight in, and they took the city" (Josh. 6:20). The soldiers of Jericho, totally shocked and bewildered by the collapse of the wall, were then easily defeated. So instead of taking months or years to conquer this walled city, Joshua and the children of Israel, with God's commander in charge, conquered it in seven days!

The Woman of Faith

Every Canaanite in Jericho perished when the city was destroyed, with the exception of one woman and her family. This woman's name was Rahab, and she was, or rather had been, a prostitute. Prior to the battle of Jericho, Joshua had sent two spies into the city to investigate it. When these two men coincidentally came to Rahab's house, instead of turning them in to the authorities, she hid them on her rooftop under stalks of flax. Then she helped them escape by letting them down a scarlet cord through the window.

As a reward for her help, the men promised her that when the army of Israel came to conquer Jericho, if they saw this scarlet cord hanging out her window, they would spare her and everyone in her house. When the fateful day of battle came, she made sure the scarlet cord was visibly hanging from the window and her family was gathered in the house. Thus Rahab and her entire family were the only Canaanites of Jericho who survived.

But the story of Rahab does not end here; it just gets better. Later in the scripture (Ruth 4, Matthew 1) we are told that Rahab went on to marry an Israeli man named Salmon. This marriage is the beginning of an interesting family tree. Please take note of the following diagram:

Salmon & Rahab

|

Boaz

|

Obed

|

Jesse

|

King David

|

(1,000 Years Later)

|

KING JESUS!

Just in case you are still questioning the goodness and mercy of God, please consider the story of Rahab. This Canaanite prostitute, who was born and raised in a wicked culture, repented of sin and placed her faith in God of Israel. As a reward for her faith, she and her family were spared. She was then allowed to marry a good man (unlike all the other men she had known). She was honored by becoming the great-great-grandmother of King David, who in turn would be the ancestral father of Jesus Christ! I would argue that every Canaanite in Jericho could have done what Rahab did. They all could have repented and turned to God, and they all would have been rewarded with His goodness and mercy. As the Apostle Peter says, "The Lord ... is not wanting anyone to perish, but everyone to come to repentance" (2 Pet. 3:9).

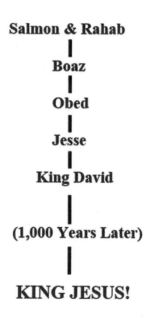

The Wonders of God During the War

God, remember, had promised Joshua that: "'No one will be able to stand up against you all the days of your life. As I was with Moses, so I will be with you; I will never leave you nor forsake you'" (Josh. 1:5). And so it came to pass. The rest of the book of Joshua is the story of an army that had God's blessing and was therefore unstoppable. Like a steamroller, Joshua and the children of Israel conquered the cities and kingdoms of Canaan, regardless of the size or strength of their armies.

During one particular battle, "the LORD hurled large hailstones down on them from the sky, and more of them died from the hailstones than were killed by the swords of the Israelites" (Josh. 10:11). On another occasion, Joshua had the opposing forces on the run, but it was getting late in the day, and the sun was going down. He needed more time to finish the battle, so

> Joshua said to the LORD in the presence of Israel: "O sun, stand still over Gibeon, O moon, over the Valley of Aijalon." So the sun stood still, and the moon stopped, till the nation avenged itself on its enemies. ... There has never been a day like it before or since. ... Surely the LORD was fighting for Israel! (Josh. 10:12–14)

The Whole Land Conquered and Divided

"So Joshua took the entire land, just as the LORD had directed Moses, and he gave it as an inheritance to Israel according to their tribal divisions. Then the land had rest from war" (Josh. 11:23). It took Joshua and the children of Israel a total of five years to conquer the land of Canaan. In Chapter 12, Joshua gives us a list of thirty-one kings who, individually or in league with other kings, fell before the army of God.

After the land was conquered, Joshua had one more assignment to complete: he was to divide the land among the twelve tribes of Israel. In Chapters 13 to 20, we read how Joshua allotted different portions of the land to the twelve tribes, with specific boundaries and borders for each tribe. Looking at the following map you will notice the names of the original twelve sons of Jacob.

THE TWELVE TRIBES OF ISRAEL

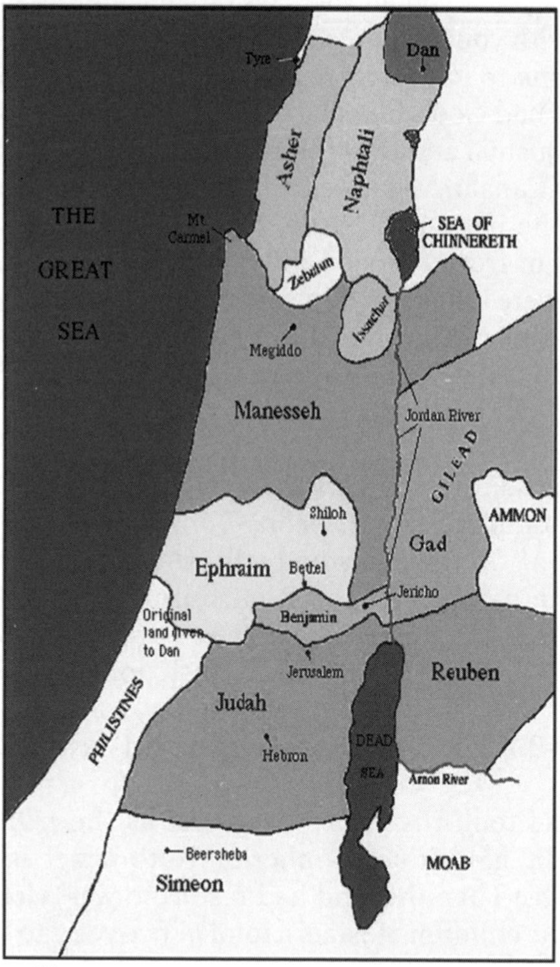

www.biblemapper.com

Somewhere around 2,000 BC, God promised this territory to Abraham and his descendants. Nearly 700 years later, these Israelites invaded, conquered, and finally inhabited this Promised Land. We are going to park the bus in Shiloh, because that is where the Tabernacle will reside for many years until the permanent Temple will be built in Jerusalem.

As you go to bed tonight, you might want to meditate on something that Joshua said at the end of his life that pretty much says it all: "Not one of all the LORD's good promises to the house of Israel failed; every one was fulfilled" (Josh. 21:45).

If you have a question about this lesson, or other questions about the Bible, please visit my website www.FredWoodwardBible.com. There you can obtain my contact information and we can communicate through email. I'll do my very best to answer your questions.

Lesson 9

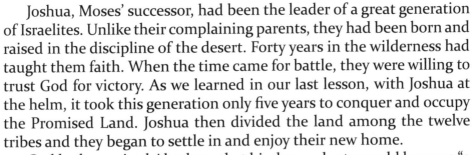

The Time of the Judges

Judges 1:1—1 Samuel 7:17

Joshua, Moses' successor, had been the leader of a great generation of Israelites. Unlike their complaining parents, they had been born and raised in the discipline of the desert. Forty years in the wilderness had taught them faith. When the time came for battle, they were willing to trust God for victory. As we learned in our last lesson, with Joshua at the helm, it took this generation only five years to conquer and occupy the Promised Land. Joshua then divided the land among the twelve tribes and they began to settle in and enjoy their new home.

God had promised Abraham that his descendants would become "a great nation" (Gen. 12:2). At Mount Sinai, God had said to them, "out of all nations you will be my treasured possession" (Exod. 19:5). Moses had said to them, "The LORD will make you the head, not the tail" (Deut. 28:13). Clearly, it was God's intention for Israel that they become not just a successful nation but a nation that would be superior to all others.

Time passed, however, and Joshua's great generation began to pass off the scene. "After that whole generation had been gathered to their fathers, another generation grew up, who knew neither the LORD nor what he had done for Israel" (Judg. 2:10). Sadly, instead of quickly becoming a successful and superior nation, Israel was about to enter into a 300-year period in which they would struggle just to survive. This period of Israel's history is known as the time of the judges.

The Reason for the 300-Year Struggle

Israel struggled through this 300-year period for a very simple reason: they did not heed the warnings God had given them concerning the Canaanites. Prior to entering the Promised Land, God, through Moses, had issued very clear instructions to Israel as to how they were to relate to and deal with these wicked people:

> When the LORD your God brings you into the land you are entering to possess and drives out before you many nations—the Hittites, Girgashites, Amorites, Canaanites, Perizzites, Hivites and Jebusites, seven nations larger and stronger than you—and when the LORD your God has delivered them over to you and you have defeated them, then you must destroy them totally. Make no treaty with them, and show them no mercy. Do not intermarry with them. Do not give your daughters to their sons or take their daughters for your sons, for they will turn your sons away from following me to serve other gods, and the LORD's anger will burn against you and will quickly destroy you. This is what you are to do to them: Break down their altars, smash their sacred stones, cut down their Asherah poles and burn their idols in the fire. (Deut. 7:1–5)

God's instructions were crystal clear: After conquering the Canaanites, Israel must destroy what was left of their corrupt culture. All remnants of their idolatrous religion were to be completely eliminated. The children of Israel must not interact or intermingle, and, especially, they must not intermarry with these people.

God's reason for these commandments was not racial; it was religious. "For they will turn your sons away from following me to serve other gods, and the LORD's anger will burn against you and will quickly destroy you" (Deut. 7:4). For Israel to remain in the Promised Land and prosper, they had to keep their hearts pure. They were told to worship no other god but God of Israel. They were, remember, in a covenant relationship with God, and the first commandment of that covenant was: "You shall have no other gods before me" (Exod. 20:3).

But after Joshua's generation passed away, the next generation of Israelites paid no attention to God's words and warnings. "When Israel became strong, they pressed the Canaanites into forced labor but never drove them out completely" (Judg. 1:28). Then we read that "the Israelites lived among the Canaanites, Hittites, Amorites, Perizzites, Hivites and Jebusites. They took their daughters in marriage and gave their own daughters to their sons, and served their gods" (Judg. 3:5–6).

From the above passage, please notice how choosing to ignore God's warnings led to the exact consequences that God had predicted. First, instead of driving out the Canaanites, Israel allowed them to dwell in the land. Next, they began to live among these people and intermingle with them socially. Shortly thereafter, they began to intermarry with them. And then, surprise, surprise, the children of Israel were seduced into worshipping and serving their false gods. God's response to this was also predictable: "They provoked the LORD to anger because they forsook him and served Baal and the Ashtoreths" (Judg. 2:12–13).

In this story, we learn a truth that will often be repeated in God's word: the danger of being "unequally yoked." While God's people are never to become arrogant "snobs," at the same time, those who believe in God must never allow themselves to become spiritually "harnessed" to those who do not believe. It is possible, and praiseworthy, to have friendships with unbelievers, but care must be taken that social friendship does not develop into spiritual fellowship. To have fellowship with someone means to be "fellow-souled" with that person, to become not just socially, but emotionally and spiritually in harmony with them.

God commands believers to avoid this situation because it almost always leads to the spiritual downfall of the believer. As the Apostle Paul warns in the New Testament, "Do not be yoked together with unbelievers. For what do righteousness and wickedness have in common? Or what fellowship can light have with darkness?" (2 Cor. 6:14).

The Repetitious Cycle

This "failure to separate" from the Canaanite people and their pagan beliefs caused the children of Israel to fall into a vicious cycle, which repeats itself many times in the book of Judges. We read about this cycle in Judges 2:14–17:

> In his anger against Israel the LORD handed them over to raiders who plundered them. He sold them to their enemies all around, whom they were no longer able to resist. Whenever Israel went out to fight, the hand of the LORD was against them to defeat them, just as he had sworn to them. They were in great distress. Then the LORD raised up judges, who saved them out of the hands of these raiders. Yet they would not listen to their judges but prostituted themselves to other gods and worshiped them.

The cycle always began when the children of Israel would FALL AWAY from God and worship other gods. In His anger about their idolatry, God would turn them over to and allow them to be OPPRESSED by a neighboring enemy nation. The misery of oppression would lead them to REPENTANCE, and they would cry out to God for help. Then God would raise up a military leader, called a "judge," and through this "judge" God would DELIVER Israel from the enemy at that time. Unfortunately, shortly after being delivered from their enemy, Israel would again FALL AWAY from God and the cycle would start all over again. A way to remember this cycle is by remembering the word "F O R D," as seen in the following image. (For all of you Ford owners, please forgive me for this comparison.)

The Vicious Cycle

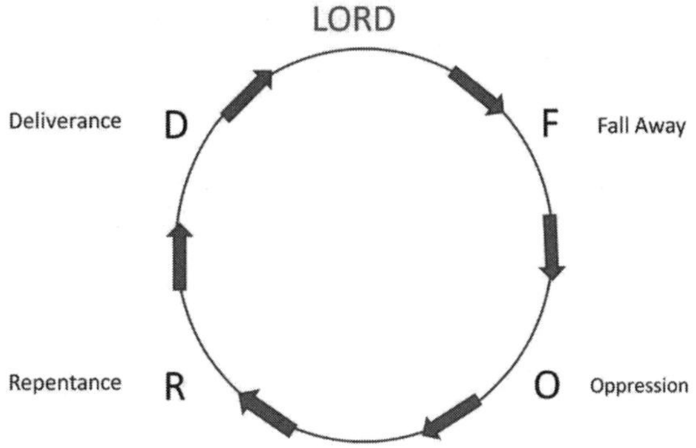

The Rescuers (Judges)

As mentioned earlier, the oppression of some neighboring nation would always bring the children of Israel to the "REPENTANCE" stage of the cycle. When they reached this stage, God would raise up what was called a "judge" to rescue them from the oppressor. Our concept of a judge in today's world is a person who dresses in a black robe, sits behind a bench, and presides over court cases. But the term "judge" in the book of Judges was used to describe a person chosen by God to serve as a temporary military leader.

Interestingly, God always insisted that the judge's military strength be small, in comparison to the strength of the enemy. For example, Gideon, one of the judges, started off with an army of 32,000 men. But "the LORD said to Gideon, 'You have too many men for me to deliver Midian into their hands. In order that Israel may not boast against me that her own strength has saved her. ...'" (Judg. 7:2). So, reluctantly, Gideon allowed 22,000 men to go home, leaving him with a mere 10,000. But to Gideon's astonishment, again "the LORD said to Gideon, 'There are still too many men'" (Judg. 7:4). Ultimately, God eliminated all but 300 Israeli men. With these 300, however, God enabled Gideon to conquer a multitude of Midianites. By insisting that Israel's army be small, God accomplished two things: (1) The children of Israel were prevented from boasting that their own power had delivered them, and (2) The miraculous deliverance served to rebuild their faltering faith.

Below is a list of the judges and the oppressing nations they encountered:

The Judges	The Oppressing Nation
Othniel (tribe of Judah)	Mesopotamians Moabites
Ehud (tribe of Benjamin)	Ammonites Amalekites
Shamgar (tribe unknown)	Philistines
Deborah (tribe of Ephraim)	Canaanites
Barak (tribe of Naphtali)	
Gideon (tribe of Manasseh)	Midianites Amalekites
Abimelech (tribe of Manasseh)	
Tola (tribe of Issachar)	
Jair (tribe of Manasseh)	
Jephthah (tribe of Manasseh)	Ammonites
Ibzan (tribe of Judah)	
Elon (tribe of Zebulun)	
Abdon (tribe of Ephraim)	
Samson (tribe of Dan)	Philistines

The Reprehensible Behavior

Please allow me to remind us all of a truth that we learned when we first began our tour of the Bible: to be truly good (by God's definition), we human beings must worship the one true God. God alone is good and is the source of our goodness. We borrow our goodness from Him. But when we fall away from God and worship something else, we immediately fall into sin. Idolatry will always be followed by iniquity (the breaking of God's laws). The God (or god) that we believe in will have an immediate and direct bearing on our moral behavior.

In the book of Judges, the children of Israel painfully remind us of this foundational truth. As they fell away from God and worshipped the false gods of the Canaanites, they also adopted their moral corruption and conduct. For example, in Judges 11:29-40, we read the shocking story of an Israeli man named Jephthah. Jephthah needed God's help in an upcoming battle with the Ammonites. But instead of simply praying for God's help, he made a pagan vow (much like the Canaanites would do with their gods):

> And Jephthah made a vow to the LORD: "If you give the Ammonites into my hands, whatever comes out of the door of my house to meet me when I return in triumph from the Ammonites will be the LORD's, and I will sacrifice it as a burnt offering." (Judg. 11:30–31)

Yes, you read those words correctly. Jephthah actually did vow that if he defeated the Ammonites, he would slay and offer as a burnt sacrifice whatever came out of his house to meet him after the battle. The "whatever" turned out to be his one and only daughter! But instead of just admitting that he had made a ridiculous vow and refusing to fulfill it, "he did to her as he had vowed" (Judg. 11:39). Where did Jephthah learn this reprehensible behavior? From the Canaanites, of course. They routinely offered their children as burnt sacrifices to their god, Baal.

In Judges 19, however, we read of behavior that is even more disturbing than what Jephthah did to his daughter. In this story, an

Israeli man, accompanied by his concubine (mistress) and a servant, were traveling through the tribe of Benjamin. Thinking he would find safety and shelter, he decided to spend the night in the town of Gibeah. He was met by a kind, elderly man who invited him and his companions to spend the night in his house. But what started out as an enjoyable, peaceful night suddenly turned into a nightmare.

> While they were enjoying themselves, some of the wicked men of the city surrounded the house. Pounding on the door, they shouted to the old man who owned the house, "Bring out the man who came to your house so we can have sex with him." (Judg. 19:22)

Yes, you read that correctly. The Israeli men of the town of Gibeah, men who were supposed to be in covenant with God, surrounded the old man's house, pounded on the door, and insisted that he send out his guest. Why? So that they could forcibly have sex with him! I can't think of any words that will sugarcoat this story. The men of Gibeah, driven by perverted desire, wanted to commit militant, homosexual rape against a fellow Israelite.

I would encourage you to go back to Genesis 19 and read the story of what had happened, 600 years earlier, to the Canaanite towns of Sodom and Gomorrah. You will notice some striking similarities between that story and the one we just discussed here from the book of Judges. And in that story, you will read that for the exact same wicked behavior, Sodom and Gomorrah were destroyed by God. The author of the book of Judges is obviously making a point: by falling away from God, Israel, during the time of the judges, became as sinful as Sodom and Gomorrah, and again, came dangerously close to destruction.

The Refreshing Story of Ruth

At this point in the Bible, it looks as if there is no hope for the children of Israel. The book of Judges ends with these discouraging words, "In those days Israel had no king; everyone did as he saw fit" (Judg. 21:25). It appears that this nation, like so many other nations, is about to disappear into the dust of history. But Israel, remember, is not like any other nation in history. This nation had entered into a covenant with God. Though the Israelites often forgot this covenant and forsook their God, God is always faithful, and He will not forget, or ever forsake, His people.

This brings us to the refreshing story of Ruth, which took place during the time of the judges. Due to a famine in the land, an Israeli man named Elimelech took his wife, Naomi, and their two sons to live in the neighboring land of Moab. While there, the two sons married two Moabite women, Ruth and Orpah. Shortly thereafter, however, the father and his two sons died, leaving Naomi and her two daughters-in-law as widows.

When Naomi decided to go back to her home in Israel, her daughter-in-law Orpah decided to stay in Moab. Ruth, however, with uncharacteristic loyalty and devotion, refused to abandon her mother-in-law. Instead, she insisted upon going back to Israel with her. In Ruth's words, "'Don't urge me to leave you or to turn back from you. Where you go I will go, and where you stay I will stay. Your people will be my people and your God my God'" (Ruth 1:16).

When the two women returned to Israel, Ruth worked in the fields to support herself and Naomi. Because of her hard work, love, and loyalty to Naomi, Ruth soon became known as "a woman of noble character" (Ruth 3:11). Her new faith in the God of Israel and her noble character were rewarded. A wealthy man by the name of Boaz took notice of her and they fell in love, got married, and had a son, whom they named Obed. At the end of the story, Naomi, who had gone through a time of bitterness for having lost her husband and two sons, once again returned to the joy in God.

In the book of Ruth, we learn that God had certainly not forgotten Israel. Instead, He had a plan that would bring an end to this period of chaos and usher in a time of blessing and peace. During the time of the judges, there had been a void of spiritual leadership. God planned to fill that void by raising up a king for Israel, a king by the name of David. (We'll talk about David in our next lesson.)

As the following diagram illustrates, David will be born from the family line of Boaz and Ruth.

BOAZ & RUTH
|
OBED
|
JESSE
|
KING DAVID

The Revival of Samuel the Prophet

In the first eight chapters of the book of 1 Samuel, we read about the miraculous birth and powerful ministry of the prophet Samuel. God used Samuel's preaching to bring Israel to repentance for a time of spiritual revival. Samuel is often referred to as "the last judge" before the time of the first king. A sampling of Samuel's preaching is found in 1 Samuel 7:3–4:

> And Samuel said to the whole house of Israel, "If you are returning to the LORD with all your hearts, then rid yourselves of the foreign gods and the Ashtoreths and commit yourselves to the LORD and serve him only, and he will deliver you out of the hand of the Philistines." So the Israelites put away their Baals and Ashtoreths, and served the LORD only.

Although we have passed through another very difficult period, we can end this lesson on a positive note. Because of the unfailing faithfulness of God, the children of Israel had hope. They were beginning to experience spiritual restoration and renewal. And I can promise you that in our next lesson life in Israel will get brighter and better. With that in mind, we're going to move our tour bus from Shiloh to Jerusalem. After we arrive in Jerusalem, we will learn about "The Golden Age of Israel."

If you have a question about this lesson, or other questions about the Bible, please visit my website www.FredWoodwardBible.com. There you can obtain my contact information and we can communicate through email. I'll do my very best to answer your questions.

Lesson 10

The United Kingdom: The Golden Age of Israel

1 Samuel 9—1 Kings 10

As we come to 1 Samuel 9, it has been nearly 400 years since God delivered the children of Israel from their bondage in Egypt. Throughout those 400 years, God faithfully raised up spiritual leaders to guide His people. First it was Moses, who led Israel from Egypt to the Promised Land. After Moses, God chose Joshua, who led the nation to conquer and divide the land of Canaan among the twelve tribes. After Joshua, God raised up a series of military leaders known as judges, who rescued Israel from various enemies. But up to this point in their history, Israel had never had a king. That's about to change.

In this lesson, we will take a look at the first three kings of Israel: Saul, David, and Solomon. Each of these men ruled for forty years. During the total 120-year period when they reigned, all twelve tribes of Israel were united under one rule. For this reason, this period is referred to as the United Kingdom. It is also known as "The Golden Age of Israel," because, as we will see, Israel, during this period, reached heights of worldwide fame, fortune, and glory.

Saul: The First King of Israel

As we learned in our last lesson, Samuel the prophet was often referred to as "the last judge" before the first king. With powerful preaching and prophecy, Samuel persuaded the children of Israel to repent of their worship of the Canaanite gods and return to God. "So the Israelites put away their Baals and Ashtoreths, and served the LORD only" (1 Sam. 7:4). Under the godly leadership of Samuel, Israel began to experience spiritual revival and renewal.

When Samuel became old, "he appointed his sons as judges for Israel" (1 Sam. 8:1). This turned out to be a mistake, however, because his sons "did not walk in his ways. They turned aside after dishonest gain and accepted bribes and perverted justice" (1 Sam. 8:3). Going on in 1 Samuel 8 we read, "So all the elders of Israel gathered together and came to Samuel at Ramah. They said to him, 'You are old, and your sons do not walk in your ways; now appoint a king to lead us, such as all the other nations have'" (1 Sam. 8:4–5). Thus, because of their dissatisfaction with Samuel's sons, the elders of Israel came to Samuel, demanding that he appoint a king to rule over them.

God decided to grant Israel their desire for a king and arranged a meeting with Samuel and a young man named Saul. God prepared Samuel for this meeting by saying, "'About this time tomorrow I will send you a man from the land of Benjamin. Anoint him leader over my people Israel'" (1 Sam. 9:16). When Samuel and Saul were alone together, "Samuel took a flask of oil and poured it on Saul's head and kissed him, saying, 'Has not the LORD anointed you leader over his inheritance?'" (1 Sam. 10:1). As seen in the illustration below, with this ceremony, Saul became "The LORD'S Anointed".

The Holy Spirit

www.biblerevival.com

As Samuel anointed Saul with a few drops of oil, something much more important also happened to Saul; the Holy Spirit of God came upon him. Saul received empowerment from on high to be the king of God's people. Hereafter, Saul would be known as "The Anointed One," "The LORD'S Anointed," or "The Anointed of the LORD." All future kings of Israel would be installed as kings by a similar anointing ceremony. The Hebrew word for "the anointed one" is Messiah. Thus, with the anointing of Saul, somewhere around 1040 BC, we are introduced to the concept of a Messiah King.

With the Spirit of God upon him, the young King Saul was off to a great start. When Israel was attacked by the Ammonites, "the Spirit of God came upon him in power, and he burned with anger" (1 Sam. 11:6). With this holy passion to protect God's people, Saul went on to raise up an army from the various tribes of Israel and lead them into a mighty victory over the Ammonites. Young Saul was thus demonstrating that when he followed God and was full of God's Spirit, he had the potential to be a great leader.

But shortly after becoming king, something happened to the heart of Saul. Perhaps the power and glory of his position went to his head. For whatever reason, Saul turned away from following the Spirit of God. He came to the point where he would no longer obey God's commandments and instructions. When it became clear that Saul had turned away from God, God revealed to Samuel the prophet that Saul would have to be rejected and a new king chosen to take his place. Because he loved Saul as a father would love a son, Samuel was grieved and distressed over Saul's fall from grace. But God cheered him up with these words: "'How long will you mourn for Saul, since I have rejected him as king over Israel? Fill your horn with oil and be on your way; I am sending you to Jesse of Bethlehem. I have chosen one of his sons to be king'" (1 Sam. 16:1).

David: The Second King of Israel

So with his flask of oil in hand, Samuel traveled to the home of a man named Jesse. You might remember from our previous lessons, that God had His hand on the development of this family of Jesse for several generations, beginning with Rahab, the Canaanite harlot from Jericho. Jesse had been blessed with eight sons.

Beginning with the eldest, "Jesse had seven of his sons pass before Samuel, but Samuel said to him, 'The LORD has not chosen these'" (1 Sam. 16:10). Finally, the youngest son, who was out keeping the sheep, was brought in to the house to pass before Samuel.

> Then the LORD said, "Rise and anoint him; he is the one." So Samuel took the horn of oil and anointed him in the presence of his brothers, and from that day on the Spirit of the LORD came upon David in power. ... Now the Spirit of the LORD had departed from Saul." (1 Sam. 16:12–14)

Thus, because Saul turned away from following God, the Spirit of God departed from him, and David, at about sixteen years old, became "The LORD'S Anointed." God allowed Saul to remain on the throne for many years, holding the position of king but without the power of the Holy Spirit. During the last several years of his life, Saul became mentally deranged and emotionally unstable. His life finally came to a tragic end when, after losing a battle to the Philistines, "Saul took his own sword and fell on it" (1 Sam. 31:4).

God Himself said that David was "a man after his own heart" (1 Sam. 13:14). Unlike Saul, David, with childlike faith, obeyed God and followed His instructions explicitly. For this reason, after the Holy Spirit came upon him, David was unstoppable. When he was about seventeen years old, he single-handedly slew a Philistine giant, named Goliath, with a slingshot. In his early twenties, he became the captain over a company of 1,000 soldiers and led them in many successful battles. At thirty years old (after Saul's death), he ascended to the throne as king.

"And he became more and more powerful, because the LORD God Almighty was with him" (2 Sam. 5:10). Within a few years, David had conquered all of the enemy nations that had threatened Israel since the time of the judges: the Jebusites, the Philistines, the Moabites, the Syrians, the Edomites, and the Ammonites. Under David's command, Israel experienced something they had not seen in centuries: peace!

Israeli soldiers finally got some much needed "R & R." And David sat safely in his own house because "the LORD had given him rest from all his enemies around him" (2 Sam. 7:1).

But for all of his accomplishments, David is remembered most of all for what is called "The Davidic Covenant." Through the prophet Nathan, God made the following promise to David:

> "The LORD declares to you that the LORD himself will establish a house for you: When your days are over and you rest with your fathers, I will raise up your offspring to succeed you, who will come from your own body, and I will establish his kingdom. He is the one who will build a house for my Name, and I will establish the throne of his kingdom forever." (2 Sam. 7:11–13)

Let me try to explain why this is one of the most important passages in the Bible. Do you remember what God promised on the very day that mankind fell into sin, way back in Genesis 3? He promised that one day in the future, an "offspring of the woman" would come to Earth to undo what Satan had done. Several centuries later, God promised Abraham that an "offspring" from him would come to Earth to be a blessing for "all peoples on earth" (Gen. 12:3). Now, here in 2 Samuel 7, God again mentioned a coming "offspring." David had been promised that his "offspring" would become an eternal king, to reign over God's kingdom forever. Though this Person would not come to Earth for another 1,000 years after David, I think you know who this promised person is. In the New Testament, He is given many titles: "the son of Mary," "the descendant of Abraham," "the son of David," "the Messiah," "the Anointed One," "the Christ." But His friends would simply call Him Jesus.

David was not only a soldier, he was also a psalm writer. The book of Psalms is a collection of Hebrew songs, put to music to worship God. Of the 150 psalms, David is thought to have written about seventy-five. In many of these psalms, David speaks prophetically of his coming "anointed" son, and for this reason, such psalms are called "Messianic." In many Bibles, a star or an asterisk is placed beside such a verse to identify it as a Messianic prophecy. In Psalm 22, for example, several verses are "Messianic."

(vs. 1) "My God, my God, why have you forsaken me?"
(vs. 7) "All who see me mock me; they hurl insults, shaking their heads."
(vs. 16) "they have pierced my hands and my feet."
(vs. 18) "They divide my garments among them and cast lots for my clothing."

When we come to the New Testament, we will see that all of the above Messianic prophecies were fulfilled as Jesus hung on the cross. Jesus' apostles often quoted verses from such Psalms to prove that Jesus is indeed the Son of David, the long-awaited Messiah King, and the fulfillment of God's covenant with King David.

Solomon: The Third King of Israel

King David eventually became "old and well advanced in years" (1 Kings 1:1). But before he died, he gave some very clear instructions as to who was to be king after him.

> King David said, "Call in Zadok the priest, Nathan the prophet and Benaiah son of Jehoiada." When they came before the king, he said to them: "Take your lord's servants with you and set Solomon my son on my own mule and take him down to Gihon. There have Zadok the priest and Nathan the prophet anoint him king over Israel. Blow the trumpet and shout, 'Long live King Solomon!'" (1 Kings 1:32-34)

Though David had many sons, he made it clear that his son Solomon was to reign in his stead. In a ceremony that included three of David's chief advisors, Nathan the prophet poured oil on Solomon's head. By now we know what this means; Solomon became the third king to be called "The LORD'S Anointed."

Solomon is perhaps best remembered for his wisdom. Shortly after Solomon ascended to the throne, God appeared to him in a dream and said, "'Ask for whatever you want me to give you'" (1 Kings 3:5). God was essentially giving Solomon a "blank check." Many men would have responded to this offer by selfishly asking for long life, riches, or perhaps death for their enemies. Instead, Solomon's response to God: was "'Give your servant a discerning heart to govern your people and to distinguish between right and wrong. For who is able to govern this great people of yours?'" (1 Kings 3:9).

God was so pleased with his unselfish request that He told Solomon, "'I will do what you have asked. I will give you a wise and discerning heart, so that there will never have been anyone like you, nor will there ever be'" (1 Kings 3:12). Thus, according to God Himself, Solomon was about to become the wisest man of all time. But in addition to great wisdom, God further promised Solomon great fame and fortune: "'Moreover, I will give you what you have not asked for—both riches and honor—so that in your lifetime you will have no equal among kings'" (1 Kings 3:13).

And so it came to pass. Solomon began to receive both honor and riches from all the nations of the world. He was honored because he "was wiser than any other man" (1 Kings 4:31). "Men of all nations came to listen to Solomon's wisdom, sent by all the kings of the world, who had heard of his wisdom" (1 Kings 4:34). And when these foreign dignitaries came to visit Solomon, they did not come empty-handed, so he garnered great wealth: "Year after year, everyone who came brought a gift—articles of silver and gold, robes, weapons and spices, and horses and mules" (1 Kings 10:25). During this time of great prosperity, "the king made silver as common in Jerusalem as stones" (1 Kings 10:27).

Solomon is also remembered for another great accomplishment: building the magnificent Temple of God. "In the four hundred and eightieth year after the Israelites had come out of Egypt, in the fourth year of Solomon's reign over Israel, in the month of Ziv, the second month, he began to build the temple of the LORD" (1 Kings 6:1).

In a previous lesson, we learned that while Israel was camped at the base of Mount Sinai, God gave Moses precise instructions for the building of the Tabernacle. The Tabernacle was basically a portable tent, made of wood and woven fabric. Though built with humble material, it was God's ordained place of worship. In their journeys, the Israelites had carried it from place to place. For many years after they conquered the land of Canaan, the Tabernacle had been in Shiloh.

But now the wise and wealthy Solomon would replace the portable Tabernacle by building a permanent Temple in Jerusalem. Solomon was careful to build the Temple according to the basic pattern that was given to Moses for the Tabernacle. Just as they had done for 480 years, the Levites would continue to serve as priests to maintain the Temple and oversee all worship services. But while the Tabernacle had been a humble facility, the Temple would be huge. The Tabernacle had been modest; the Temple would be magnificent. Without comparison, Solomon's Temple was one of the most magnificent and ornate buildings of the ancient world. It became "a house of prayer for all nations" (Isa. 56:7).

It's easy to see why this period was known as "The Golden Age of Israel." People from all over the world came to hear Solomon's wisdom and to worship the God of Israel at the Temple. One such foreign dignitary, the Queen of Sheba, summed it up best by saying,

> "The report I heard in my own country about your achievements and your wisdom is true. But I did not believe these things until I came and saw with my own eyes. Indeed, not even half was told me; in wisdom and wealth you have far exceeded the report I heard. How happy your men must be! How happy your officials, who continually stand before you and hear your wisdom! Praise be to the LORD your God, who has delighted in you and placed you on the throne of Israel." (1 Kings 10:6–9)

The Queen of Sheba was overwhelmed by Solomon's wisdom and wealth. Seeing the blessing of God upon Israel, she became a believer in the God of Israel. We can safely assume that after visiting King Solomon in Jerusalem, many foreign kings, queens, and dignitaries had the same experience. When they left Israel to go back home, they took their new faith in the God of Israel with them.

As we conclude this lesson, let's park our bus on a high hill overlooking the city of Jerusalem, and take a few minutes to reflect on Israel's history. Let's remember that about 500 years earlier, the children of Israel worked in the mud pits of Egypt. Now they have become the wealthiest people on earth. They were a nation of slaves. Now they have become a nation of spiritual leaders for all nations. Jerusalem had become "a city on a hill" that "cannot be hid" (Matt. 5:14), not just because of its high elevation, but because God exalted the nation above all others.

If you have a question about this lesson, or other questions about the Bible, please visit my website www.FredWoodwardBible.com. There you can obtain my contact information and we can communicate through email. I'll do my very best to answer your questions.

Lesson 11

The Divided Kingdom

1 Kings 11—2 Kings 25

We ended our last lesson on a mountain top. Because of the accomplishments of the first three kings, Saul, David, and Solomon, the nation of Israel had entered into its Golden Age. Saul and David, as warrior kings, had successfully conquered all of Israel's enemies and eliminated the threat of foreign attack. There was peace and rest from war. Then, because of his God-given gift of wisdom, Solomon became the wisest and the wealthiest king on earth.

> King Solomon was greater in riches and wisdom than all the other kings of the earth. The whole world sought audience with Solomon to hear the wisdom God had put in his heart. Year after year, everyone who came brought a gift—articles of silver and gold, robes, weapons and spices, and horses and mules. (1 Kings 10:23–25)

Indeed, during this Golden Age, Israel reached its peak of success in power, prosperity, and worldwide prestige. But when we come to 1 Kings 11, the first three words of verse 1 are: "King Solomon, however." Whenever we see the word "however," we all say "uh oh," because we know that something bad is about to happen. And in this case, that is correct. Let's read a few more verses in Chapter 11 to find out what bad thing happened.

The Women of Solomon

> King Solomon, however, loved many foreign women besides Pharaoh's daughter—Moabites, Ammonites, Edomites, Sidonians and Hittites. They were from nations about which the LORD had told the Israelites, "You must not intermarry with them, because they will surely turn your hearts after their gods." Nevertheless, Solomon held fast to them in love. He had seven hundred wives of royal birth and three hundred concubines. (1 Kings 11:1–3)

For all of his great wisdom, in one area of his life Solomon was very weak and foolish: his obsession with women. It was already a violation of God's will that he loved "many" women. Even more serious was his sin of loving many "foreign" women. You may recall that during the time of the judges, this was the very issue that caused Israel to repeatedly fall from God. They intermarried with the idolatrous Canaanites and ended up worshipping the Canaanite gods. Now Solomon (supposedly the wisest man on Earth) was committing the same sin. (SIGH.)

The Waywardness of Solomon

Marrying these foreign women had the exact effect on Solomon that God had warned of: "'You must not intermarry with them, because they will surely turn your hearts after their gods'" (1 Kings 11:2). So we are not the least surprised to read what happened to Solomon after he ignored this warning:

> and his wives led him astray. As Solomon grew old, his wives turned his heart after other gods, and his heart was not fully devoted to the LORD his God, as the heart of David his father had been. He followed Ashtoreth the goddess of the Sidonians, and Molech the detestable god

> of the Ammonites. (1 Kings 11:3–5)

It gets worse. Solomon craved the approval of his wives so much that he would do anything to please them. And I mean anything. For example:

> On a hill east of Jerusalem, Solomon built a high place for Chemosh the detestable god of Moab, and for Molech the detestable god of the Ammonites. He did the same for all his foreign wives, who burned incense and offered sacrifices to their gods. (1 Kings 11:7–8)

Hard to believe, isn't it? This is the man who built the Temple of God in Jerusalem, so that all nations could come and worship the true God. That same man was now building pagan temples in Jerusalem just to please his pagan wives!

When the leader of a nation falls into sin, his people typically follow him. And this is exactly what happened in Israel. Because King Solomon became an idol worshipper, many Israelites, following his example, turned away from God and became idol worshippers. A plague of idolatry, beginning with Solomon, began to permeate the entire nation. (Well played, Mr. Satan.)

The Woes of Solomon

Understandably: "The LORD became angry with Solomon because his heart had turned away from the LORD, the God of Israel, who had appeared to him twice" (1 Kings 11:9). The fact that God had previously honored Solomon by personally appearing to him twice made his sin of turning away all the more grievous. God went on to inform Solomon that, because of this influx of idolatry in Israel, God would have to discipline the entire nation. God announced what that discipline would be in the following verses:

> So the LORD said to Solomon, "Since this is your attitude and you have not kept my covenant and my decrees,

> which I commanded you, I will most certainly tear the kingdom away from you and give it to one of your subordinates. Nevertheless, for the sake of David your father, I will not do it during your lifetime. I will tear it out of the hand of your son. Yet I will not tear the whole kingdom from him, but will give him one tribe for the sake of David my servant and for the sake of Jerusalem, which I have chosen." (1 Kings 11:11–13)

Thus God announced that He would discipline Israel by allowing a division to take place in the nation. God tore ten tribes away from the house of David, leaving it to reign over just two tribes. While this would not happen in Solomon's lifetime, it happened when his son, Rehoboam, came to the throne, as God said.

And so it came to pass. In 1 Kings 13, we read that ten tribes from the northern region rebelled against the house of David and separated from the two southern tribes. I know it's a little confusing, because up to this time the name "Israel" has referred to all twelve tribes. But during this particular period, the ten tribes that made up the "Northern Kingdom" became known as "Israel." The two tribes in the south formed the "Southern Kingdom" and became known as "Judah." Of these two tribes, Judah was by far the bigger and more influential. It might interest you to know that the name "Jew" is thought to originate from "Judah." The map below will illustrate the divided kingdom.

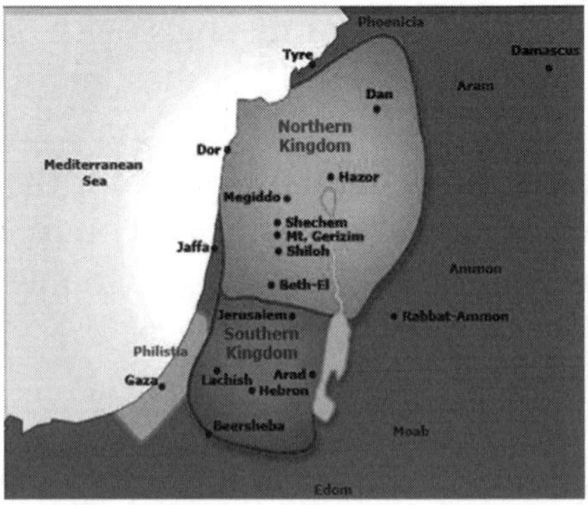

www.biblemapper.com

The Work of God

A good question at this point would be: "Since it was God who told Solomon that He would 'tear' ten tribes away from the house of David, what was God trying to accomplish with this division?" I believe God was planning to salvage one faithful nation from two faltering ones. As an illustration, suppose you owned two identical cars. And let's suppose that both cars are involved in accidents, with one car suffering more damage than the other. Why (if you are a car enthusiast) might you keep the more damaged one in your backyard? For spare parts. You can take parts off the more damaged car to restore the other, thus making one good car from two wrecks.

And so we read, "The priests and Levites from all their districts throughout Israel sided with him [King Rehoboam]. The Levites even abandoned their pasturelands and property, and came to Judah" (2 Chron. 11:13–14). In other words, many faithful worshippers of God in the Northern Kingdom, desiring to accurately worship God, left their homes and moved south to Judah, the Southern Kingdom, thus strengthening it spiritually.

The Wickedness of the Kings

The diagram that follows illustrates the two kingdoms and their kings. Notice that during the collective time (120 years) of Saul, David, and Solomon, the kingdom was united. The division came during the reign of Solomon's son, Rehoboam. It's important to understand that the kings of the Southern Kingdom (Judah) were all descendants of David, while the kings of the Northern Kingdom (Israel) came from various tribes. God, remember, made a promise to David: "'Your house and your kingdom will endure forever before me; your throne will be established forever'" (2 Sam. 7:16).

Saul
David
Solomon

Northern Kingdom (Israel)		Southern Kingdom (Judah)	
King	**Prophet**	**King**	**Prophet**
*Jeroboam		Rehobaom	
Nadab		Abijah	
• Baasha		Asa (Good)	
Elah		Jehoshaphat (Good)	
•Zimri		Jehoram	
• Omri		Ahaziah	
Ahab	Elijah	Athaliah	
Ahaziah		Joash (Mostly Good)	Joel
Joram	Elisha	Amaziah (Mostly Good)	
• Jehu		Uzziah (Good)	Isaiah
Jehoahaz		Jotham (Good)	Micah
Joash			Obadiah
Jeroboam II	Jonah	Ahaz	
Zechariah	Amos		
• Shallum	Hosea	Hezekiah (Great)	
• Menahem		Manasseh	Nahum
Pekahiah		Amon	
• Pekah		Josiah (Great)	Jeremiah
• Hoshea		Jehoahaz	Habakkuk
Assyrian Captivity (722 BC)		**The Exile Into Babylonia**	
		Jehoiakim	Zephaniah
* New Dynasty		Jehoiachin	Daniel
		Zedekiah	Ezekiel
		Babylonian Captivity (586 BC)	

The Northern Kingdom had a total of nineteen kings, and they were all bad. By "bad," I mean that none of them were worshippers of God. Quite the contrary, they even introduced and supported idol worship. Right off the bat, Jeroboam, fearing that some of his people would return to worship God in Jerusalem, established two alternative places to worship idols.

> After seeking advice, the king made two golden calves. He said to the people, "It is too much for you to go up to Jerusalem. Here are your gods, O Israel, who brought you up out of Egypt." One he set up in Bethel, and the other in Dan. And this thing became a sin; the people went even as far as Dan to worship the one there. (1 Kings 12:28–30)

Notice how Jeroboam strategically located these golden calves, one at the southern border (Bethel), and the other at the northern border (Dan) of Israel. Unfortunately, all of the eighteen kings who came after Jeroboam followed his terrible example. They worshipped idols and even ordered their people to do the same. For example, when we go down the list to the sixteenth king, Menahem, it is said of him: "He did evil in the eyes of the LORD. During his entire reign he did not turn away from the sins of Jeroboam son of Nebat, which he had caused Israel to commit" (2 Kings 15:18).

Let me also point out that beside the names of some of the kings of the Northern Kingdom I have placed an asterisk. This is to mark the beginning of a new "dynasty." A dynasty refers to a particular ruling family. You will notice that there were nine different dynasties in the Northern Kingdom. Often the change of dynasty came about as a result of an assassination. A man with a following would assassinate the king and take the throne. This new king and his descendant(s) would rule until there was another assassination and another family would come to power.

As we have observed already many times in our tour of the Bible, when a society departs from God, they are on a slippery slope, and there's no place to go but down. So it was with the Northern Kingdom. The further they fell from God, the deeper they sank into spiritual, moral, and political chaos. The selected verses that follow contain a summary of what eventually happened to the Northern Kingdom.

> The king of Assyria invaded the entire land, marched against Samaria and laid siege to it for three years. In the ninth year of Hoshea, the king of Assyria captured Samaria and deported the Israelites to Assyria. ... All this took place because the Israelites had sinned against the LORD their God, who had brought them up out of Egypt from under the power of Pharaoh king of Egypt. They worshiped other gods and followed the practices of the nations the LORD had driven out before them, as well as the practices that the kings of Israel had introduced. ... The LORD warned Israel and Judah through all his prophets and seers: "Turn from your evil ways. Observe my commands and decrees, in accordance with the entire Law that I commanded your fathers to obey and that I delivered to you through my servants the prophets." But

> they would not listen and were as stiff-necked as their fathers, who did not trust in the LORD their God. ... They sacrificed their sons and daughters in the fire. They practiced divination and sorcery and sold themselves to do evil in the eyes of the LORD, provoking him to anger. So the LORD was very angry with Israel and removed them from his presence. (2 Kings 17:5–8, 13–14, 17–18)

So there you have it. Despite all of the warnings of God's prophets, the Israelites in the Northern Kingdom, generation after generation, fell further and further away from God. They worshipped the gods of the Canaanite people and adopted their ways: idolatry, witchcraft, sorcery, and yes, even child sacrifice. Therefore in the year 722 BC, God allowed the king of Assyria (the world power at the time) to invade, conquer, and carry away thousands of people from the ten northern tribes. Thus the Northern Kingdom came to a complete end. Those Israelites in the north who were carried away would never again return to their homeland, the Promised Land that God had given to their fathers.

As we turn our attention now to the Southern Kingdom, we will see that these "Judeans" would experience a similar, but thankfully not exactly the same, fate as that of the Northern Kingdom. This line of kings in the south, remember, was the descendants of David, and God had promised to preserve the house of David, and his throne, forever.

Whereas the Northern Kingdom had nineteen kings, all bad, the Southern Kingdom would have twenty kings, and eight of them would be either "mostly good" or "good," and two were even "great." I mean, of course, that these eight kings, to some lesser or greater degree, worshipped God and encouraged their people to do likewise. When these good kings reigned, God would bless Judah with prosperity and protection from her enemies.

When the bad kings reigned, however, they led the people away from God and into sin. Judah imitated "her sister" Israel by falling into the same error of idolatry. Through the prophet Jeremiah, God said, "'I gave faithless Israel her certificate of divorce and sent her away because of all her adulteries. Yet I saw that her unfaithful sister Judah had no fear; she also went out and committed adultery'" (Jer. 3:8). God is lamenting that, though they saw what had happened to the Northern Kingdom, the people of the Southern Kingdom did not learn from this. They also persisted in the sin of idolatry, which God calls "adultery."

The Words of the Prophets

I think we all would understand if God had just given up on these people. After all, for almost 700 years, ever since He had brought them out of Egypt, they had been stubborn and stiff-necked, and God had to repeatedly forgive them and put up with their rebellious ways. But instead of giving up on them, God sent them a series of prophets, to plead with them to repent and return to Him.

Again, looking at the diagram on page 108, you will notice in both kingdoms a column entitled "Prophet." For example, the five prophets that God sent to the Northern Kingdom were Elijah, Elisha, Jonah, Amos, and Hosea. Likewise, in the Southern Kingdom, beginning with Joel, God sent several prophets. The names of the prophets are placed adjacent to the kings to whom they were sent. God led most of these prophets to record their messages, and their exact words can be found in the books of the prophets at the end of the Old Testament.

Since both kingdoms were falling away from God, the primary message of all the prophets was repentance. They tirelessly pleaded with the people to repent and return to God. As proof that they were speaking the word of God, God often gave them the ability to work miracles. They called for droughts and famines, and then, when they saw repentance, called for rain. They brought down fire from Heaven, healed the sick, multiplied food, and raised the dead, all to get the attention of God's people and reawaken their faith in Him.

But in addition to the message of repentance, the prophets had another message; they spoke often of the coming of the Messiah, the son promised to David. The prophets said that "the Anointed One" would be coming soon, and He would bring to Earth the kingdom of God. To paraphrase their message, "Repent, O Israel, and get ready for the coming of the Messiah!"

Time prevents us from making a list of all the predictions that the prophets made of the coming son of David. Perhaps more than any of the other prophets, Isaiah "foresaw" the coming of "the Anointed One." What follows is one of Isaiah's Messianic prophecies:

> For to us a child is born, to us a son is given, and the government will be on his shoulders. And he will be called Wonderful Counselor, Mighty God, Everlasting Father, Prince of Peace. Of the increase of his government and peace there will be no end. He will reign on David's throne and over his kingdom, establishing and upholding it with justice and righteousness from that time on and forever. The zeal of the LORD Almighty will accomplish this. (Isa. 9:6–7)

When Isaiah spoke these words, all of the kings, from both kingdoms, had in one way or another failed God. Saul turned away from God. David committed adultery and murder. Solomon married foreign women and worshipped their idols. Jeroboam made golden calves, etc., etc., etc. Every king so far in Israel, because they were just sinners (like you and me), had, in some way, failed God. Their "shoulders" were just not big enough to carry the weight of God's kingdom.

But God gave Isaiah the ability to look 700 years into the future. And Isaiah saw that one would be coming to Israel who would not be a sinner. In fact, one of His titles would be "Mighty God," meaning that He will be God in human form. He will have big "shoulders," big enough to carry the government of God. And, unlike all the other kings, this coming King will not fail, and His kingdom will endure forever.

If you have a question about this lesson, or other questions about the Bible, please visit my website www.FredWoodwardBible.com. There you can obtain my contact information and we can communicate through email. I'll do my very best to answer your questions.

Lesson 12

The Babylonian Captivity

2 Kings 25, Daniel, Ezekiel, Esther

The last time we rode in our tour bus, it was to travel from the town of Shiloh to Jerusalem. We made that trip because we wanted to follow the movement of the Tabernacle. Somewhere around 1,000 BC, King David made Jerusalem the capital city of Israel and moved the Tabernacle there. In the last few lessons, we have had no need to move the bus, because we were able to learn about several centuries of Israel's history while staying right in "the holy city."

But now we're going to have to get back on the bus and travel to a faraway land called Babylon. The straight line distance from Jerusalem to Babylon is about 500 miles, but we can't go that way because it's desert. We'll have to take the same trade route that the ancient travelers took, up through Syria and then southeast following the Euphrates River, a total journey of about 900 miles. "Why," you may ask, "do we have to leave the Promised Land and go to Babylon?" Well, that's what I hope to explain to you in this lesson. I'll tell you the story on the way there.

ALL ABOARD.

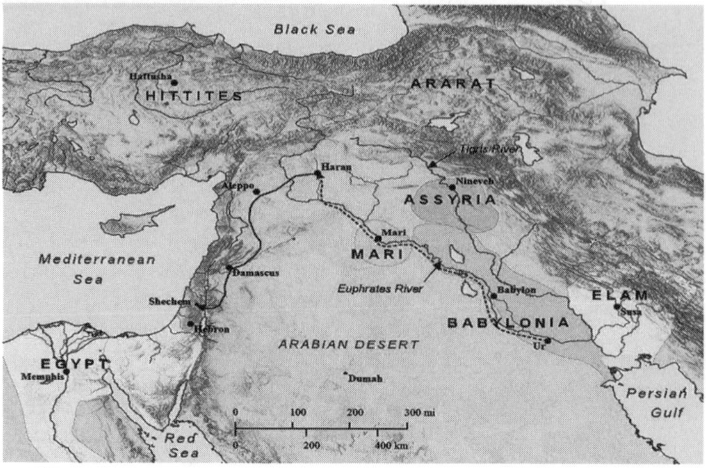

www.biblemapper.com

The Destruction of Jerusalem

In our last lesson we learned that, as a result of the idolatry that Solomon had introduced into Israel, God allowed a division to take place in what had been a united kingdom. Ten tribes in the northern region broke away from the house of David and (for this period) retained the name of "Israel." The two remaining tribes in the south together became known as "Judah." Because of the influence of nineteen bad kings, the Northern Kingdom fell very quickly into ever deeper levels of idolatry and sin. For nearly 200 years, God sent prophets to the ten northern tribes to call them back to God, but they would not listen. Because they refused to repent, God, in the year 722 BC, allowed the Assyrians to conquer and carry away captive the people of Israel. Thus the Northern Kingdom came to a complete end.

The Southern Kingdom, Judah, suffered a similar fate, only not quite as quickly. Because of the godly influence of a few good kings, destruction was often prevented and the life of the nation prolonged. Ultimately, however, Judah became just like "her sister," Israel, and also fell into idolatry and sin. And, like her sister, she refused to listen to the prophets that God sent to her. In the following passage, we learn what ultimately happened to the Southern Kingdom and the capital city of Jerusalem as a result of her rebellion against God:

> So in the ninth year of Zedekiah's reign, on the tenth day of the tenth month, Nebuchadnezzar king of Babylon marched against Jerusalem with his whole army. He encamped outside the city and built siege works all around it. The city was kept under siege until the eleventh year of King Zedekiah. By the ninth day of the [fourth] month the famine in the city had become so severe that there was no food for the people to eat. Then the city wall was broken through, and the whole army fled at night. (2 Kings 25:1–4)

As the above passage reveals, Nebuchadnezzar, king of Babylon (the new world power after Assyria), brought his army against Jerusalem and put the city under siege. Eventually, after about a year and a half, both the citizens of the city and its soldiers began to starve. When the Israeli soldiers fled for their lives, Jerusalem was left unprotected, and Babylon's army easily broke through the wall and took the city. About one month after this, even more destruction came.

> Nebuzaradan commander of the imperial guard, an official of the king of Babylon, came to Jerusalem. He set fire to the temple of the LORD, the royal palace and all the houses of Jerusalem. Every important building he burned down. The whole Babylonian army, under the commander of the imperial guard, broke down the walls around Jerusalem. (2 Kings 25:8–10)

As stated above, the Babylonian army broke down the walls of Jerusalem and burned the royal palace, all the houses of Jerusalem, and every important building. Worst of all, they set fire to the Temple of God, the dwelling place of God's glory. This destruction of Jerusalem took place in the year 586 BC, 136 years after the fall of the Northern Kingdom in 722 BC.

The Deportation of God's People

But the king of Babylon was not finished yet:

> the commander of the guard carried into exile the people who remained in the city, along with the rest of the populace and those who had gone over to the king of Babylon. But the commander left behind some of the poorest people of the land to work the vineyards and fields. ... So Judah went into captivity, away from her land. (2 Kings 25:11–12, 21)

Several hundred leading citizens of Judah were taken captive to Babylon. These were the wealthy, the aristocratic, and the educated people of Jerusalem and surrounding areas. Notice the Babylonian commander "left behind some of the poorest people of the land to work the vineyards and fields." This was a common tactic used in the ancient world to completely destroy a culture of people. First, conquer the nation, and then carry away captive all of the leading citizens and leave behind the poor. All of this came to pass because Judah "mocked God's messengers, despised his words and scoffed at his prophets until the wrath of the LORD was aroused against his people and there was no remedy" (2 Chron. 36:16).

The Different Plan for Judah

But something different must happen to the Southern Kingdom than what had happened to the Northern Kingdom. Because the ten northern tribes fell from God into idolatry, they were conquered and carried away captive by the Assyrians, never to return. Likewise, the Southern Kingdom, because they also fell from God into idolatry, was conquered and carried away captive by the Babylonians. But Judah must return!

Why must the Southern Kingdom (Judah) return to the Promised Land? Because of God's promise to David. God had promised David that his son would sit on the throne of the kingdom forever. Therefore to keep His promise, God must somehow preserve the tribe of Judah and the family of David until the coming of the promised "son of David," "the Anointed One," the "Messiah King." When He comes, He will reign throughout eternity.

So rather than allowing the Judeans to be destroyed, God had a plan to discipline them, much like a father would correct his children. Long before it happened, God revealed through the prophets what this discipline for Judah would be. Isaiah the prophet, for example, saw it coming at least 100 years before it happened. Speaking to King Hezekiah, Isaiah said, "'The time will surely come when everything in your palace, and all that your fathers have stored up until this day, will be carried off to Babylon. Nothing will be left, says the LORD'" (Isa. 39:6).

But Jeremiah the prophet was even more specific. "This whole country will become a desolate wasteland, and these nations will serve the king of Babylon seventy years" (Jer. 25:11). Isaiah predicted where Judah would be taken captive: Babylon. Jeremiah predicted how long they would be captives in Babylon: seventy years.

That, then, was the plan. God would allow Judah to be carried away captive to Babylon and remain there in exile for seventy years. God would not cast them off (as with the Northern Kingdom), but He would certainly correct them. This seventy-year "time out" was to have a tremendous effect on the Judeans. They would miss all of the goodness of the Promised Land and the God of their fathers. Being exiles in a strange land would cause them to seek their God. When the seventy years were over and they had learned their lesson about idolatry, God would allow them to return to the Promised Land. After the captivity, they would never again bow down to pagan idols. In this way, God preserved the tribe of Judah and fulfilled His promise to David.

The Devotion to God During the Captivity

It's been a long, hot trip since we left Jerusalem, but our tour bus has finally arrived in Babylon. After we get off the bus, we're going to spend a little time looking at a few of God's people and what became of them during the seventy years of exile. I think you're going to be amazed at what you see. God used this time in Babylon to raise up some men and women who had tremendous faith and devotion to God. In some cases, it was a devotion to God even unto death!

Let's start with Daniel.

> Then the king [Nebuchadnezzar] ordered Ashpenaz, chief of his court officials, to bring in some of the Israelites from the royal family and the nobility—young men without any physical defect, handsome, showing aptitude for every kind of learning, well informed, quick to understand, and qualified to serve in the king's palace. He was to teach them the language and literature of the Babylonians. The king assigned them a daily amount of food and wine from the king's table. They were to be trained for three years, and after that they were to enter the king's service. Among these were some from Judah: Daniel, Hananiah, Mishael and Azariah. (Dan. 1:3–6)

As the above passage indicates, Daniel and three of his friends were some of the first Judean captives to arrive in Babylon. To help him rule over the countries he had conquered, King Nebuchadnezzar liked having advisors in his court who had come from these foreign countries. So his policy was to secure bright young men and induct them into a three-year training program that would prepare them to serve in his court. Young Daniel and his three Israeli friends were chosen for this training.

Right away, Daniel's faith and devotion to God were put to the test. The king himself had "assigned them a daily amount of food and wine from the king's table" (Dan. 1:5). But this was a problem for Daniel and his friends because some of the food from the king's table was prohibited by the dietary laws that God had given through Moses. At this point, it would have been easy for Daniel to just compromise, not make waves, and go with the flow. "But Daniel resolved not to defile himself with the royal food and wine, and he asked the chief official for permission not to defile himself this way" (Dan. 1:8).

Daniel's devotion to his God created a problem for the chief official, who said to Daniel, "'I am afraid of my lord the king, who has assigned your food and drink. Why should he see you looking worse than the other young men your age? The king would then have my head because of you'" (Dan. 1:10). So Daniel made a deal with the chief administrator:

> "Please test your servants for ten days: Give us nothing but vegetables to eat and water to drink. Then compare our appearance with that of the young men who eat the royal food, and treat your servants in accordance with what you see." So he agreed to this and tested them for ten days. At the end of the ten days they looked healthier and better nourished than any of the young men who ate the royal food. So the guard took away their choice food and the wine they were to drink and gave them vegetables instead. (Dan. 1:12–16)

After the ten-day test period, when the chief administrator saw how healthy these four boys looked, he was persuaded to allow Daniel and his friends to eat only the food that agreed with the Law of Moses for the duration of the training period. The following passage tells us what happened at the end of the three years.

> At the end of the time set by the king to bring them in, the chief official presented them to Nebuchadnezzar. The king talked with them, and he found none equal to Daniel, Hananiah, Mishael and Azariah; so they entered the king's service. In every matter of wisdom and understanding about which the king questioned them, he found them ten times better than all the magicians and enchanters in his whole kingdom. (Dan. 1:18–20)

Thus, because of their faith and devotion to God, these four boys were greatly blessed. Let me point out to you that when the king questioned them, they not only had more wisdom and understanding than their fellow trainees, they were "*ten times better than all the magicians and enchanters in his whole kingdom.*"

This initial story in Daniel sets the tone for the rest of the book.

Time and time again, the faith of Daniel and his three friends would be severely tested. But because of their deep devotion to God, He always delivered them. In Chapter 3, for example, for refusing to bow to the king's golden idol, Shadrach, Meshach, and Abednego were thrown alive into a fiery furnace. But God sent an angel to be with them and protect them from the flames. When they emerged from the furnace, the king, along with several governors and royal advisors, "saw that the fire had not harmed their bodies, nor was a hair of their heads singed; their robes were not scorched, and there was no smell of fire on them" (Dan. 3:27).

And of course there is the famous story of Daniel in the lion's den. In Chapter 6, under threat of being thrown to lions, Daniel was ordered to stop praying to his God. Did Daniel "cave," or compromise his faith? No, instead, "he went home to his upstairs room where the windows opened toward Jerusalem. Three times a day he got down on his knees and prayed, giving thanks to his God, just as he had done before" (Dan. 6:10). As warned, for praying to his God, Daniel was thrown into a lion's den and spent the night with a pride of hungry lions. But God honored Daniel's faith by sending yet another angel who "'shut the mouths of the lions'" (Dan. 6:22) and delivered Daniel from a horrific death.

Another Israelite who was taken captive to Babylon was the prophet Ezekiel. His assignment from God was to prophesy to his fellow captives, making it very clear to them that God had allowed this captivity because of their stubborn refusal to turn away from idolatry. Through Ezekiel, forty-two times God made the statement, "'And you will know that I am the LORD'" (Ezek. 6:7 is the first time). God wanted there to be no doubt that this seventy-year period in Babylon was to discipline them for their unfaithfulness to Him.

Ezekiel's assignment was not easy. Many of the Israelites were still rebellious and unrepentant. God commanded Ezekiel, however, to remain strong and courageous:

> "And you, son of man, do not be afraid of them or their words. Do not be afraid, though briers and thorns are all around you and you live among scorpions. Do not be afraid of what they say or terrified by them, though

> they are a rebellious house. You must speak my words to them, whether they listen or fail to listen, for they are rebellious." (Ezek. 2:6–7)

Throughout the rest of his life, all of which was spent in Babylon, Ezekiel never wavered. He remained true to his calling from God. So as not to leave you ladies out, let's also take a brief look at Esther. Esther's family was also among the Jewish families taken to Babylon. In fact, the first time the word "Jew" is used in the Bible is in Esther 2:5. It was during this period of exile that the Gentile world began referring to the children of Israel as "the Jews."

When we come to the time of Esther, there had been a shift in world power. The great kingdom of Babylon had fallen to the Persians. Because of her great poise and beauty, Esther was chosen to become the wife of the Persian king, Ahasuerus. Thus a captive became a queen! Her position as queen, of course, gave her great access to the king.

As the story unfolds, a wicked man named Haman, who had an intense hatred for all Jews (but not knowing that Esther was a Jew), devised a plan to exterminate all Jews in the kingdom. (I seem to remember another man, named Hitler, who had a similar plan.) Haman intended to send out murderous thugs throughout the whole realm "to destroy, kill and annihilate all the Jews—young and old, women and little children—on a single day, the thirteenth day of the twelfth month, the month of Adar, and to plunder their goods" (Esther 3:13).

When Esther learned about the plot against her people, she was, of course, distressed. But even though she was the queen, she could not approach the king uninvited. Anyone who dared to approach the king without his invitation could, at his whim, be executed. But Esther, with tremendous faith and courage, "put on her royal robes and stood in the inner court of the palace, in front of the king's hall" (Esther 5:1). When the king saw her standing in his court, instead of being angry at her, he "was pleased with her and held out to her the gold scepter that was in his hand. So Esther approached and touched the tip of the scepter" (Esther 5:2).

Esther went on to tell the king of Haman's wicked plot. The king then, enraged at Haman, had him hanged on a seventy-five-foot set of gallows. His wicked plot was thus prevented. To this day, once a year, Jewish people around the world celebrate the Feast of Purim to remember the story of Esther and how God used her to deliver the Jews.

Thus, by looking at Daniel, Ezekiel, and Esther, we see that God had certainly not given up on His people. During the seventy years of captivity, He did a mighty work in their hearts. He cured them of their craving for idols. He caused them to sincerely repent and return to Him. He raised up men and women of tremendous faith and devotion. And, most important, He prepared the children of Israel to go back home, to rebuild their blessed Promised Land.

We'll spend the night here in Babylon. I have rooms reserved at The Babylonian Bed and Breakfast. In our next lesson, we'll get on our bus and go with the children of Israel, back home, to the Promised Land.

If you have a question about this lesson, or other questions about the Bible, please visit my website www.FredWoodwardBible.com. There you can obtain my contact information and we can communicate through email. I'll do my very best to answer your questions.

Lesson 13

The Return from Captivity

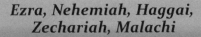

Ezra, Nehemiah, Haggai, Zechariah, Malachi

I'm going to have to ask you to do something that you probably won't want to do. Please get back on the bus. "But," you protest, "it took two, long, hot days on the bus to get here from Jerusalem. And now that we're finally here in Babylon, we're going to turn right around and go back to Jerusalem? Why?" Because we've seen all the important sights in Babylon that we need to see.

We've seen how God used this seventy-year period of captivity to discipline the children of Israel. Here in Babylon, God brought them to repentance. He cured them of their craving for idols and created in their souls a hunger and thirst for His Spirit. Now they would be ready to return home, to rebuild their blessed Promised Land.

In the Bible, the number seven (or a multiple of seven) always signifies God's perfection or completion. Therefore, during the seventy years in Babylon, God did a perfect and complete work in their hearts. Since God was done here in Babylon, so are we. With all apologies for your aching back, please get back on the bus.

The Proclamation of King Cyrus

> In the first year of Cyrus king of Persia, in order to fulfill the word of the LORD spoken by Jeremiah, the LORD

> moved the heart of Cyrus king of Persia to make a proclamation throughout his realm and to put it in writing. (Ezra 1:1)

Nearly twenty years before it happened, the prophet Jeremiah had predicted that Judah, the Southern Kingdom, would be taken captive to Babylon and after seventy years would be set free to return home. In the above passage, the seventy years are over, and Ezra is telling us how they were officially released from captivity and even encouraged to return to Jerusalem. God "*moved the heart*" of the most powerful man in the world at the time to issue a worldwide proclamation. Below is the proclamation of Cyrus, king of Persia:

> This is what Cyrus king of Persia says: "The LORD, the God of heaven, has given me all the kingdoms of the earth and he has appointed me to build a temple for him at Jerusalem in Judah. Anyone of his people among you—may his God be with him, and let him go up to Jerusalem in Judah and build the temple of the LORD, the God of Israel, the God who is in Jerusalem. And the people of any place where survivors may now be living are to provide him with silver and gold, with goods and livestock, and with freewill offerings for the temple of God in Jerusalem." (Ezra 1:2–4)

You may recall the magnificent Temple that Solomon had built, which was destroyed when the Babylonians conquered Jerusalem. Now Cyrus, a Gentile (non-Jew) king, is claiming that God has appointed *him* to build a temple in Jerusalem to replace the one that had been destroyed. He further encouraged all Jews in the realm to return to Jerusalem, and those who chose to stay were encouraged to provide money and material resources for those who chose to return. Thus God allowed a Gentile king (Nebuchadnezzar) to destroy the Temple. Now, seventy years later, God is ordering a Gentile king (Cyrus) to build the Temple.

Many Israelites were anxious to go home. "Then the family heads of Judah and Benjamin, and the priests and Levites—everyone whose heart God had moved—prepared to go up and build the house of the LORD in Jerusalem" (Ezra 1:5). It's estimated that at this time about 50,000 Jews, "*whose heart God had moved*," decided to return to their homeland.

The Restoration of Spiritual Duties

As our bus enters the city of Jerusalem (see, that bus trip wasn't so bad), let's pretend it's somewhere around 538 BC. Let's try to imagine what the Israelites saw as they returned to the city. The Babylonian army, remember, had completely destroyed Jerusalem. So the first thing they would have noticed would have been the condition of the surrounding wall. In many places, the wall had been completely torn down, while other sections had been left standing. Jerusalem, therefore, was completely defenseless.

As they continued making their way into the heart of the city, they were probably shocked to see that all the houses had been broken down and burned. There was debris everywhere. Finally, as they approached the area where the Temple had been, no doubt they wept. The glorious Temple of Solomon was gone. In the place where it used to stand there were broken stones, burned wood, and ashes. This is where we will park our bus, in the place where the Temple of Solomon used to be.

With Jerusalem in this terrible state, the returning captives probably asked themselves, "Where do we begin? Our country, our capital city, and our culture have all been destroyed. We want to rebuild our nation, but where do we start?" With the encouragement of the priests and the Levites, they began with the restoration of their spiritual duties to God. They had been taken to Babylon because they had forsaken God. The first thing to do, then, was to restore their relationship with Him. Sound wisdom for any nation!

The ultimate plan, of course, was to build another Temple to replace the one Solomon had built. Then they would be able to worship God according to all the laws given by Moses. But that was going to be a big project that would take a long time. So in the meantime they built a temporary altar to offer sacrifices to God, as the passage indicates:

> Then Jeshua son of Jozadak and his fellow priests and Zerubbabel son of Shealtiel and his associates began to build the altar of the God of Israel to sacrifice burnt offerings on it, in accordance with what is written in the Law of Moses the man of God. ... Then in accordance with what is written, they celebrated the Feast of Tabernacles with the required number of burnt offerings prescribed for each day. After that, they presented the regular burnt offerings, the New Moon sacrifices and the sacrifices for all the appointed sacred feasts of the LORD, as well as those brought as freewill offerings to the LORD. ... though the foundation of the LORD's temple had not yet been laid. (Ezra 3:2, 4–6)

This altar would suffice as a temporary place of worship until the official temple could be built. Seven months later, they began the work of building the Temple. They used the money that their fellow Jews in Babylon had given them to "bring cedar logs by sea from Lebanon to Joppa, as authorized by Cyrus king of Persia" (Ezra 3:7). On the day that they laid the foundation of the Temple, the priests put on their vestments and called for a celebration. "With trumpets and cymbals they worshipped the LORD. With praise and thanksgiving they sang to the LORD: 'He is good; his love to Israel endures forever.' And all the people gave a great shout of praise to the LORD, because the foundation of the house of the LORD was laid" (Ezra 3:10–11).

The Opposition of the Surrounding Nations

But not everybody was happy about the building of the Temple in Jerusalem, and I'm sure you can guess who that was. Yes, our old archenemy, the adversary of the ages, Satan. The devil will never allow any work of God to go unchallenged. He is particularly opposed to the building of a temple where all men can find and worship the true God. So, using evil men, Satan set out to stop the work, as the following passage indicates.

> When the enemies of Judah and Benjamin heard that the exiles were building a temple for the LORD, the God of Israel, they came to Zerubbabel and to the heads of the families and said, "Let us help you build because, like you, we seek your God. ..." (Ezra 4:1–2)

At first, these enemies attempted to interrupt the work by infiltration. They pretended that they wanted to "help" the Jews build the temple. What they really wanted to do was pollute God's temple by bringing into it their own pagan forms of worship. It's worth noting how the Jewish leadership responded to this offer: "'You have no part with us in building a temple to our God. We alone will build it for the LORD, the God of Israel, as King Cyrus, the king of Persia, commanded us'" (Ezra 4:3). Here we notice what effect the Babylonian Captivity had on the Jews. Before the captivity, they were all too happy to be "unequally yoked" with foreigners and to incorporate all forms of idol worship. Now, after the captivity, we notice that the returning Jews were resolved to keep the Temple pure and free from pagan influences. God knows how to discipline His children.

When the attempt to infiltrate the work failed, the enemies of the Jews

> set out to discourage the people of Judah and make them afraid to go on building. They hired counselors to work against them and frustrate their plans during the entire reign of Cyrus king of Persia and down to the reign of Darius king of Persia. Thus the work on the house of God in Jerusalem came to a standstill until the second year of the reign of Darius king of Persia. (Ezra 4:4–5; 24)

Satan was temporarily successful. For about fifteen years, no further work was done on the Temple.

The Exhortation of Two Prophets

But as we have seen so many times already, when Israel falls, God finds a way to raise them back up. In this instance, God spoke through two prophets to inspire the people to resume building the Temple, Haggai and Zechariah. Both of these men wrote down their words and we have their books in the Old Testament. Below is a small sampling from Haggai.

> Then the word of the LORD came through the prophet Haggai: "Is it a time for you yourselves to be living in your paneled houses, while this house remains a ruin?" ... Go up into the mountains and bring down timber and build the house, so that I may take pleasure in it and be honored," says the LORD. "You expected much, but see, it turned out to be little. What you brought home, I blew away. Why?" declares the LORD Almighty. "Because of my house, which remains a ruin, while each of you is busy with his own house. Therefore, because of you the heavens have withheld their dew and the earth its crops. I called for a drought on the fields and the mountains, on the grain, the new wine, the oil and whatever the ground produces, on men and cattle, and on the labor of your hands." (Hag. 1:3–4, 8–11)

God was displeased with His people because while they were already living in "*paneled houses*," God's house was still in ruins. To show his displeasure, God had called for a drought on the land and upon the work of their hands.

God used Haggai's message to stir up "the spirit of the whole remnant of the people. They came and began to work on the house of the LORD Almighty, their God, on the twenty-fourth day of the sixth month in the second year of King Darius" (Hag. 1:14–15). Thus the building of the Temple resumed. About six years later, the work was done. The house of the living God was again standing in the holy city, and once again, the world was invited to come to Jerusalem and worship Him.

The Reconstruction of the Wall

With the Temple built, the Jews could now worship God in accordance with the laws of Moses. But the walls of the city were still in shambles and Jerusalem was still completely vulnerable to enemy attack. This brings us to the book and the story of Nehemiah. Nehemiah's family was among those taken captive to Babylon. While in this region, Nehemiah (like Daniel and Esther) had risen to a place of prominence. He was the "cupbearer" to the then-ruling king of Persia, Artaxerxes, which made Nehemiah a trusted and important official. He begins telling us his story in the following verses:

> Hanani, one of my brothers, came from Judah with some other men, and I questioned them about the Jewish remnant that survived the exile, and also about Jerusalem. They said to me, "Those who survived the exile and are back in the province are in great trouble and disgrace. The wall of Jerusalem is broken down, and its gates have been burned with fire." (Neh. 1:2–3)

Having come from Judah, Hanani, Nehemiah's brother, gave him a report of the sorry state of Jerusalem. After hearing this sad news, Nehemiah said, "When I heard these things, I sat down and wept. For some days I mourned and fasted and prayed before the God of heaven" (Neh. 1:4). Nehemiah was heartbroken over the condition of Jerusalem and his fellow Jews who lived there. He was so heartbroken, in fact, that he went into an extended period of prayer and fasting to seek the help of God.

His prayer was answered when one day King Artaxerxes saw the sadness on Nehemiah's face. The king said to him, "'Why does your face look so sad when you are not ill? This can be nothing but sadness of heart'" (Neh. 2:2). This was the open door for Nehemiah to share with the king his concern for Jerusalem. "'May the king live forever! Why should my face not look sad when the city where my fathers are buried lies in ruins, and its gates have been destroyed by fire?'" (Neh. 2:3). To which the king responded, "'What is it you want?'" (Neh. 2:4).

Having received this blank check from the king, Nehemiah went on to request that he be allowed to take time off from his duties in order to return to Jerusalem and rebuild the wall. Further, he requested that the king sign official letters that he could carry with him to Jerusalem, authorizing him to take charge of the work once he arrived there. Nehemiah tells us that "because the gracious hand of my God was upon me, the king granted my requests" (Neh. 2:8). Now we see why God had led Nehemiah to hold such a high position in this Gentile kingdom. He was God's man of the hour to rebuild the walls of Jerusalem.

Nehemiah goes on to tell us that when he arrived in Jerusalem, he was able to inspire his fellow Jews to rise up and rebuild the wall. "I also told them about the gracious hand of my God upon me and what the king had said to me. They replied, 'Let us start rebuilding.' So they began this good work" (Neh. 2:18). Being thus motivated and led by Nehemiah, the Jews of Jerusalem rallied together and rebuilt the wall in an amazingly short period of fifty-two days.

The Reformation of the People

After the Temple was built and the work on the wall completed, Ezra and Nehemiah worked together to bring about a much-needed spiritual and moral reformation of the people. For most of the people, it had been a very long time since they had listened to the Law of Moses. Now, after the captivity, they were hungry to hear God's word.

> They told Ezra the scribe to bring out the Book of the Law of Moses, which the LORD had commanded for Israel. So on the first day of the seventh month Ezra the priest brought the Law before the assembly, which was made up of men and women and all who were able to understand. He read it aloud from daybreak till noon as he faced the square before the Water Gate in the presence of the men, women and others who could understand. And all the people listened attentively to the Book of the Law. (Neh. 8:1–3)

As Ezra was reading the Book of the Law, "the Levites ... instructed the people in the Law while the people were standing there ... so that the people could understand what was being read" (Neh. 8:7–8). After the people heard the words of God, the Levites had to comfort them, and tell them not to weep, "for all the people had been weeping as they listened to the words of the Law" (Neh. 8:9). Thus we see the effect that God's word had on this crowd. They came under conviction and guilt for their sins and sincerely repented. God forgave their sins and wanted them to be comforted. A true revival and spiritual reformation had taken place in Jerusalem.

The Prediction of the Last Prophet

About 100 years after the Jews had returned from Babylon, after the Temple had been built and the wall rebuilt, God found it necessary to raise up one last Old Testament prophet, Malachi. Another prophet was necessary because, by this time, the Israelites had (again) begun to fall back into some of their old familiar sins. The priests had become lax and derelict in their duties at the Temple and were offering inferior animal sacrifices. The people had (again) become apathetic about worshipping at the House of God. They were disobeying God's commandment to tithe (give a tenth) of their income to God. They were divorcing their wives to marry pagan women. God sent Malachi to rebuke the people for these sins and urge them to repent.

I would especially like us to look at the last two verses of Malachi's message, which also happen to be the last two verses of the Old Testament:

> "See, I will send you the prophet Elijah before that great and dreadful day of the LORD comes. He will turn the hearts of the fathers to their children, and the hearts of the children to their fathers." (Mal. 4:5–6)

This prophecy is a mystery. God promised that, before the coming of God (Messiah), He would first send "*Elijah*," who would preach a message of repentance to "*turn the hearts*" of the children of

Israel. This message of repentance was to prepare the way for the coming *"day of the LORD."* But how could this be? When Malachi spoke this prophecy, Elijah had finished his ministry and gone to Heaven nearly 450 years earlier! I guess we'll just have to wait until we get to the New Testament to understand this prophecy of Elijah.

Believe it or not, dear friends, we have come to the end of our tour of the Old Testament. At this point in time, Israel is not the nation it could have been. With God's blessing, Israel could have been the most powerful and prosperous nation on earth, as we saw in the glory days of Solomon. Instead, because of their stubbornness and lack of faith, they became a powerless and impoverished little country, struggling just to survive. But, because of the faithfulness of God, they did survive. And from this struggling little nation, the Savior of the world was yet to come.

We have traveled through about 3,600 years of history. If I were to ask you to describe the tour so far, you would probably say, "It's been a religious roller coaster," and you would be right. The unfolding story of God and Man is filled with ups and downs. As we have seen countless times, when man trusts in God, he is lifted up to heights of glory. But when man turns from God, he falls into depravity, despair, and destruction.

But, dear friends, the tour's not over yet. In fact, we're just now getting to the good part! We are headed for the New Testament. In the New Testament, God, the Creator of all things, will create and make available to the whole world a new medicine, a medicine that will cure everything that is wrong with man. You don't want to miss that!

So one more time (pretty please with sugar on it) get back on the bus. This next trip will only take a couple of hours. We are going to leave Jerusalem and head to the northern region of Israel, where we will stop and park our bus in a little town called Nazareth.

If you have a question about this lesson, or other questions about the Bible, please visit my website www.FredWoodwardBible.com. There you can obtain my contact information and we can communicate through email. I'll do my very best to answer your questions.

Lesson 14

Jesus: From Birth to Age Thirty

Matthew, Mark, Luke, John

The Intertestamental Period

From the last book of the Old Testament, Malachi, to the first book of the New Testament, Matthew, there was a silent period of 400 years. By silent, I don't mean to say that God abandoned Israel in any way. He remained ever-faithful to His people as they struggled to survive as a nation. But during this 400-year period, no more prophets were sent from God. Malachi's inspired words were the last words that Israel would hear from God until the New Testament.

The 66 Books of the Bible

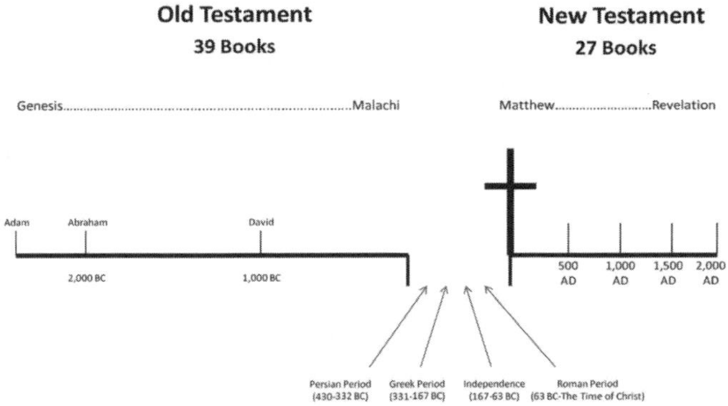

As the previous time line indicates, between the Old and New Testaments, Israel was tossed to and fro with the rise and fall of various world powers. First it was the Persians, then the Greeks, a period of independence, and then the Romans. This explains why we read about so many Roman governors and Roman soldiers in the New Testament. Israel (and the entire world) was under Roman domination and occupation when the events of the New Testament took place.

The Introduction to the New Testament

As we toured the Old Testament, I'm sure you remember the many times I pointed out to you the pictures, the poems (psalms), and the prophecies of the coming Messiah. And I kept promising that these would all be fulfilled when we came to the New Testament. Well, dear friends, we are here! As I hope to show you, the New Testament, from beginning to end, has one main goal: to give an accurate account of the person and work of Jesus, the Messiah.

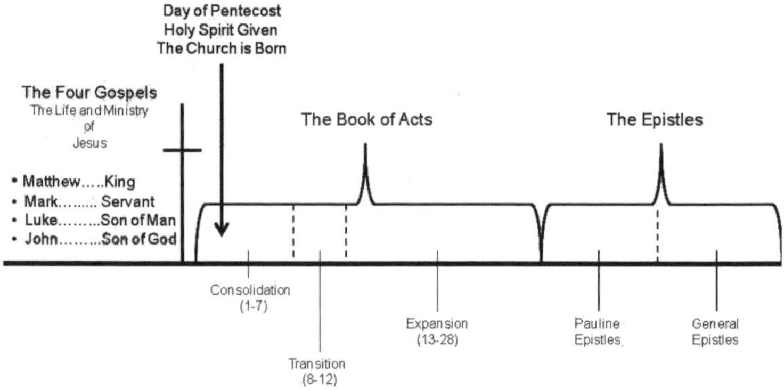

As we see in the above illustration, the New Testament can be divided into three major sections: the four Gospels, the book of Acts, and the Epistles. The word "epistle" simply means "letter." This last section is further divided into the Pauline letters and the General letters. You will probably be happy to hear that the New Testament is much shorter than the Old Testament.

Whereas the Old Testament covered approximately 3,600 years of history, all of the events of the New Testament occurred and were recorded in fewer than 100 years. We'll start our tour of the New Testament with the first section, the four Gospels.

The first four books of the New Testament are called the *Gospels*. These inspired books give us an accurate account of the life and ministry of Jesus. Though these Gospels all tell the same basic story, they each tell it from a different perspective, with different details. Also, each Gospel has its own theme. For example, Matthew stresses that Jesus is the King, while Mark shows that Jesus is also a Servant. Luke wants us to know that Jesus was a real human being, so he will often use the term "Son of Man." But John reveals that Jesus is not only human, He is also divine. Jesus is not just a man; He is also the Son of God.

It's much like what happens when four eyewitnesses view the same event. Each witness sees the event from a different point of view and can provide his/her own information. Their accounts do not conflict with each other; they complement each other. So it is with the four Gospels. By letting us view Jesus from four vantage points, we are given a fuller, more complete picture of Him. But the authors of the Gospels do not want us to just know about Jesus; they want us to come to know Jesus, so that we might have a personal relationship with Him, by faith. John, the author of the fourth Gospel, tells us that he has written his account of Jesus "that you may believe that Jesus is the Christ, the Son of God, and that by believing you may have life in his name" (John 20:31).

The Incarnation

At the end of our last lesson, I mentioned that we would have to get on our bus, leave Jerusalem, and travel a short distance north to the little town of Nazareth. That's because the story of Jesus begins with a couple in Nazareth who were betrothed (engaged) to be married. They both were descendants of King David, and they both were given an assignment from God that would require great faith. Their names, of course, were Joseph and Mary.

Luke tells us that Mary was the first to hear about the (almost unbelievable) miracle that was about to happen in her life. God sent the archangel, Gabriel, to Mary with these words:

> "Do not be afraid, Mary, you have found favor with God. You will be with child and give birth to a son, and you are to give him the name Jesus. He will be great and will be called the Son of the Most High. The Lord God will give him the throne of his father David, and he will reign over the house of Jacob forever; his kingdom will never end." (Luke 1:30–33)

To paraphrase Gabriel's words, "Mary, you will become the mother of the Messiah!" Mary, quite naturally, asked Gabriel how this could be possible, "'since I am a virgin?'" (Luke 1:34). Gabriel answered, "'The Holy Spirit will come upon you, and the power of the Most High will overshadow you. So the holy one to be born will be called the Son of God'" (Luke 1:35). With incredible faith, Mary responded, "'I am the Lord's servant. ... May it be to me as you have said'" (Luke 1:38).

But when Mary actually became pregnant, Joseph, her betrothed husband, was quite naturally distressed. He could only conclude that Mary, even before the official marriage ceremony, had cheated on him and was pregnant by some other man. Joseph, not wanting to expose Mary to public disgrace, decided to quietly call off the wedding.

> But after he had considered this, an angel of the Lord appeared to him in a dream and said, "Joseph son of David, do not be afraid to take Mary home as your wife, because what is conceived in her is from the Holy Spirit. She will give birth to a son, and you are to give him the name Jesus, because he will save his people from their sins." (Matt. 1:20–21)

After hearing this explanation from the angel (we assume Gabriel), Joseph, with incredible faith, "did what the angel of the Lord had commanded him and took Mary home as his wife. But he had no union with her until she gave birth to a son. And he gave him the name Jesus" (Matt. 1:24–25).

Matthew, quoting Isaiah 7:14, reminds us that this unique birth of Jesus was not an accident. Somewhere around 740 BC, Isaiah the prophet had spoken of it: "'The virgin will be with child and will give birth to a son, and they will call him Immanuel—which means, God with us'" (Matt. 1:23).

Thus, Jesus, the Son of God, through this miraculous virgin birth, "took on" a human body and human nature. Bible scholars refer to this act of "taking on flesh" as the incarnation. Joseph and Mary had the faith to believe it could happen. I strongly encourage you, dear friends, to have the faith to believe that it did happen.

The Infancy of Jesus

Because Matthew and Luke give us different details, we can go back and forth between these two Gospels and piece together the story of Jesus' infancy. Luke tells us that toward the end of Mary's pregnancy, the Roman emperor Caesar Augustus gave orders for a worldwide census. Though Joseph and Mary lived in the northern town of Nazareth, they were required to register in Joseph's home town of Bethlehem, "the town of David, because he belonged to the house and line of David" (Luke 2:4). This would have been a trip of about ninety miles and would have taken Joseph and pregnant Mary about a week.

This brings us to the well-known Christmas story of Jesus' birth in Bethlehem: "While they were there, the time came for the baby to be born, and she gave birth to her firstborn, a son. She wrapped him in cloths and placed him in a manger, because there was no room for them in the inn" (Luke 2:6–7). Matthew, quoting from Micah 5:2, wants us to know that Jesus' birth in Bethlehem was itself a fulfillment of prophecy. Micah had said, "'But you, Bethlehem, in the land of Judah, are by no means least among the rulers of Judah; for out of you will come a ruler who will be the shepherd of my people Israel'" (Matt. 2:6). That night, when Jesus was born, Luke tells us that a great company of angels appeared to a group of shepherds keeping their flocks in the hills near Bethlehem. The angelic choir sang: "'Glory to God in the highest, and on earth peace to men on whom his favor rests'" (Luke 2:14).

On the eighth day after His birth, the baby Jesus was circumcised, just as His ancestor Abraham had been nearly 2,000 years earlier. On the fortieth day after His birth, according to the Law of Moses, Joseph and Mary brought Him to the Temple in Jerusalem to be presented to God. Again, obeying the Law of Moses, they offered a pair of doves as a sacrifice, which was the usual offering of poor people.

While Joseph, Mary, and Baby Jesus were performing these prescribed ceremonies at the Temple, they encountered two elderly people who were not there by accident: a man named Simeon and a woman named Anna. They may have been senior citizens, but they were Spirit-filled senior citizens. The Holy Spirit had revealed to Simeon that before he died he would be allowed to see God's Messiah. And so it came to pass.

> Moved by the Spirit, he [Simeon] went into the temple courts. When the parents brought in the child Jesus to do for him what the custom of the Law required, Simeon took him in his arms and praised God, saying: "Sovereign Lord, as you have promised, you now dismiss your servant in peace. For my eyes have seen your salvation, which you have prepared in the sight of all people, a light for revelation to the Gentiles and for glory to your people Israel." (Luke 2:27–32)

Likewise, Anna was an eighty-four-year-old prophetess who

> never left the temple but worshiped night and day, fasting and praying. Coming up to them at that very moment, she gave thanks to God and spoke about the child to all who were looking forward to the redemption of Jerusalem. (Luke 2:37–38)

Obviously, the Holy Spirit had led these two godly people to be at the right place at the right time. They were there to confirm to Joseph and Mary, and those who happened to be at the Temple, that this child was indeed Israel's promised Messiah. And of course, Matthew would not have us miss the famous visit of the Magi (also known as "the wise men") from the east.

> After Jesus was born in Bethlehem in Judea, during the time of King Herod, Magi from the east came to Jerusalem and asked, "Where is the one who has been born king of the Jews? We saw his star in the east and have come to worship him." (Matt. 2:1–2)

Many Bible scholars believe that these Magi had come from Babylon and were possibly remnants of the royal advisory group that Daniel had been a part of during the captivity. If so, they may have first learned of the coming Messiah from Daniel's prophecies, which he had written hundreds of years earlier. Then, at the right time, God revealed to them "*his star in the east.*" After the guiding star led them to the house where the holy child was, "they bowed down and worshiped him. Then they opened their treasures and presented him with gifts of gold and of incense and of myrrh" (Matt. 2:11). These were gifts, of course, that were fit for a king.

But not everyone was happy about the birth of the king of the Jews. That would be, of course, our old familiar foe, Satan. We've already seen many times how the devil works through wicked men to accomplish his evil purposes. This time, Satan used the wicked King Herod of Jerusalem.

When Herod heard the news of a newborn king, he was irate. He viewed this as a threat to his throne. To eliminate this threat, Herod sent a company of soldiers to Bethlehem and the surrounding area with orders to kill every newborn male child. But, thanks be to God,

> an angel of the Lord appeared to Joseph in a dream. "Get up," he said, "take the child and his mother and escape to Egypt. Stay there until I tell you, for Herod is going to search for the child to kill him." So he got up, took the child and his mother during the night and left for Egypt, where he stayed until the death of Herod. (Matt. 2:13–15)

Matthew, to let us know that this escape to Egypt was also a fulfillment of Old Testament prophecy, quotes from Hosea 11:1: "And so was fulfilled what the Lord had said through the prophet: 'Out of Egypt I called my son'" (Matt. 2:15).

So the baby Jesus was rescued from Herod's wrath. Many other baby boys, however, were not spared. We don't know the exact number, but many mothers were left weeping and grief-stricken after the soldiers had carried out their unthinkable orders. This event is sometimes referred to as "The Slaughter of the Innocents" and, according to Matthew, it too was a fulfillment of Old Testament prophecy: "Then what was said through the prophet Jeremiah was fulfilled: 'A voice is heard in Ramah, weeping and great mourning, Rachel weeping for her children and refusing to be comforted, because they are no more'" (Matt. 2:17–18).

When King Herod was dead, Joseph was instructed by an angel: "'Get up, take the child and his mother and go to the land of Israel, for those who were trying to take the child's life are dead'" (Matt. 2:20). But when Joseph and his little family arrived back in Judea, he discovered that it was still not safe to live in that region because Herod's son was now on the throne. One final time, Joseph was warned in a dream to leave the Bethlehem area and go back up north to Nazareth, where he and Mary had first met.

This explains why Jesus, though born in Bethlehem, would grow up in Nazareth. Matthew would have us know that this, too, was not an accident: "And he went and lived in a town called Nazareth. So was fulfilled what was said through the prophets: 'He will be called a Nazarene'" (Matt. 2:23).

The following is a list of what one might refer to as the spiritual, supernatural, or Heavenly things that took place before, during, and immediately after Jesus' birth.

Angelic Visit to Mary (Luke)
Angelic Visit to Joseph (Matthew)
Isaiah's Prophecy of the "Virgin Birth" Fulfilled (Matthew)

Micah's Prophecy of "Messiah's Birth in Bethlehem" Fulfilled (Matthew)
Angelic Visit to Shepherds (Luke)
Prophecies from the Holy Spirit by Simeon and Anna (Luke)
Star-Guided Visit of Magi (Matthew)
Angelic Order to Escape to Egypt (Matthew)
Jeremiah's Prophecy of the "Slaughter of the Innocents" Fulfilled (Matthew)
Angelic Order to Go Back to Israel (Matthew)
Hosea's Prophecy That "Out of Egypt I Have Called My Son" Fulfilled (Matthew)
Joseph Warned in a Dream to Move to Nazareth (Matthew)
Isaiah's Prophecy That "Messiah Would Be Called a Nazarene" Fulfilled (Matthew)

Now I'm not a historian, but I'm pretty sure you cannot find any baby in all of earth's history that ever received so much "Heavenly" attention. No doubt it's because Jesus came from Heaven and is the most important Person to ever walk the earth.

The Incident at the Temple

We have only one story that tells us what Jesus was like as a child. It happened when Jesus was twelve years old and is recorded for us in the Gospel of Luke.

> Every year his parents went to Jerusalem for the Feast of the Passover. When he was twelve years old, they went up to the Feast, according to the custom. After the Feast was over, while his parents were returning home, the boy Jesus stayed behind in Jerusalem, but they were unaware of it. Thinking he was in their company, they traveled on for a day. Then they began looking for him among their relatives and friends. When they did not find him, they

> went back to Jerusalem to look for him. (Luke 2:41–45)

As did all devout Jewish families, Jesus' family faithfully attended the yearly Feast of the Passover. They probably made this pilgrimage from Nazareth to Jerusalem as one big extended clan, which included fathers, mothers, brothers, sisters, aunts, uncles, cousins, etc. One week later, after Passover Week was finished, no doubt they returned to Nazareth the same way, as one big happy family.

After walking for one day on the way back to Nazareth, Joseph and Mary discovered that Jesus was missing. They had assumed that He had been walking safely with relatives, but when they looked for Him, He was nowhere to be found. (If you've ever seen the movie *Home Alone* then you know how Mary must have reacted...JESUS!!!) Returning to Jerusalem, they searched for Jesus for three days.

> After three days they found him in the temple courts, sitting among the teachers, listening to them and asking them questions. Everyone who heard him was amazed at his understanding and his answers. When his parents saw him, they were astonished. His mother said to him, "Son, why have you treated us like this? Your father and I have been anxiously searching for you." (Luke 2:46–48)

To which Jesus replied (these, by the way, are the first recorded words of Jesus), "'Why were you searching for me? ... Didn't you know I had to be in my Father's house?'" (Luke 2:49). Mary and Joseph, however, "did not understand what he was saying to them" (Luke 2:50).

His parents did not understand what He meant by "*my Father's house*." Joseph was a carpenter. If Jesus wanted to be in his "*father's house*," he should have been in Joseph's workshop back in Nazareth, not in the Temple of Jerusalem. Of course looking back, it's obvious to us that Jesus was referring not to Joseph, His earthly father, but to God, His Heavenly Father. At this point, without further discussion, young Jesus "went down to Nazareth with them and was obedient to them" (Luke 2:51).

There are several things that we can take away from this story. First, we would notice that even though He is the Son of God, knowledge and wisdom did not come to Jesus automatically. He was required to submit to the same learning process that all human beings must go through: studying, memorization, asking questions of adults, etc. Also, we should notice how amazingly mature Jesus was for a boy His age. Here was a child who actually did know more than his parents.

But I think the most important truth to see from this story is simply this: at this point in His young life, Jesus knew His true identity. It's possible that this truth was revealed to Him as He had worshipped at the Feast of the Passover. At twelve years old, Jesus knew who He was. He was the unique, one and only, Son of God. Eighteen years later, when He turned thirty, the whole world would begin to know it as well.

To be where we need to be for our next lesson, we have to leave Nazareth. So, you know the drill, time to get back on the bus. We're headed south to the western shore of the Jordan River.

If you have a question about this lesson, or other questions about the Bible, please visit my website www.FredWoodwardBible.com. There you can obtain my contact information and we can communicate through email. I'll do my very best to answer your questions.

Lesson 15

Before the Ministry

Matthew, Mark, Luke, John

Aside from the incident that we looked at in Luke 2, we have no other information about Jesus' childhood. In that story, after searching for Him for three days, His parents found Him in the Temple at Jerusalem. His question to them was, "'Why were you searching for me? ... Didn't you know I had to be in my Father's house?'" (Luke 2:49). Mary and Joseph, however, "did not understand what he was saying to them" (Luke 2:50). Thus, Jesus at twelve years old understood who He was, but when He saw that His parents did not understand, He submitted to their authority and "went down to Nazareth with them and was obedient to them" (Luke 2:51).

And so it was for the next eighteen years. We can certainly assume that Jesus was an obedient child and a good son while living with His parents. He did not, however, do anything spectacular or out of the ordinary that would draw attention to Himself. During those years at home, He didn't perform miracles, preach sermons, heal the sick, or cast out demons. But, dear friends, that's about to change! When He turned thirty, He would begin His world-changing ministry. In this lesson, we will look at some events that took place just before Jesus began doing the work that His Father had sent Him to do.

The Baptizer

Six months before the birth of Jesus, another baby had been born, also the result of a miraculous conception. In this case, the miracle came to an elderly couple, Elizabeth and Zechariah, who up until that time had been childless. Zechariah was a priest, and on an occasion when he was ministering in the Temple, the angel Gabriel (who later was sent to Mary) appeared to him with the following message:

> "Do not be afraid, Zechariah; your prayer has been heard. Your wife Elizabeth will bear you a son, and you are to give him the name John. He will be a joy and delight to you, and many will rejoice because of his birth, for he will be great in the sight of the Lord. He is never to take wine or other fermented drink, and he will be filled with the Holy Spirit even from birth. Many of the people of Israel will he bring back to the Lord their God. And he will go on before the Lord, in the spirit and power of Elijah, to turn the hearts of the fathers to their children and disobedient to the wisdom of the righteous—to make ready a people prepared for the Lord." (Luke 1:13–17)

Let me fulfill a promise I made to you. When we ended our tour of the Old Testament, I promised that in the New Testament we would come to understand the mysterious prophecy of Malachi, in which God promised to send Elijah before the coming of God: "'See, I will send you the prophet Elijah before that great and dreadful day of the LORD comes. He will turn the hearts of the fathers to their children, and the hearts of the children to their fathers'" (Mal. 4:5, 6). But the question is, how could this be, since Elijah had left the earth and gone to Heaven nearly 450 years before Malachi spoke this prophecy?

We find the answer in the angel's message to Zechariah. Gabriel said that Zechariah's son "*will go on before the Lord, in the spirit and power of Elijah.*" In other words, God was not planning to bring Elijah back to Earth; rather He was going to raise up another prophet that would be similar to Elijah in spirit and power. This prophet's message would also be similar to Elijah's. It would be a message of repentance that would "turn the hearts" of the children of Israel back to their God. This child, then, born to Elizabeth and Zechariah, would be the fulfillment of Malachi's prophecy. Many years later, Jesus confirmed this by saying of John, "'He is the Elijah who was to come'" (Matt. 11:14).

As instructed by the angel Gabriel, Zechariah and Elizabeth named the baby John. "And the child grew and became strong in spirit; and he lived in the desert until he appeared publicly to Israel" (Luke 1:80). When he became an adult, John left his parents' home to live in the desert, alone with God. He became very similar to the Old Testament prophet Elijah in spirit and appearance. His "clothes were made of camel's hair, and he had a leather belt around his waist. His food was locusts and wild honey" (Matt. 3:4). When John turned thirty years old, he began his preaching ministry, about six months before Jesus began His work. Israel, and eventually the whole world, would know him as John the Baptist.

Let us fast-forward to the time when John began preaching his message. "The word of God came to John son of Zechariah in the desert. He went into all the country around the Jordan, preaching a baptism of repentance for the forgiveness of sins" (Luke 3:2–3).

Luke would have us know that, in addition to Malachi's prophecy, another Old Testament prophet had also predicted John's ministry of repentance. So Luke quotes from Isaiah 40:3: "As is written in the book of the words of Isaiah the prophet: A voice of one calling in the desert, 'Prepare the way for the Lord, make straight paths for him. Every valley shall be filled in, every mountain and hill made low. The crooked roads shall become straight, the rough ways smooth'" (Luke 3:4–5).

His assignment from God was very clear. John, as a forerunner, was to go ahead of the Messiah and build a spiritual road for Him. Before the children of Israel could come to faith in the Messiah, they must first repent of their sins. John would build a road of repentance to prepare the way.

According to Isaiah, as he was building his road, John would encounter several types of spiritual terrain. He was to lift up some folks who were in a "valley" (the lame, the poor, and the blind). Others who came to him on a "mountain" (the rich, the self-righteous, and the proud) would have to be made low. He would have to straighten out some who were "crooked" (thieves, dishonest merchants, tax collectors), and he would have to smooth out others who had rough ways (violent criminals, abusive soldiers, prostitutes). There is one thing that all of these people had in common: to be ready to receive the Messiah, every one of them had to repent and turn away from their sins.

John faithfully carried out his assignment. With all the power of an Old Testament prophet, he preached his message to the children of Israel. When people responded by coming forward, John had them confess their sins publicly, and then he baptized them in the Jordan River. We don't know the exact number of Jews who were baptized, but we do know that all who sincerely repented were ready to move on to the next phase of their spiritual journey of faith in the Messiah, who, John said, would be coming soon.

Not everyone in Israel, however, was ready to repent at John's preaching. In particular, two powerful religious groups, known as the Pharisees and Sadducees, came to hear John but they came with unrepentant hearts. John had stern words of warning for them.

> "You brood of vipers! Who warned you to flee from the coming wrath? Produce fruit in keeping with repentance. And do not think you can say to yourselves, 'We have Abraham as our father.' I tell you that out of these stones God can raise up children for Abraham." (Matt. 3:7–9)

From John's words, we see the fundamental error of the Pharisees and Sadducees: since they were the biological offspring of Abraham, they believed that they were automatically righteous and had no need of repentance. But by calling them "*vipers*" (poisonous snakes), John made it clear that their hearts were full of wickedness. If they did not repent, they would face the wrath of God. We will encounter these two religious groups many more times in the New Testament.

John's preaching was so powerful that many people thought that he might be the Messiah: "The people were waiting expectantly and were all wondering in their hearts if John might possibly be the Christ" (Luke 3:15). But John was always quick to remind them: "'After me will come one more powerful than I, the thongs of whose sandals I am not worthy to stoop down and untie. I baptize you with water, but he will baptize you with the Holy Spirit'" (Mark 1:7–8).

The Baptism

And then one day while he was preaching and baptizing, the one John had said was coming came to the bank of the Jordan River.

> Then Jesus came from Galilee to the Jordan to be baptized by John. But John tried to deter him, saying, "I need to be baptized by you, and do you come to me?" Jesus replied, "Let it be so now; it is proper for us to do this to fulfill all righteousness." Then John consented. As soon as Jesus was baptized, he went up out of the water. At that moment heaven was opened, and he [John] saw the Spirit of God descending like a dove and lighting on him. And a voice from heaven said, "This is my Son, whom I love; with him I am well pleased." (Matt. 3:13–17)

There are so many interesting things to say about the above passage that it's hard to know where to start. Let's begin with a question that is often asked. Since we believe that Jesus was sinless and had nothing to repent of, why did He submit to John's baptism of repentance? Even John, knowing Jesus to be a righteous person, was reluctant to perform this baptism, saying, "*I need to be baptized by you.*" I believe the answer is this: Though we are now studying in the New Testament, Israel in the days of John the Baptist was still under the Old Testament Law of God, established by Moses on Mount Sinai. This would mean that John was the last Old Testament prophet. Therefore, to obey the Law and to fulfill all the requirements of the old covenant, Jesus needed to submit to John's prophetic authority. He persuaded John by saying, "*Let it be so for now; it is proper for us to do this to fulfill all righteousness.*"

Also, in this account of Jesus' baptism, we notice that all three members of the *Trinity* were present. The Bible teaches that God exists in three persons: the *Father*, the *Son*, and the *Holy Spirit*. After John performed the baptism, the Son came up out of the water, the Father spoke from Heaven in an audible voice, and the Spirit came down upon Jesus in the likeness of a dove.

This leads us to yet another question. Why did the Holy Spirit descend upon Jesus in the likeness of a dove? This one is pretty easy. The dove represents gentleness, quietness, and peace. About 750 years earlier, the prophet Isaiah had said that the Messiah would be called the "Prince of Peace" (Isa. 9:6).

But the most important thing for us to see in this story is that on this day, God the Father officially declared His Son Jesus to be the long-awaited "Anointed One", the Messiah. Now, in the power of the Holy Spirit, Jesus is ready to begin the work that His Father sent Him to do. Notice I didn't say He became the Son of God, because He has always been, and forever shall be, the Son of God. But it was on this day that the Holy Spirit came upon Jesus, to empower Him for His work on Earth.

You might remember that in a previous lesson we learned about the anointing of the Spirit when Saul was anointed to be the first king of Israel. Likewise David, Solomon, and all the kings of Israel were anointed. And surely you remember the promise that God made to David that his future son would sit on the throne at the right hand of God and reign forever! Well, dear friends, here He is, coming up out of the water of Jordan, having been baptized by John the Baptist, anointed by the Holy Spirit, and blessed by God the Father: Jesus the Messiah, the son of David, the King who would reign forever, the Prince of Peace!

Up to this point in our tour of the Bible, I have used the word "Messiah" because it is the Hebrew word for "the anointed one" and the term most frequently used by Jewish people. The New Testament, however, is written in Greek and the Greek word for "the anointed one" is CHRISTOS, or when translated into English, "Christ". So the words "Messiah" and "Christ" have the exact same meaning and can be used interchangeably.

The Battle

Before Jesus could begin His ministry, there was one more thing He had to do. He had to face and overcome the devil. Matthew, Mark, and Luke all tell us what happened immediately after Jesus was baptized. Matthew says, "Then Jesus was led by the Spirit into the desert to be tempted by the devil. After fasting forty days and forty nights, he was hungry" (Matt. 4:1–2). As we see from Matthew's account, Jesus did not accidently wander into the wilderness; He was led there "*by the Spirit*." Therefore, this battle with Satan was not optional. Rather, it was ordained by God. In short, it was something Jesus had to do.

Why was it so necessary for Jesus to fight and win this battle? Because He had to show the world that He could do it. Let me remind you that from the first sin in the Garden of Eden, when Satan successfully tempted Adam and Eve, no human being had been able to resist the devil and remain totally free from sin. As King Solomon once said, "There is not a righteous man on earth who does what is right and never sins" (Eccles. 7:20). To prove that He was worthy to become God's eternal king, Jesus first had to demonstrate that He was able to overcome Satan, the king of darkness.

We might think of this battle between Jesus and Satan as the "boxing match" of the ages. In one corner, with a record of millions of wins and no losses, having held the title for thousands of years, the undefeated champion of the world, Satan. And in the other corner, a newcomer to the ring, fighting His first fight, the challenger, Jesus of Nazareth. This will be a three-round fight.

Why only three rounds? Because of all the different kinds of sin that Satan might tempt us to commit, there are only three basic categories of sin: gratification, greed, and greatness. We saw these three forms of seduction when Satan tempted Eve to eat the forbidden fruit. "When the woman saw that the fruit of the tree was good for food [gratification] and pleasing to the eye [greed], and also desirable for gaining wisdom [greatness], she took some and ate it. She also gave some to her husband, who was with her, and he ate it" (Gen. 3:6).

There's a lot riding on this fight. If Jesus is still standing after three rounds, He wins. But if Satan can tempt Jesus to sin, he wins. If that had happened, there would have been no hope for the human race. We all, including Jesus, would have been sinners forever and the eternal slaves of Satan. Jesus is our only hope. Since I knew you would want to see this title fight of the ages, I got us all ringside seats.

(ding ding) **Round 1...The Temptation to Gratification**

"The tempter came to him and said, 'If you are the Son of God, tell these stones to become bread.' Jesus answered, 'It is written: "Man does not live on bread alone, but on every word that comes from the mouth of God"'" (Matt. 4:3–4). Since Jesus had not eaten for forty days, every cell in His body was crying out for food. Satan, knowing this, tempted Him to abuse His newly acquired power by turning stones into bread. The Lord had been anointed with power to serve, but the devil suggested He should use this power for selfish gratification. Jesus quickly recognized Satan's lie and resisted it by quoting Deuteronomy 8:3. Our Lord thus demonstrated that He would not give in to bodily cravings of any kind. Round 1, therefore, goes to Jesus.

(ding ding) **Round 2...The Temptation to Greatness**

Satan also knows that human beings experience a perverted form of pleasure whenever they feel superior. For the sin of pride, remember, Satan (originally Lucifer) was cast out of Heaven. Now, the devil tempts us to commit this same sin by taking us to "high places," causing us to exalt ourselves in pride to the point where we think we can give orders to God! Satan thought he could fool the Lord with this lie.

> Then the devil took him to the holy city and had him stand on the highest point of the temple. "If you are the Son of God," he said, "throw yourself down. For it is written: 'He will command his angels concerning you, and they will lift you up in their hands, so that you will not strike your foot against a stone.'" Jesus answered him, "It is also written: 'Do not put the Lord your God to the test.'" (Matt.4:5–7)

Jesus was not deceived. He resisted this second temptation, by again quoting from Old Testament scripture, Deuteronomy 6:16. Jesus wins Round 2.

(ding ding) **Round 3...The Temptation to Greed**

Satan had one more trick up his sleeve. He would have us believe that instead of filling our lives with the good things of God, we should try to satisfy our souls with stuff: money, material possessions, things, toys, property, etc. In God's word, such craving for the things of earth is called "covetousness" and is forbidden by one of the Ten Commandments: "You shall not covet" (Exod. 20:17). The devil tried to tempt Jesus to commit this sin.

> Again, the devil took him to a very high mountain and showed him all the kingdoms of the world and their splendor. "All this I will give you," he said, "if you will bow down and worship me." Jesus said to him, "Away from me, Satan! For it is written: 'Worship the Lord your God, and serve him only.'" Then the devil left him, and angels came and attended him. (Matt. 4:8-11)

As with the previous temptations, Jesus recognized the devil's deception and resisted it with a quote from the Old Testament scripture, Deuteronomy 6:13.

(ding ding ding ding ding)

The fight is over! Because Jesus was still on His feet after three rounds, He won. Our Lord has done what no man has ever done (before or since). He kept His soul pure by resisting Satan's most powerful suggestions. He went toe to toe with the tempter and took a terrible beating, but He ended up still standing! Enraged with hate and humiliation, the devil "*left him*" and slithered away.

But while Jesus has won this battle, the war with the wicked one is far from over. In a little over three years, Satan would demand a rematch. Since I knew you would be anxious to see the outcome of that future fight, I have already reserved ringside seats for all of us. But let me prepare you ahead of time: the next bout between these two will be much more brutal and barbaric. Jesus will be beaten beyond recognition and His blood will be shed.

Please notice Matthew's last comment: "*and angels came and attended him.*" After forty days of fasting, and then this battle with Satan, Jesus was completely spent physically, spiritually, and emotionally. He was so exhausted that angels from God had to come and help him make His way back to civilization. Isn't it sad that after this tremendous accomplishment, Jesus was all alone in the desert? There was no one there to lift His hand in victory, no cheering crowd, no one to thank Him for standing up to the bully of the universe. But this can be seen often during His lifetime. Jesus would often be left alone, to do for us what He alone could do.

Since the Lord needed some time to rest and heal, we will leave our bus parked right here, near the Jordan River. As we will see in our next lesson, when He recuperated from this ordeal in the desert, Jesus, who was now officially the Christ, would begin His public ministry.

If you have a question about this lesson, or other questions about the Bible, please visit my website www.FredWoodwardBible.com. There you can obtain my contact information and we can communicate through email. I'll do my very best to answer your questions.

Lesson 16

The Ministry of Jesus, Part 1

Matthew, Mark, Luke, John

When Jesus reached the age of thirty, everything necessary to prepare Him for His work on Earth had been accomplished. He had grown up in the godly home of Joseph and Mary. When baptized by John the Baptist, He received the anointing of the Holy Spirit and was empowered to do the work of God. Then He faced the devil and demonstrated His ability to resist temptation. At this point, He was ready to begin His ministry.

Considering that Jesus would change the world and the course of history, His public life was surprisingly short, lasting only about three and a half years. In this lesson, we will look at some important events that took place during the first year and a half of His work.

The First Witness

When John baptized Jesus, God allowed John to see the Holy Spirit come upon the Lord in the form of a dove. In John's own words,

> "I saw the Spirit come down from heaven as a dove and remain on him. I would not have known him, except that the one who sent me to baptize with water told me, 'The man on whom you see the Spirit come down and remain

> is he who will baptize with the Holy Spirit.' I have seen and I testify that this is the Son of God." (John 1:32–34)

After His battle with the devil, Jesus again returned to the bank of the Jordan River where John was busy preaching and baptizing repentant sinners. When John looked up and saw Jesus passing by, he said, "'Look, the Lamb of God!'" (John 1:36).

Why did John refer to Jesus as the "Lamb of God"? The nation of Israel was looking and longing for a military messiah, a king who would lead them in battle against the oppressive Roman Empire. If John wanted to publicly introduce Jesus, why not use a more impressive declaration like, "Look, the Mighty Messiah"? Or, "Look, the Conquering Christ"? Or, "Look, the Son of David, Who Will Deliver Us from Rome"? To the Jews, "Lamb of God" would have sounded awfully tame. In fact (Heaven forbid) this title suggested gentleness and peace.

At this point, we can benefit from our tour of the Old Testament. In Lesson 5, we discussed the story of the Passover Lamb. To deliver Israel from their Egyptian bondage, God sent a death angel upon Egypt. The households of Israel, however, escaped this plague of death by slaying a lamb and putting the blood of the lamb on their houses. When the death angel saw blood on a house, he passed over it, but the plague came upon every house that was without blood. Thus, because of the blood of the lamb, the children of Israel were protected from the judgment and wrath of God.

Clearly, when John the Baptist declared the Lord to be the Lamb of God, he was thinking of this Old Testament story. With John's introduction of Jesus, we are already beginning to see Israel's misconception of the coming Messiah. In contrast to Israel's expectations, "the Anointed One" would not be a military messiah or a conquering king. Rather, He would be a sacrificial Lamb who would be slain. His blood would pay for the sin of the world and protect those who believe in Him from the judgment and wrath of God. At the Jordan River when he pointed to Jesus, John became the first witness for Christ.

The First Five Followers

It's amazing how quickly John's ministry began to bear fruit. At the very moment that he said to the crowd, "*Look, the Lamb of God!*" two of his own disciples (a disciple is a learner) who had repented and been baptized were standing there with him.

> When the two disciples heard him say this, they followed Jesus. Turning around, Jesus saw them following and asked, "What do you want?" They said, "Rabbi" (which means Teacher), "where are you staying?" "Come," he replied, "and you will see." So they went and saw where he was staying, and spent that day with him. (John 1:37–39)

One of these two men was John (not the Baptist, but John who wrote the fourth Gospel), and the other man's name was Andrew.

> The first thing Andrew did was to find his brother Simon and tell him, "We have found the Messiah" (that is, the Christ). And he brought him to Jesus. Jesus looked at him and said, "You are Simon son of John. You will be called Cephas" (which, when translated, is Peter). (John 1:41–42)

The next day, Jesus, finding Philip, said to him, "'Follow me'" (John 1:43). "Philip found Nathaniel and told him, 'We have found the one Moses wrote about in the Law and about whom the prophets also wrote—Jesus of Nazareth, the son of Joseph'" (John 1:45).

Thus begins the transfer of disciples from John the Baptist to Jesus. John had accomplished his mission. He had led these men to repentance and now they were ready to place their faith in the Christ. Later on, Jesus would promote these first five men, John, Andrew, Peter, Philip, and Nathaniel, to the position of apostle, and they would become members of the famous group known as the twelve apostles.

As the transfer of disciples from John to Jesus continued, some thought that John would somehow be troubled, maybe even jealous.

They could not have been more wrong. Concerning this, John said,

> "A man can receive only what is given him from heaven. You yourselves can testify that I said, 'I am not the Christ but am sent ahead of him.' The bride belongs to the bridegroom. The friend who attends the bridegroom waits and listens for him, and is full of joy when he hears the bridegroom's voice. That joy is mine, and it is now complete. He must become greater; I must become less." (John 3:27–30)

As he watched people leave him to follow Jesus, John's joy was complete. He was born to prepare for and point to the coming Messiah. Now that the Messiah had come, John understood completely why he must "*become less*" while Jesus "*must become greater*." John the Baptist—what an amazing and wonderful man of God!

The First Miracle

Jesus and these five followers left John at the Jordan River and traveled north to the region that was home to all of them: Galilee. Shortly after their arrival, the Lord, His disciples, and His mother were all invited to a wedding in the town of Cana. "When the wine was gone, Jesus' mother said to him, 'They have no more wine.' 'Dear woman, why do you involve me?' Jesus replied. 'My time has not yet come.' His mother said to the servants, 'Do whatever he tells you'" (John 2:3–5).

For thirty years, Mary, Jesus' mother, had cherished in her heart the words she had heard from the angel Gabriel concerning this most unusual son: "'He will be great and will be called the Son of the Most High'" (Luke 1:32). Apparently Mary, knowing what her son was capable of, decided it was time to give Him a little prompting to show His power. After a gentle reminder that His "*time*" had not yet come, Jesus granted His mother's request.

> Nearby stood six stone water jars, the kind used by the Jews for ceremonial washing, each holding from twenty

> to thirty gallons. Jesus said to the servants "Fill the jars with water"; so they filled them to the brim. Then he told them, "Now draw some out and take it to the master of the banquet." (John 2:6–8)

When the master of the banquet tasted the water that had been changed into wine, he was surprised at how good it tasted. He complimented the bridegroom by saying,

> "Everyone brings out the choice wine first and then the cheaper wine after the guests have had too much to drink; but you have saved the best till now." This, the first of his miraculous signs, Jesus performed at Cana in Galilee. He thus revealed his glory, and his disciples put their faith in him. (John 2:10–11)

Let us notice that when Jesus changed the water into wine, it was not only *abundant* (180 gallons), it was also "the best." While this was Jesus' first miracle, it would certainly not be His last. The four Gospels record approximately thirty-five miracles that Jesus performed. But John tells us that this was just a small sampling of the overall number: "Jesus did many other things as well. If every one of them were written down, I suppose that even the whole world would not have room for the books that would be written" (John 21:25). The Lord's miracles always had a twofold purpose. They were always to meet some practical need, and, more important, they demonstrated His divine authority and revealed His glory. Or, as John put it, "*He thus revealed his glory and his disciples put their faith in him.*"

The First Principle

In the previous lesson, we learned that a particular religious group, the Pharisees, came to hear John's message of repentance, but after hearing they refused to repent. Generally speaking, the Pharisees were unrepentant. There was, however, one exception to this general rule: a man named Nicodemus. Probably fearing the wrath of his fellow Pharisees, he came to Jesus at night for a private meeting.

> Now there was a man of the Pharisees named Nicodemus, a member of the Jewish ruling council. He came to Jesus at night and said, "Rabbi, we know you are a teacher who has come from God. For no one could perform the miraculous signs you are doing if God were not with him." In reply Jesus declared, "I tell you the truth, no one can see the kingdom of God unless he is born again." "How can a man be born when he is old?" Nicodemus asked. "Surely he cannot enter a second time into his mother's womb to be born!" Jesus answered, "I tell you the truth, no one can enter the kingdom of God unless he is born of water and the Spirit. Flesh gives birth to flesh, but the Spirit gives birth to spirit. You should not be surprised at my saying, 'You must be born again.'" (John 3:1–7)

In the above conversation between Jesus and Nicodemus, we clearly see the fundamental flaw in Pharisee thinking. Though they saw themselves as teachers of the Law of God, the Pharisees literally did not know the first thing about God. According to Jesus, the first thing every human being must know about God is that "'*no one can see the kingdom of God unless he is born again.*'" The Lord also said to Nicodemus, "'You should not be surprised at my saying, *"You must be born again."*'" But Nicodemus was surprised and confused about this term "born again." He was confused because all of his life he had been taught that his natural birth into the family of Abraham made him automatically righteous in God's sight. But what Nicodemus failed to notice was that Abraham himself had been born *twice*. Like all men, Abraham had been born "from the flesh" when he came out of his mother's womb. This natural birth, however, just made him another member of the fallen human race, spiritually dead and unrighteous. Abraham experienced his second birth, and was declared righteous, when his heart came to faith in God's word. Do you remember that we discussed this principle at length in Lesson 4? "Abram believed the LORD, and he

[God] credited it to him as righteousness" (Gen. 15:6).

Just as Abraham 2,000 years earlier had been made righteous by faith in God's spoken word, now, with the coming of the Messiah, men could be born again and made righteous by faith in God's Living Word, Jesus Christ. The principle, however, that men pass from death to life by faith remains the same.

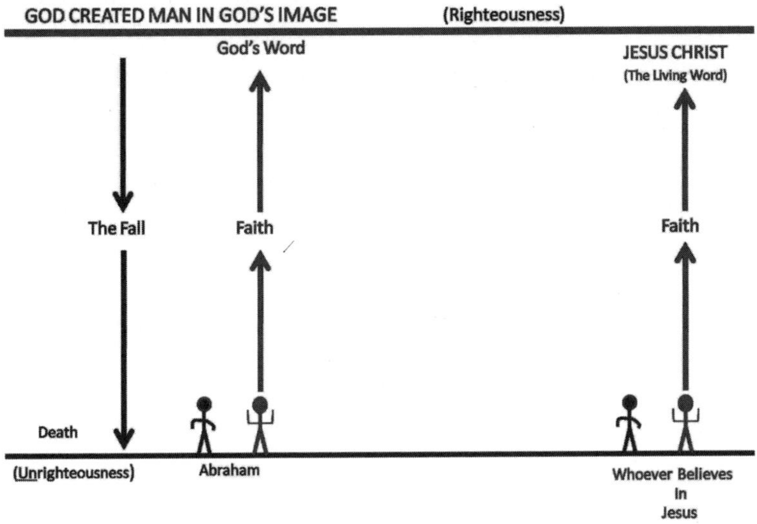

As the above illustration shows, God originally created mankind in His own image and in the state of righteousness. When Adam and Eve sinned, they not only fell from God themselves, they also took the entire human race with them into the state of spiritual death and unrighteousness. With the example of Abraham, we learn that by faith an unrighteous person becomes righteous by God's declaration. Now, in the New Testament era, all mankind can have the same "born again" experience that Abraham had 4,000 years ago by placing their faith in Jesus Christ.

The First Bad Sign

After the Lord officially began His work, He instructed His disciples to baptize the people who had become His followers. At the same time,

John the Baptist also continued preaching and baptizing at the Jordan River. For a few months, they had complementary ministries in and around Jerusalem. According to God's plan, Jesus' work began to grow while John's began to diminish.

It was during this period that John's ministry came to an abrupt end when he was arrested by Herod the Tetrarch, son of the wicked King Herod. This Herod had married his brother's wife, which was a violation of the Law of Moses. As mentioned before, John thundered against sin. He pulled no punches and played no favorites, not even with kings! So "when John rebuked Herod the tetrarch because of Herodias, his brother's wife, and all the other evil things he had done, Herod added this to them all: He locked John up in prison" (Luke 3:19–20). Herod did this with the approval of Israel's religious leaders, the Pharisees and Sadducees.

This, my friends, was a bad sign and a scary preview of things to come. For if the ruling powers of Israel were now arresting and persecuting a man of God such as John, what would they do in the future to Jesus?

The First Foreigners

"When Jesus heard that John had been put in prison, he returned to Galilee" (Matt. 4:12). This meant that the Lord "had to go through Samaria" (John 4:4), since Galilee was in the northern region of Israel.

> So he came to a town in Samaria called Sychar, near the plot of ground Jacob had given to his son Joseph. Jacob's well was there, and Jesus, tired as he was from the journey, sat down by the well. It was about the sixth hour. When a Samaritan woman came to draw water, Jesus said to her, "Will you give me a drink?" (His disciples had gone into the town to buy food.) The Samaritan woman said to him, "You are a Jew and I am a Samaritan woman. How can you ask me for a drink?" (For Jews do not associate with Samaritans.) (John 4:5–9)

Before we take a closer look at the encounter between Jesus and the Samaritan woman, let me say a few words about the region of Samaria and the Samaritans who lived there. Again, our tour of the Old Testament should come in handy. As you may recall, Israel went through a period in which the twelve tribes were divided. In the days of the division, the ten northern tribes were called the Northern Kingdom, while the two remaining southern tribes were known as the Southern Kingdom, or Judah. Because the Northern Kingdom fell into incurable corruption, God allowed the nation of Assyria to invade, conquer, and carry away thousands of Israelites from the ten northern tribes in the year 722 BC.

But in addition to exporting thousands of Jews from their homeland, the king of Assyria also imported thousands of foreigners into this region. "The king of Assyria brought people from Babylon, Cuthah, Avva, Hamath and Sepharvaim and settled them in the towns of Samaria to replace the Israelites. They took over Samaria and lived in its towns" (2 Kings 17:24). When these foreign people moved in, they did two things: they brought with them their pagan gods, and they began intermarrying with the remaining Jews in the land.

Thus the region of Samaria became a place of mixed races and mixed religions. For this reason, the Jews of Jerusalem considered the Samaritans to be of "impure blood." They looked (down) upon them with contempt and disgust. They had no dealings with them. When traveling from north to south, or vice versa, most Jews would take a detour to bypass this region. This explains why the Samaritan woman at the well was so surprised that Jesus would even speak to her. *"You are a Jew and I am a Samaritan woman. How can you ask me for a drink?"*

We, of course, know the answer to the woman's question. Jesus did not have a prejudicial bone in His whole body. He had come to Earth to bring the love and forgiveness of God to all people, including this sad Samaritan woman. Sad, I say, because she had been married five times and was now living with her sixth man. But none of these men had brought her any real happiness, joy, or fulfillment. No doubt she suffered from very low self-esteem.

She had come to the well to draw water, but Jesus told her that what she really needed was a different kind of water: "'If you knew the gift of

God and who it is that asks you for a drink, you would have asked him and he would have given you living water'" (John 4:10). By living water, the Lord was referring to the thirst-quenching, life-giving, soul-satisfying water of God, the Holy Spirit.

After just a few minutes of talking with Him, the Samaritan woman came to believe in Jesus. She was so excited that she left her water jar at the well, went back into town, and encouraged the people of the city to go out to the well and talk to Him themselves.

> So when the Samaritans came to him, they urged him to stay with them, and he stayed two days. And because of his words many more became believers. They said to the woman, "We no longer believe just because of what you said; now we have heard for ourselves, and we know that this man really is the Savior of the world." (John 4:40–42)

And this, my friends, was a very good sign and a preview of wonderful things to come. The good news of Jesus Christ would not be just for Jews, it would also be for the Gentiles (nations). In a few years, after the Lord had finished His work on Earth, the gospel of Christ would spread throughout all the world. Men, women, and children of every nation would be invited to drink the living water. In Jesus' words, "'If anyone is thirsty, let him come to me and drink. Whoever believes in me, as the Scripture has said, streams of living water will flow from within him'" (John 7:37–38).

If you have a question about this lesson, or other questions about the Bible, please visit my website www.FredWoodwardBible.com. There you can obtain my contact information and we can communicate through email. I'll do my very best to answer your questions.

Lesson 17

The Ministry of Jesus, Part II

Matthew, Mark, Luke, John

During His three and a half years of ministry (forty-two months), Jesus would spend the majority of His time in the northern region of Israel, doing God's work in towns and villages near the Sea of Galilee. The only time He would journey south to Jerusalem would be to observe one of the three required annual feasts of God. According to the Law of Moses, every year, all Jewish men were commanded to attend the Feast of the Passover, the Feast of Pentecost, and the Feast of Tabernacles.

At the close of our last lesson, after attending the Feast of Passover, Jesus and His disciples were making their way north to Galilee. They had stopped at a well near a little village of Samaria, and while there, Jesus had a very positive experience with a Samaritan woman and the people of the town. Since the Lord would spend most of His time further north, we are going to go ahead of Him, park our bus on the western shore of the Sea of Galilee, and leave it there for quite a while.

At this point, Jesus had been preaching, teaching, working miracles, and gathering disciples for about eighteen months. In this lesson, we will look at some important events and experiences that took place from the eighteenth month to the thirtieth month of His ministry.

The Miracles of Jesus

As you may recall from an earlier lesson, God empowered the Old Testament prophets with the ability to work miracles. This was to endorse the prophet and affirm that he was truly speaking "the Word of the LORD." Moses, for example, performed many acts of power over a forty-year period to confirm the old covenant. Likewise, Jesus performed countless miracles to confirm the new covenant. These supernatural signs demonstrated the Lord's power and authority over three specific areas: sickness, Satan, and the natural world.

When we discussed the Fall of Man, we learned that when sin came into the world through Adam and Eve, sickness came with it. As a result of the Fall, our human body is now a "body of death" (Rom. 7:24), subject to every form of infirmity, decay, and disease. To show His power over all disease, Jesus healed countless people from any and all forms of illness. No one with any infirmity ever came to Jesus and went away dissatisfied. He healed them all!

To demonstrate His power over the devil, Jesus cast out many demons from people who were "possessed." At this point you might be asking, "What is a demon, and how does a person become demon-possessed?" To briefly explain, let me remind you of what we learned about the devil himself. Originally, God did not create Satan; He created a holy and good angelic being named Lucifer. For his sin of pride and rebellion, Lucifer was expelled from Heaven and his name was changed to Satan. But, unfortunately, he was not alone in his rebellion against God. The devil was able to persuade a multitude of other angelic beings (some think as many as one-third of the angelic host) to join him. These fallen angels now faithfully serve Satan in various ways and are referred to in the Bible as "evil spirits," "unclean spirits," or "demons."

As to how a person becomes "demon-possessed," there are various theories. Some suggest that it is the result of a psychological wound that may have occurred in childhood, such as a terribly frightening experience or sexual abuse. Others, who study this area, believe demon possession is the result of experimenting with satanic rituals or witchcraft. While we may not know the exact cause of demon possession, we do know that in such cases demons have somehow invaded the body, soul, and mind of the affected person. The symptoms of demon possession are usually extreme mental and emotional torment.

In one of His first miracles, while teaching in a Jewish synagogue, Jesus dealt with a demon-possessed man.

> Just then a man in their synagogue who was possessed by an evil spirit cried out, "What do you want with us, Jesus of Nazareth? Have you come to destroy us? I know who you are—the Holy One of God!" "Be quiet!" said Jesus sternly. "Come out of him!" The evil spirit shook the man violently and came out of him with a shriek. (Mark 1:23–26)

Another example of demon possession was when Jesus dealt with a young woman named Mary Magdalene. After Jesus cast out "seven demons" (Luke 8:2) from her, she became a faithful follower of the Lord. (Mary, in fact, was the first person to see Jesus after His resurrection.) We could cite many more examples that would all make the same point: Jesus has complete power and authority over Satan and all the evil spirits that serve him.

Finally, Jesus performed miracles to demonstrate His authority over the natural world. In the famous miracle of the fishes, Simon (Peter) and his brother had fished all night on the Sea of Galilee and had caught nothing.

> When he [Jesus] had finished speaking, he said to Simon, "Put out into deep water, and let down the nets for a catch." Simon answered, "Master, we've worked hard all night and haven't caught anything. But because you say so, I will let down the nets." When they had done so, they caught such a large number of fish that their nets began to break. So they signaled their partners in the other boat to come and help them, and they came and filled both boats so full that they began to sink. When Simon Peter saw this, he fell at Jesus' knees and said, "Go away from me, Lord; I am a sinful man!" For he and all

> his companions were astonished at the catch of fish they had taken, and so were James and John, the sons of Zebedee, Simon's partners. (Luke 5:4–10)

After witnessing this miracle, Peter was so amazed at what he had seen that he was actually afraid to be in the presence of such a godly and holy man. But in His unique ability to use the natural world to teach about the spiritual world, Jesus said, "'Don't be afraid; from now on you will catch men'" (Luke 5:10).

In addition to the sheer power of Jesus' miracles, let me point out to you that there was a progression to His miracles. As time went on, the signs and wonders that the Lord performed became increasingly more spectacular. For example, sometime after the miracle of the fishes, He performed another act of power on the Sea of Galilee. Jesus and His disciples were in a boat crossing the Sea of Galilee when suddenly

> a furious storm came up on the lake, so that the waves swept over the boat. But Jesus was sleeping. The disciples went and woke him, saying, "Lord, save us! We're going to drown!" He replied, "You of little faith, why are you so afraid?" Then he got up and rebuked the winds and the waves, and it was completely calm. The men were amazed and asked, "What kind of man is this? Even the winds and the waves obey him!" (Matt. 8:24–27)

The disciples were astonished at this because they no doubt recalled Psalm 89:8–9, which says, "O LORD God Almighty, who is like you? You are mighty, O LORD, and your faithfulness surrounds you. You rule over the surging sea; when its waves mount up, you still them." Since only God can still the raging sea, the disciples were right to ask, *"What kind of a man is this?"*

After the miracle of calming the sea, Jesus performed another spectacular sign when He miraculously fed a multitude of people. All four Gospel writers record that on one occasion a multitude of men, women, and children had come to hear Jesus teach. Rather than send them away hungry, Jesus said to His disciples, "'They do not need to go away. You give them something to eat.' 'We have here only five loaves of bread and two fish,' they answered. 'Bring them here to me,' he said" (Matt. 14:16–18).

After Jesus blessed the five loaves of bread and two fish, He gave them to His disciples who, in turn, gave them to the people. Miraculously, the disciples kept giving and giving and giving until "they all ate and were satisfied, and the disciples picked up twelve basketfuls of broken pieces that were left over. The number of those who ate was about five thousand men, besides women and children" (Matt. 14:20–21). Why were there exactly twelve baskets of food left over? To demonstrate that if all twelve tribes of Israel had been there that day, they would have all eaten and been satisfied!

Immediately after the feeding of the 5,000, Jesus did something yet more amazing. He instructed His disciples to get into a boat and go to the other side of the Sea of Galilee, while He went to a nearby mountainside to be alone and pray. After several hours, and the disciples had rowed a considerable distance, "Jesus went out to them, walking on the lake. When the disciples saw him walking on the lake, they were terrified. 'It's a ghost,' they said, and cried out in fear. But Jesus immediately said to them: 'Take courage! It is I. Don't be afraid'" (Matt. 14:25–27).

Again, please notice not only the power but also the progression of Jesus' miracles. With His very first miracle (John 2), Jesus changed water into wine. Now, approximately two years later, He is walking on water!

The Mentoring of Jesus

Along with the miracles, an even more important part of Jesus' ministry was His mentoring. Everywhere Jesus went, He was constantly teaching and preaching the word of God. Sometimes He spoke privately to just one person (as with Nicodemus). At other times He taught quietly with a few chosen disciples. Then there were times when He lifted His voice to crowds numbering in the thousands.

In order to understand the teachings of Jesus, we must first understand the relationship between the old covenant that Moses brought and the new covenant that Jesus was bringing. Do you remember when we were touring the Old Testament we parked our bus for a couple of days at Mount Sinai? While there, we learned that somewhere around 1400 BC, Moses, acting as mediator, brought from God a covenant of LAW to the nation of Israel. Actually, this was not just one law, it was a collection of about 640 statutes, judgments, and commandments. When the people agreed to obey all these laws, Moses sprinkled the congregation with the blood of young bulls and the covenant between God and Israel was sealed.

At this point you may be asking, "Since the children of Israel already have 640 laws to keep, and for fourteen centuries failed miserably at keeping them, do they really need any more? And didn't we learn that it was forbidden to add to or take away from the Law of Moses? Does Jesus plan to alter the Law of God or will He add more commandments to the 640 already given?"

The answer to that question is an emphatic NO. Jesus did not come to add to or alter the Law of Moses. Please notice what He said about this: "'Do not think that I have come to abolish the Law or the Prophets; I have not come to abolish them but to fulfill them. I tell you the truth, until heaven and earth disappear, not the smallest letter, not the least stroke of a pen, will by any means disappear from the Law until everything is accomplished'" (Matt. 5:17–18).

Jesus did not come to Earth to bring more commandments to keep. He came to bring a different kind of covenant, one that would enable sinful mankind to keep the laws of the old covenant. Moses brought a covenant of LAW. Jesus will bring a covenant of GRACE. The word "grace" means unmerited favor. When God gives us his grace, He is giving us help and blessings that we do not deserve. The Apostle John pointed out the difference between Moses and Jesus when he said, "For the law was given through Moses; grace and truth came through Jesus Christ" (John 1:17).

To further explain the relationship between the LAW of Moses and the GRACE of Jesus, please allow me to share a couple of illustrations. A while back, I went to my doctor complaining that I was experiencing pain in my right shoulder. He instructed me to have my shoulder x-rayed. The x-ray revealed that there was something wrong with my rotator cuff.

Now this may sound a little too obvious, but after the x-ray had revealed the problem, there was nothing more it could do. The x-ray had revealed the problem, but it could not heal it. At that point, my doctor had to prescribe the proper medication and treatment. In a similar way, the Old Testament LAW of God functions like an x-ray machine. When a sinner (like us) looks toward it, the Law penetrates into the heart and reveals the problem within—sin! The LAW enables a person to see the flaws in their character that God already sees. And, like the x-ray machine, the LAW reveals sin but it cannot heal it. For sin to be healed, some type of medicine will be required. Jesus came to Earth to bring that medicine: the GRACE of God.

As another example, suppose you go to your doctor for a yearly check-up. You think this check-up is totally unnecessary because you feel "fit as a fiddle." You see yourself as a perfect specimen of physical fitness. Your doctor, however, suspecting there is something wrong with your heart, orders you to take a treadmill test. The doctor sets the machine to the speed you ought to be able to walk if, in fact, your heart is healthy. But after just a few minutes of walking, your heart is pounding at a dangerous rate. Now you realize what the doctor suspected—you have a bad heart! The doctor shuts off the treadmill because it has served its purpose. It has revealed there is a problem with your heart, but it cannot heal it. At this point, some type of heart medication and treatment will be necessary.

Likewise, the Old Testament LAW is God's treadmill. We human beings don't see ourselves as God sees us. We initially see ourselves as perfect specimens of spiritual health. So God says to us (sinners), "Here, step up on my treadmill and we'll see how spiritually healthy you really are." When we try to keep God's commandments, we fail miserably, and experientially we learn what God already knows: that our innermost being is infected with the disease called *sin*. But, like the treadmill, the LAW of God has served its purpose. It has revealed the sin within us, but it cannot heal it. Some type of medication is needed. Jesus came to bring that medicine, which is the GRACE of God.

I have spent quite a bit of time on the contrast between LAW and GRACE because this will be the underlying theme in all of Jesus' teachings. Jesus will never tell His disciples that they should try harder to keep the LAW. Instead, He will instruct them to take the medicine of God's GRACE and become spiritually healthy. Jesus will reaffirm what the LAW of Moses has revealed, that the heart of man is corrupt, sick with sin, and in desperate need of healing. In His words, "For from within, out of men's hearts, come evil thoughts, sexual immorality, theft, murder, adultery, greed, malice, deceit, lewdness, envy, slander, arrogance and folly. All these evils come from inside and make a man 'unclean'" (Mark 7:21–23).

Jesus also said, "Make a tree good and its fruit will be good, or make a tree bad and its fruit will be bad, for a tree is recognized by its fruit" (Matt. 12:33). On our property here in Michigan, we have many apple trees. Those trees do not "try real hard" to produce apples. They produce apples because, at their core, they are apple trees. Likewise, Jesus is teaching us that we must become a different person at the very core of our being. We must become a person whose heart has been made pure and good by the grace of God. The fruit of that grace will be outward behavior that is also pure and good.

And how do we take this medicine of grace that Jesus is bringing? You already know the key words, repentance and faith. A very sinful woman (possibly a prostitute) once came to Jesus and fell at His feet. With tears of repentance, she washed His feet, dried them with her hair, and then poured perfume on them. Jesus said to her, "'Your sins are forgiven. ... Your faith has saved you; go in peace'" (Luke 7:48, 50). Please notice that she did not receive salvation from sin by doing good works, by giving aid to the poor, or by a observing a religious ceremony. It was by her sincere repentance and her faith in Jesus that this woman received the grace of God.

The Chosen Men of Jesus

We have already learned the meaning of the word "disciple." A disciple is a person who follows a rabbi (teacher), sits at his feet, and learns his teachings. After Jesus had been teaching, preaching, and ministering for over a year and a half, He had attracted many disciples. At this point, He did something very significant.

> Jesus went up on a mountainside and called to him those he wanted, and they came to him. He appointed twelve—designating them apostles—that they might be with him and that he might send them out to preach and to have authority to drive out demons. These are the twelve he appointed: Simon (to whom he gave the name Peter); James son of Zebedee and his brother John (to them he gave the name Boanerges, which means Sons of Thunder); Andrew, Philip, Bartholomew, Matthew, Thomas, James son of Alphaeus, Thaddaeus, Simon the Zealot and Judas Iscariot, who betrayed him. (Mark 3:13–19)

The term "apostle" comes from the Greek word APOSTOLOS and means something entirely different than the word "disciple." A disciple is a follower, but an apostle is an ambassador. An apostle is a disciple who has been fully trained, equipped, and empowered to represent his master. An apostle can speak and act in the authority of his master.

These twelve chosen men received special treatment from the Lord. He did not just teach them, He trained them. He often called the Twelve aside to give them advanced instruction. He allowed them to watch Him as He preached, healed, and cast out demons. He taught them how to pray, worship, and work in the power of the Holy Spirit. Obviously, the Lord had a plan. Knowing His time on Earth would be short, Jesus was preparing this group of men to carry on His mission after His departure to Heaven. After His death, burial, and resurrection, He will pass the mantle of ministry to them.

After about six months of this special attention, the Lord sent the twelve apostles out on their first ministry mission. "Calling the Twelve to him, he sent them out two by two and gave them authority over evil spirits" (Mark 6:7). "They went out and preached that people should repent" (Mark 6:12). When they completed their mission, "the apostles gathered around Jesus and reported to him all they had done and taught" (Mark 6:30).

It was during this period in His ministry that Jesus became "full of joy through the Holy Spirit" (Luke 10:21). The Lord rejoiced to see that His twelve apostles were learning and acquiring His ministry skills.

This was evidence that Jesus' work on Earth would certainly continue even after His departure to Heaven, which, as He knew, was only about twelve months away.

And we should rejoice as well. For this, dear friends, was the beginning of a trend that continues to this day. For over 2,000 years, people have been receiving the grace of God by placing their faith in Jesus. They, in turn, are anxious to go out and share this life-giving good news with a lost and dying world.

If you have a question about this lesson, or other questions about the Bible, please visit my website www.FredWoodwardBible.com. There you can obtain my contact information and we can communicate through email. I'll do my very best to answer your questions.

Lesson 18

The Ministry of Jesus, Part III

Matthew, Mark, Luke, John

When Jesus first began His public ministry, He did not come bursting on the scene, proclaiming Himself to be Israel's long-awaited Messiah. Quite the contrary, He was deliberately evasive concerning the title of "Christ" and even took steps to conceal this part of His identity. For example, on one occasion in the early days of His ministry, "a man in their synagogue who was possessed by an evil spirit cried out, 'What do you want with us, Jesus of Nazareth? Have you come to destroy us? I know who you are—the Holy One of God!' 'Be quiet!' said Jesus sternly. 'Come out of him!'" (Mark 1:23–25).

Because demons have angelic insight, the demon in this man actually did know who Jesus was: *"the Holy One of God."* But when the evil spirit (speaking through the man) said this publicly, the Lord ordered him: *"Be quiet!"*

In another incident early on, Jesus healed a man of leprosy. But afterward, "Jesus sent him away at once with a strong warning: 'See that you don't tell this to anyone. But go, show yourself to the priest and offer the sacrifices that Moses commanded for your cleansing, as a testimony to them'" (Mark 1:43–44).

Leprosy was a dreaded, incurable disease. To be healed of it was virtually unheard of. Clearly, at this point, the Lord did not want Israel to know that He had this kind of power. Why was the Lord reluctant to reveal that He was "the Anointed One"? Because the people of Israel were misled and misinformed about the coming Messiah. Overlooking many Old Testament prophecies and misinterpreting others, they had come to believe that the Christ would be a conquering king, a man of war who would lead Israel in victory, not just over Rome but over the rest of the world as well. His kingdom would be an earthly kingdom, bringing power, glory, and prosperity to Israel. They had been taught to believe that the Christ could never suffer or die.

As we will see, there came a time toward the end of His ministry when Jesus did acknowledge that He is indeed the Christ, first privately to His twelve apostles, and then publicly to all of Israel. But before that time, the Lord endeavored to teach His followers that He was a different kind of king, bringing a different kind of kingdom. Unlike all the other kingdoms of the world, Jesus' kingdom would be neither visible, material, nor earthly. It would be invisible, spiritual, and eternal. And His followers would not be superior to the world, they would be the servants of the world. As Jesus proclaimed this message, the people of Israel responded in two distinct ways: Some opened their hearts, received Him, and loved Him. Others hardened their hearts, rejected Him, and hated Him.

The Repentant Crowd That Received Jesus

There were thousands of people in Israel who came to love Jesus and chose to follow Him because they were convinced that He loved them. He proved His love over and over again by His care, kindness, healing, and, most important, His acceptance of them. So many in Israel had felt rejected. They had been rejected by the hypocritical religious leaders (the scribes, the Pharisees, and Sadducees) who called the common people "sinners." This rejection, coming from the priests and rulers of Israel, caused this group of people to feel that God had rejected them, too.

But the Lord accepted them. He reached out in love to the social outcasts: beggars, the lame, the blind, prostitutes, thieves, crooked tax collectors, mentally challenged individuals, the demon-possessed, lepers, etc. He intermingled with them, he ate with them, and, most surprising of all, unlike the religious leaders who considered them unclean, Jesus touched them.

In so many of His teachings, Jesus convinced the people that not only had God not rejected them, God was actually looking for them and anxiously longing for their return to Him. One of the Lord's favorite tools for teaching was the parable. A parable is an analogy, a visible story that contains spiritual truth. In Luke 15, for example, we find three back-to-back parables that all carry the same message: "Though you are lost in sin, you are valuable to God. He loves you and He's looking for you."

The Parable of the Lost Sheep

> "Suppose one of you has a hundred sheep and loses one of them. Does he not leave the ninety-nine in the open country and go after the lost sheep until he finds it? And when he finds it, he joyfully puts it on his shoulders and goes home. Then he calls his friends and neighbors together and says, 'Rejoice with me; I have found my lost sheep.' I tell you that in the same way there will be more rejoicing in heaven over one sinner who repents than over ninety-nine righteous persons who do not need to repent." (Luke 15:4–7)

The Parable of the Lost Coin

> "Or suppose a woman has ten silver coins and loses one. Does she not light a lamp, sweep the house and search carefully until she finds it? And when she finds it, she calls her friends and neighbors together and says, 'Rejoice with me; I have found my lost coin.' In the same way, I tell you, there is rejoicing in the presence of the angels of God over one sinner who repents." (Luke 15:8–10)

The Parable of the Lost Son

> "There was a man who had two sons. The younger one said to his father, 'Father, give me my share of the estate.' So he divided his property between them. Not long after that, the younger son got together all he had, set off for a distant country and there squandered his wealth in wild living. After he had spent everything, there was a severe famine in that whole country, and he began to be in need. ... When he came to his senses, he said, 'How many of my father's hired men have food to spare, and here I am starving to death! I will set out and go back to my father and say to him: Father, I have sinned against heaven and against you. I am no longer worthy to be called your son; make me like one of your hired men.' So he got up and went to his father. But while he was still a long way off, his father saw him and was filled with compassion for him; he ran to his son, threw his arms around him and kissed him. The son said to him, 'Father, I have sinned against heaven and against you. I am no longer worthy to be called your son.' But the father said to his servants, 'Quick! Bring the best robe and put it on him. Put a ring on his finger and sandals on his feet. Bring the fattened calf and kill it. Let's have a feast and celebrate. For this son of mine was dead and is alive again; he was lost and is found.'" (Luke 15:11–14, 17–24)

In the parable of the lost son, a young man, foolishly deciding that he no longer needed his father, set off for a "*distant country*," where he quickly squandered all his money. "*When he came to his senses*," he realized how much he missed and needed his father. So he decided to return home, accept punishment for his sins, and become one of his father's slaves. But when he arrived back home, instead of rejecting him for his mistakes, the father ran to him and hugged him. Instead of making him a servant, he gave him the new (and best) garments for a son. Instead of punishing the son for his sins, the father gave a party in his honor!

Likewise, the Lord is teaching that this is exactly the way God the Father feels about sinners (like all of us) who have gone astray and departed from Him. He wants us back! If we return to the Father with sincere repentance, He will run to us, welcome us with open arms, forgive us of all our sins, and give us assurance that we are forever His children. This was the message of God's love that Jesus conveyed to the common people. In return, they loved Him.

The Unrepentant Crowd That Rejected Jesus

But while Jesus loved everybody in Israel, not everybody in Israel loved Him. By now you already know that this was the same group of men who had refused to repent and be baptized by John the Baptist. It was the Pharisees, the Sadducees, the scribes, and the so-called "experts" of the Mosaic Law. Just as they had rejected John, they rejected Jesus. Every conversation that Jesus had with these men turned into a confrontation. When they came to the Lord, it was not to ask sincere questions but to make accusations. They were not interested in His teachings. They wanted only to trap Him with His words.

"Why," you may ask, "would anyone (then or now) reject Jesus? After all, what's not to love?" As we read the four Gospels, we can see at least three reasons why these men rejected the Lord. They argued with Him about tradition. They disagreed with Him on the subject of religion, and, because of Him, they were worried about losing their position. Let's consider these three issues.

The Pharisees and Sadducees frequently condemned Jesus for not keeping their man-made traditions. The Law of Moses, remember, was to be Israel's guidebook for worshipping and serving God. However, after the return from the Babylonian captivity and during the 400 inter-testament years, Jewish rabbis began adding their own oral traditions to the written Law of Moses. The religious leaders of Israel considered these traditions of the elders to be sacred and of equal authority to the written Law. And anyone who did not keep these traditions was a sinner. For example, concerning the observance of the Sabbath (our Saturday), the Law of God said,

> "Remember the Sabbath day by keeping it holy. Six days you shall labor and do all your work, but the seventh day is a Sabbath to the LORD your God. On it you shall not do any work, neither you, nor your son or daughter, nor your manservant or maidservant, nor your animals, nor the alien within your gates." (Exod. 20:8–10)

Indeed, the Law called for a general ceasing of labor on the Sabbath day. It was to be a day of rest and refreshment. Such things as burden bearing, traveling, trading, and marketing would have been violations of God's Law. But not satisfied with God's written word about the Sabbath, Jewish rabbis added their own long list of unwritten do's and don'ts. For example, according to the tradition of the elders:

- You should not look in a mirror on the Sabbath because you might be tempted to pull out a gray hair and that would be reaping.
- A donkey could be led out of the stable on the Sabbath, but the harness and saddle had to be placed on him the day before.
- It was unlawful to move furniture on the Sabbath. One exception to this was a ladder could be moved, but only four steps.
- It was not permitted to wear jewelry on the Sabbath as that would be "burden bearing."
- It was fine to spit on a rock on the Sabbath, but you could not spit on the ground because that made mud and mud was mortar, and that was work.

In short, the rabbis turned God's day of rest into a day of (foolish) man-made rules! Jesus, however, always obedient to the word of God, did not even pretend to care about their Sabbath traditions. Instead He said, "'it is lawful to do good on the Sabbath'" (Matt. 12:12). Frequently the Lord healed people of various ailments on the Sabbath. But when He did so, instead of rejoicing that a suffering person had been made well, the Pharisees were enraged because Jesus was "breaking the

Sabbath" (John 5:18). Some of the Pharisees actually said, "'This man is not from God, for he does not keep the Sabbath'" (John 9:16).

Mark records another clash between Jesus and Israel's religious leaders over their tradition of hand washing. "The Pharisees and teachers of the law asked Jesus, 'Why don't your disciples live according to the tradition of the elders instead of eating their food with "unclean" hands?'" (Mark 7:5). Once again, Jewish rabbis had gone beyond the Law of God to add a tradition. The Law certainly called for bodily cleanliness. The priests were required to wash their hands and feet before entering into the Temple sanctuary (Exod. 30:19–21). But the Pharisees had turned routine hand washing into a religious ritual. A ceremonial technique had to be observed. (Probably rubbing the fist of one hand into the palm of the other and then washing.) Again, when Jesus ignored this unnecessary tradition, the Pharisees accused Him of sinning.

The Lord not only ignored the traditions of the elders, He condemned them. According to Jesus, these man-made rules were not just harmless additions to God's Law, they were dangerous distractions from it! For example, the Jewish rabbis established a tradition that if a man donated money to the Temple as a gift, he then was excused from his obligation to honor or help his parents with financial support. Jesus pointed out to the Pharisees that this was a clear violation of one of the Ten Commandments. In His words,

> "You have let go of the commands of God and are holding on to the traditions of men." And he said to them: "You have a fine way of setting aside the commands of God in order to observe your own traditions! For Moses said, 'Honor your father and your mother,' and, 'Anyone who curses his father or mother must be put to death.' But you say that if a man says to his father or mother: 'Whatever help you might otherwise have received from me is Corban' (that is, a gift devoted to God), then you no longer let him do anything for his father or mother. Thus you nullify the word of God by your tradition that you have handed down. And you do many things like that." (Mark 7:8–13)

The disagreement that Jesus had with Israel's leaders over tradition led to another controversy on the subject of religion. We might summarize the difference this way: To the Pharisees, Sadducees, and scribes, religion was all about rules, regulations, and rituals. But to Jesus, true religion was about relationships, loving relationships toward God and man. The Lord once taught that man's duty to God could be summarized with just two commandments:

> "'Love the Lord your God with all your heart and with all your soul and with all your mind.' This is the first and greatest commandment. And the second is like it: 'Love your neighbor as yourself.' All the Law and the Prophets hang on these two commandments." (Matt. 22:37–40)

According to Jesus, the purpose of religion was to cleanse the heart and make it pure. But to the Pharisees and Sadducees, religion was a cloak to hide an evil heart. Please notice a comment the Lord once made to them: "'Now then, you Pharisees clean the outside of the cup and dish, but inside you are full of greed and wickedness. You foolish people! Did not the one who made the outside make the inside also?'" (Luke 11:39–40). On another occasion He said, "'Woe to you, teachers of the law and Pharisees, you hypocrites! You are like whitewashed tombs, which look beautiful on the outside but on the inside are full of dead men's bones and everything unclean'" (Matt. 23:27).

The religion of the Pharisees, Sadducees, and scribes was one of works. They believed that by obeying the commandments of God and keeping the traditions of the elders, a person could earn favor with God and be deserving of Heaven. Since, in their opinion, they were doing all these things perfectly, they did not need the message of repentance and faith that John the Baptist had preached and now Jesus was preaching. But Jesus warned them of their need of repentance by saying, "'unless you repent, you too will all perish'" (Luke 13:5). He also warned them of their need for faith. "'If you do not believe that I am [the one I claim to be], you will indeed die in your sins'" (John 8:24).

Perhaps the biggest reason of all for rejecting and hating Jesus was simply that He was a threat to their position. These hypocritical men loved the spotlight. They loved the status of being looked upon as the spiritual leaders of Israel. According to the Lord, "'Everything they do is done for men to see: They make their phylacteries wide and the tassels on their garments long; they love the place of honor at banquets and the most important seats in the synagogues; they love to be greeted in the marketplaces and to have men call them 'Rabbi'"(Matt. 23:5–7).

As Jesus became more and more popular with the people, the religious leaders became envious of Him. They saw their position and status slipping away. They even admitted as much: "'Here is this man performing many miraculous signs. If we let him go on like this, everyone will believe in him, and then the Romans will come and take away both our place and our nation'" (John 11:47–48).

Although they had heard the Lord say so many amazing things, and they had seen Him perform so many spectacular signs, this crowd of unrepentant men adamantly refused to believe that Jesus was from God. On one occasion, a demon-possessed man who was both blind and mute was brought to Jesus. After the Lord healed the man, most of the crowd was astonished and glorified God. But the Pharisees responded with, "'It is only by Beelzebub, the prince of demons, that this fellow drives out demons'" (Matt. 12:24). "Beelzebub" is another term for the devil. Unable to deny that an amazing miracle had taken place, the Pharisees resorted to accusing Jesus of being the servant of Satan!

The Revelation That Jesus Is the Christ

As mentioned earlier, Jesus fully intended to acknowledge His identity as the Christ. But this revelation would come in His time and in His way, with or without the approval of wicked men. His time to do this was almost at the end of His ministry, with only about four months remaining of His earthly life. His way of doing it was in a private setting with His twelve apostles.

> When Jesus came to the region of Caesarea Philippi, he asked his disciples, "Who do people say the Son of Man is?" They replied, "Some say John the Baptist; others say Elijah; and still others, Jeremiah or one of the prophets."

> "But what about you?" he asked. "Who do you say I am?" Simon Peter answered, "You are the Christ, the Son of the living God." Jesus replied, "Blessed are you, Simon son of Jonah, for this was not revealed to you by man, but by my Father in Heaven." (Matt. 16:13–17)

This was Jesus' time and way. Rather than proclaim His own identity, He chose to reveal it to His disciples by allowing them to watch Him, observe Him, and listen to Him for over three years. He wanted them to reach the conclusion that He was the Christ as a result of God's teaching influence in their own hearts. Peter was the first apostle to acknowledge that Jesus was truly "the Anointed One". But immediately after Peter's wonderful confession, the Lord "warned his disciples not to tell anyone that he was the Christ" (Matt. 16:20).

While the apostles had come to believe that Jesus was the Messiah, they were still very confused about His mission on Earth, as demonstrated by the passage below.

> From that time on Jesus began to explain to his disciples that he must go to Jerusalem and suffer many things at the hands of the elders, chief priests and teachers of the law, and that he must be killed and on the third day be raised to life. Peter took him aside and began to rebuke him. "Never, Lord!" he said. "This shall never happen to you!" Jesus turned and said to Peter, "Get behind me, Satan! You are a stumbling block to me; you do not have in mind the things of God, but the things of men." (Matt. 16:21–23)

Thus we see that even Peter, who had been the first apostle to perceive that Jesus was the Christ, still believed (like all Israel) that the Christ could NEVER suffer or die. Six days later, to provide even more convincing proof that He was "*the Christ, the Son of the living God*," Jesus took three of His apostles, Peter, James, and John, to a nearby mountain. "There he was transfigured before them. His face shone like the sun, and his clothes became as white as the light" (Matt. 17:2).

Jesus did not at this time go to Heaven; Heaven came upon Him! He glistened with the splendor and glory of God. Then the three apostles heard a voice from Heaven. It was the same audible voice that the children of Israel had heard 1,400 years earlier at Mount Sinai, and the same Heavenly voice that John the Baptist heard at the Jordan River when he had baptized Jesus. This time the voice said, "'This is my Son, whom I love; with him I am well pleased. Listen to him!'" (Matt. 17:5).

As we approach the end of Jesus' earthly life, we observe a very sad and serious situation. As a result of the Lord's three-and-a-half-year ministry, the nation of Israel was divided. It was divided over Him! There were thousands of people in Israel who had humbled themselves and repented of sin. Though they did not yet fully understand His mission on Earth, they had come to love Jesus and believe that He was truly the Son of God. But there was another crowd in Israel, made up of proud, powerful men who, because of the hardness of their hearts, had not repented and had come to have an intense hatred for Him. In our next lesson, when we look at the last week of our Lord's earthly life, we will see just how serious this situation really was.

If you have a question about this lesson, or other questions about the Bible, please visit my website www.FredWoodwardBible.com. There you can obtain my contact information and we can communicate through email. I'll do my very best to answer your questions.

Lesson 19

Passion Week: Palm Sunday to Thursday

Matthew, Mark, Luke, John

As mentioned previously, because He felt so much animosity coming from the religious leaders in Jerusalem, Jesus did most of His teaching, healing, and disciple-making in northern Israel. And for that reason, our tour bus has been parked for quite some time on the western shore of the Sea of Galilee. But once again, we need to get onboard the bus and travel south for a trip that will take about three hours.

We are headed for a specific location. There is a road that leaves the ancient town of Jericho and leads to the eastern border of Jerusalem. As the road makes its way along the eastern slope of the Mount of Olives, there is a scenic overlook from which we will be able to view the entire city of Jerusalem. As we will see, Jesus Himself once stopped at this very spot and beheld the city. We will park the bus at this location so that we can observe the last week of our Lord's earthly life. This week is referred to as "Passion Week." The word "passion" means suffering.

On our bus ride south, let me encourage you to take a nap, drink some coffee, or perhaps eat a candy bar. In short, please do whatever you need to do to make sure you are awake and alert by the time we reach our destination. Because, without any exaggeration, of all the things we have observed on our tour of the Bible, the events of Passion Week are the most important.

The King Comes to Jerusalem (Sunday)

It was not at all unusual for Jesus to visit Jerusalem. According to the Law of Moses, all Jewish men were required to attend three of the seven annual feasts of God. Even by a conservative estimate, during His thirty-three years on earth, the Lord probably visited the holy city well over one hundred times. As Jesus approached the end of His earthly life, He came to Jerusalem one last time to attend the annual Feast of Passover.

The Lord had stayed for two days with some dear friends, Mary, Martha, and their brother Lazarus, who lived in Bethany, a small village on the Jericho road about two miles east of Jerusalem. On the first day of the week (Sunday), with the Feast of Passover just four days away, Jesus and His disciples began walking toward Jerusalem.

As they approached the city, Jesus instructed two of His disciples to "'go to the village ahead of you, and at once you will find a donkey tied there, with her colt by her. Untie them and bring them to me'" (Matt. 21:2). Matthew would have us know that the Lord did this to fulfill prophecy, so he quoted from Zechariah 9:9: "This took place to fulfill what was spoken through the prophet: 'Say to the Daughter of Zion, "See, your king comes to you, gentle and riding on a donkey, on a colt, the foal of a donkey"'"(Matt. 21:4–5).

"When they brought the colt to Jesus and threw their cloaks over it, he sat on it" (Mark 11:7). After this, "the great crowd that had come for the Feast heard that Jesus was on his way to Jerusalem. They took palm branches and went out to meet him" (John 12:12–13). And then came the shouting from the crowd.

"Hosanna to the Son of David!"
"Blessed is he who comes in the name of the Lord!"
"Hosanna in the highest!" (Matt. 21:9)

"Hosanna!"
"Blessed is he who comes in the name of the Lord!"
"Blessed is the coming kingdom of our father David!"
"Hosanna in the highest!" (Mark 11:9–10)

"Blessed is the king who comes in the name of the Lord!"
"Peace in heaven and glory in the highest!" (Luke 19:38)

"Hosanna!"
"Blessed is he who comes in the name of the Lord!"
"Blessed is the King of Israel!" (John 12:13)

What the crowd was shouting said it all.

- "Hosanna" is a Hebrew word that means "Save Now!"
- "Blessed is he who comes in the name of the Lord!" is Psalm 118:26, a Messianic prophecy.
- "Blessed is the coming kingdom of our father David!" is an acknowledgment that Jesus is the promised son of David.
- "Peace in heaven and glory in the highest!" fulfills Isaiah's prophecy of the "Prince of Peace" (Isaiah 9:6).
- "Blessed is the King of Israel!" is an acknowledgment that Jesus is the long-awaited Messiah King.

Just as Jesus had privately acknowledged His identity to His twelve apostles a few months earlier, now He was publicly declaring Himself to be the Christ to all Israel! Bible scholars refer to this event as "The Triumphal Entry." Because the crowd spread palm leaves on the road ahead of Jesus, every year Christians celebrate "Palm Sunday" one week before Easter Sunday.

The King Cries for Jerusalem

It will not surprise you to learn that not everyone was thrilled that Jesus was being honored and welcomed into Jerusalem as the Christ. Yes, you guessed it: the Pharisees were not at all happy. Angered that the Lord was being hailed as the Son of David, "some of the Pharisees in the crowd said to Jesus, 'Teacher, rebuke your disciples!'" (Luke 19:39). But Jesus responded by saying, "'I tell you ... if they keep quiet, the stones will cry out'" (Luke 19:40). The coming of God's King to Jerusalem was an event for all of creation (stones included) to celebrate, whether the Pharisees liked it or not!

This hostility that the Pharisees felt toward Jesus helps to explain what happened next. Still riding the donkey colt, the Lord came to the place (where our bus is parked) that allowed Him to view the entire city of Jerusalem. When He "saw the city, he wept over it" (Luke 19:41). Now this indeed must have been a strange sight. While a huge crowd of people was smiling, shouting, clapping, and celebrating, Jesus, who was the reason for all this rejoicing, was weeping.

Why, on what should have been such a happy occasion, was the Lord weeping? The answer is found in His own words.

> "If you, [Jerusalem], even you, had only known on this day what would bring you peace—but now it is hidden from your eyes. The days will come upon you when your enemies will build an embankment against you and encircle you and hem you in on every side. They will dash you to the ground, you and the children within your walls. They will not leave one stone on another, because you did not recognize the time of God's coming to you." (Luke 19:42–44)

With His unique ability, Jesus was not just looking at Jerusalem, He was looking into Jerusalem's future. And what He saw troubled Him. Jesus saw the spiritual division that we have observed, between the repentant crowd in Israel that loved Him and the unrepentant crowd that hated Him. He saw that the powerful religious leaders would ultimately prevail and persuade the people of Jerusalem to reject Him. Instead of crowning Him as their king, they would crucify Him as a common criminal. And He saw that instead of being on the threshold of global greatness, Israel was on the threshold of national disaster. And, according to Jesus, it was all because they *"did not recognize the time of God's coming."* Foreseeing Jerusalem's tragic future, Jesus wept.

The King Cleanses the Temple

After His moment of sorrow, the Lord resumed riding the donkey colt toward Jerusalem. He rode through the eastern gate of the city and all the way to the steps of the Temple. By doing so, He fulfilled a prophecy that Malachi had made some 400 years earlier: "'Then suddenly the Lord you are seeking will come to his temple; the messenger of the covenant, whom you desire, will come,' says the LORD Almighty" (Mal. 3:1).

But when Jesus entered the Temple, He was very angry at what He saw. In what probably looked like a "flea market," several merchants had set up shop right in the Temple compound. They were selling doves, sheep, and bulls, and they had set up tables to exchange various kinds of foreign currency.

In order to understand why the Lord was so angry, we must remember that in those days, Jewish people (because of the Assyrian and Babylonian captivities) were scattered all over the known world. To attend the Passover Feast in Jerusalem, some would have had to travel hundreds of miles. It would have been impractical, if not impossible, for them to bring with them the animals needed for sacrifice at the Temple. They also would have needed to exchange their foreign currency in order to make a donation to God. Obviously, they would have had to obtain these things once they arrived in Jerusalem.

In short, it wasn't what these merchants were doing that was so wrong, it was where they were doing it. By conducting their business in a place that Jesus considered sacred, they were desecrating and defiling His Father's House. His anger led to immediate action.

> Jesus entered the temple area and began driving out those who were buying and selling there. He overturned the tables of the money changers and the benches of those selling doves, and would not allow anyone to carry merchandise through the temple courts. And as he taught them, he said, "Is it not written: 'My house will be called a house of prayer for all nations'? But you have made it 'a den of robbers.'" (Mark 11:15–17)

This act of cleansing the Temple, however, infuriated the Pharisees, Sadducees, and other religious leaders. In their minds, they were in charge of the Temple, and they had given these merchants permission to conduct business there. Just who did this young rabbi think He was? And why did He think He had the authority to do these things?

The King Confounds His Enemies (Tuesday)

By Tuesday, Jerusalem's religious elite had had enough. They had stood helplessly by as multitudes of people came to the Temple to hear Jesus and be healed by Him. Now it was time for them to take action. They decided that the best way to stop this "Messiah madness" was to confront the Lord publicly and ask Him theological (pertaining to God) questions. In this way, they would humiliate and discredit Him in front of the people. Since they were educated and learned men, and this Jesus fellow was just an uneducated peasant, how hard could it be?

So, one by one, the various groups came to Jesus with their questions. First, it was the chief priests and the elders of the people. Next, "the Pharisees went out and laid plans to trap him in his words" (Matt. 22:15). And then the Sadducees took their turn. And after the Sadducees, "an expert in the law, tested him" (Matt. 22:35).

But their plan completely backfired. They obviously did not know whom they were dealing with. With His profound wisdom and insight of the scriptures, Jesus not only answered their questions, He amazed them (and the crowd) with His answers. Instead of publicly humiliating Him, they were humiliated by Jesus. Understandably, "from that day on no one dared to ask him any more questions" (Matt. 22:46).

The King is Conspired Against

Having failed in their attempt to embarrass and discredit Him in front of the people, Jesus' enemies decided that there was just one thing left to do. They must kill Him. The chief priests, the scribes, and the elders "plotted to arrest Jesus in some sly way and kill him" (Matt. 26:4). The reason they had to arrest the Lord "in some sly way" was because they were afraid that if they arrested Him publicly "'there may be a riot among the people'" (Matt. 26:5).

Enter the Dragon! Do you remember that three and a half years earlier Jesus had battled and defeated the devil by resisting all of his temptations? After that fight was over, the devil "left him until an opportune time" (Luke 4:13). Well, he came back. Satan's "opportune time" had come.

> Then Satan entered Judas, called Iscariot, one of the Twelve. And Judas went to the chief priests and the officers of the temple guard and discussed with them how he might betray Jesus. They were delighted and agreed to give him money. He consented, and watched for an opportunity to hand Jesus over to them when no crowd was present. (Luke 22:3–6)

This, then, was the plan. Judas, one of the Twelve, promised the chief priests that he would (for a price) watch "for an opportunity" when Jesus was away from the crowds. When that opportunity presented itself, Judas would run back to the religious leaders to let them know where Jesus could be safely apprehended. From that moment on, Satan would be actively involved in the conspiracy to kill the Son of God.

The King Establishes the New Covenant (Thursday)

The Feast of Passover was scheduled to begin on Thursday evening of Passion Week. So that they might prepare for the Feast, Jesus gave two of His disciples the following instructions.

> "Go into the city, and a man carrying a jar of water will meet you. Follow him. Say to the owner of the house he enters, 'The Teacher asks: Where is my guest room, where I may eat the Passover with my disciples?' He will show you a large upper room, furnished and ready. Make preparations for us there." (Mark 14:13–15)

Later that evening, when Jesus and the rest of His apostles came to the upper room, they all sat down to enjoy the Passover meal, which would have included, of course, the Passover lamb. What the Lord did next was what His Heavenly Father had sent Him to do. He had come from Heaven to establish a new covenant between God and man. Luke tells us what Jesus did as He and His disciples were finishing the Passover meal.

> And he took bread, gave thanks and broke it, and gave it to them, saying, "This is my body given for you; do this in remembrance of me." In the same way, after the supper he took the cup, saying, "This cup is the new covenant in my blood, which is poured out for you." (Luke 22:19–20)

Thus in this upper room, the old covenant, established by Moses on Mount Sinai between God and Israel, which had been in effect for 1,400 years, came to an end. The new covenant, which would be between God and whoever believes in His Son, had come. "'For God so loved the world that he gave his one and only Son, that whoever believes in him shall not perish but have eternal life'" (John 3:16). Here, also, the Lord initiated what was to be called the Lord's Supper. For this reason, to remember Jesus and to recommit themselves afresh to the new covenant, Christians for over 2,000 years have observed this holy ordinance by taking "the bread and the cup."

"But," you may ask, "where's the blood? When Moses mediated the old agreement between God and Israel on Mount Sinai, he sprinkled animal blood on the people to seal the covenant. Here, in the upper room, we see Jesus, the mediator, and His disciples who believe in Him, but where's the blood?" Don't worry, my friends. In about twelve hours Jesus will supply the necessary blood for the new covenant: His own!

If you have a question about this lesson, or other questions about the Bible, please visit my website www.FredWoodwardBible.com. There you can obtain my contact information and we can communicate through email. I'll do my very best to answer your questions.

Lesson 20

Passion Week: Thursday Night to Sunday

Matthew, Mark, Luke, John

You might remember that after Jesus won His first battle with Satan, I said that the war with the wicked one was far from over and that one day the devil would demand a "rematch." That time had now come. The fight started sometime late Thursday night and continued until three o'clock Friday afternoon. For approximately eighteen hours, Satan would beat, bruise, and bludgeon our Lord. As promised, I have obtained front-row seats for this fight. But be warned, this battle will be brutal. If sometime during the fight you feel like crying, go ahead.

The King Confronts His Betrayer

On Thursday night, as Jesus and His disciples were finishing their meal, the Lord surprised the Twelve by saying,

> "I tell you the truth, one of you will betray me—one who is eating with me." They were saddened, and one by one they said to him, "Surely not I?" "It is one of the Twelve," he replied, "one who dips bread into the bowl with me. The Son of Man will go just as it is written about him. But woe to that man who betrays the Son of Man! It would be better for him if he had not been born." (Mark 14:18–21)

This seems to be a veiled warning to Judas of the horrors that awaited him if he carried out his wicked intentions. As Jesus explained, His own death was prophesied in the holy scriptures and was a part of God's plan. To destroy Jesus, Satan would inevitably find someone to work through. But Judas, Jesus warned, don't let it be you!

Moments later, the Lord said to Judas, "'What you are about to do, do quickly'" (John 13:27). The other disciples at the table just thought that Jesus was sending Judas on an errand. But in reality, Judas was leaving the upper room to betray the Lord. In a statement full of symbolic meaning, John relayed, "As soon as Judas had taken the bread, he went out. And it was night" (John 13:30). Much more than just leaving a room and going out into the night, Judas was leaving the Lord and stepping out into eternal darkness. A thousand years earlier, King David, inspired by the Holy Spirit, had prophesied of this betrayal of friendship: "Even my close friend, whom I trusted, he who shared my bread, has lifted up his heel against me" (Ps. 41:9).

The King Seeks Comfort from His Father

Jesus then led His (eleven) disciples to one of His favorite places, a quiet garden on the Mount of Olives called the Garden of Gethsemane. Knowing that in the next few hours He would face unspeakable suffering, the Lord wanted to spend time in prayer to prepare Himself. Unfortunately, Judas also "knew the place, because Jesus had often met there with his disciples" (John 18:2). So while Jesus and His disciples were on their way to the Garden of Gethsemane, Judas was on his way to the Lord's enemies, to reveal to them that Jesus would be at this garden and could be arrested there without incident.

At this point, Jesus told His disciples: "'This very night you will all fall away on account of me, for it is written: "I will strike the shepherd, and the sheep of the flock will be scattered"'" (Matt. 26:31). All of the disciples objected to this, insisting that their loyalty to the Lord was to the death. Peter even boasted, "'Even if all fall away on account of you, I never will'" (Matt. 26:33).

After arriving at the Garden of Gethsemane, the Lord "took Peter, James and John along with him, and he began to be deeply distressed and troubled. 'My soul is overwhelmed with sorrow to the point of death,' he said to them. 'Stay here and keep watch'" (Mark 14:33–34). According to Luke:

> He withdrew about a stone's throw beyond them, knelt down and prayed, "Father, if you are willing, take this cup from me; yet not my will, but yours be done." An angel from heaven appeared to him and strengthened him. And being in anguish, he prayed more earnestly, and his sweat was like drops of blood falling to the ground." (Luke 22:41-44)

Matthew and Mark tell us that Jesus went to His Heavenly Father three times, with the same words, making the same request, "*take this cup from me.*" The Lord was not only divine, He was also very human. As such, He recoiled from the prospect of unimaginable pain, suffering, and death. He did not want to die. But all three times, He also added, "*yet not my will, but yours be done.*" After the third time, the Lord accepted the harsh truth that it was His Father's will that He suffer rejection, shame, humiliation, and an excruciating death on a Roman cross.

The King Becomes a "Criminal"

And it was at that same moment that "Judas, one of the Twelve, appeared. With him was a crowd armed with swords and clubs, sent from the chief priests, the teachers of the law, and the elders" (Mark 14:43). Because it was dark and the men in this mob did not know Jesus, Judas "arranged a signal with them: 'The one I kiss is the man; arrest him and lead him away under guard.' Going at once to Jesus, Judas said, 'Rabbi!' and kissed him. The men seized Jesus and arrested him" (Mark 14:44–46). Then, just as Jesus had predicted, "all the disciples deserted him and fled" (Matt. 26:56).

The King Is Condemned

After being arrested, Jesus was taken to the Sanhedrin, the highest court in Israel. The Sanhedrin was composed of seventy Jewish men and had authority over all religious matters. The acting high priest of Israel served as the president of the group. But for Jesus' case, this particular Sanhedrin was made up of the very men who hated Him most and had already conspired to kill Him. So this trial of Jesus would not be a quest for truth. These wicked men had already decided that the Lord would die; they just wanted to "make it legal."

To their great dismay, "the chief priests and the whole Sanhedrin were looking for evidence against Jesus so that they could put him to death, but they did not find any. Many testified falsely against him, but their statements did not agree" (Mark 14:55–56). Finally, in frustration, Caiaphas the high priest asked Jesus, "'Are you the Christ, the Son of the Blessed One?'" (Mark 14:61). The Lord responded with "'I am'" (Mark 14:62).

In a show of righteous indignation (actually he was rejoicing), "the high priest tore his clothes. 'Why do we need any more witnesses?' he asked. 'You have heard the blasphemy. What do you think?' They all condemned him as worthy of death" (Mark 14:63–64). With Jesus' acknowledgment that He was "*the Son of the Blessed One*," the Sanhedrin had all they needed. Anyone claiming to be equal with God was committing the sin of blasphemy, and in Israel, blasphemy was a crime punishable by death. Trial over!

At this point, the members of the Sanhedrin would have liked nothing better than to just take Jesus out and stone Him to death. But for one very irritating reason they could not do that. The irritating reason was Rome. Israel, at the time, was under Roman occupation, and the Romans did not allow the nations they occupied to exercise the death penalty. Not that the Romans were opposed to the death penalty; they just wanted to be the ones to administer it. To terrorize and control the nations they had conquered, the Romans had invented one of the cruelest, most tortuous forms of execution: crucifixion. For this reason, to put Jesus to death, the members of the Sanhedrin were forced to take Jesus to the Roman governor, Pontius Pilate.

> Then the Jews led Jesus from Caiaphas to the palace of the Roman governor. By now it was early morning, and to avoid ceremonial uncleanness the Jews did not enter the palace; they wanted to be able to eat the Passover. So Pilate came out to them and asked, "What charges are you bringing against this man?" "If he were not a criminal," they replied, "we would not have handed him over to you." Pilate said, "Take him yourselves and judge him by your own law." "But we have no right to execute anyone," the Jews objected. (John 18:28–31)

Pilate immediately realized that the members of the Sanhedrin had no legitimate charges to bring against Jesus. He also perceived that "it was out of envy that the chief priests had handed Jesus over to him" (Mark 15:10). After he had personally interrogated the Lord, Pilate went back out to the crowd and said, "'I find no basis for a charge against him'" (John 18:38). Convinced that the Lord was an innocent man, Pilate actually appealed to the crowd because he wanted "to release Jesus" (Luke 23:20).

Every year at the Passover, it was Pilate's custom to release one Jewish prisoner, who was chosen by the crowd. At the time, a notorious criminal named Barabbas had been arrested and charged with insurrection (against Rome) and murder. In one last attempt to rescue Jesus, Pilate asked the crowd, "'Which one do you want me to release to you: Barabbas, or Jesus who is called Christ?'" (Matt. 27:17). At the urging of the chief priests and elders, the crowd answered, "'Give us Barabbas!'" (John 18:40). "'What shall I do, then, with Jesus who is called Christ?' Pilate asked. They all answered, 'Crucify him!' 'Why? What crime has he committed?' asked Pilate. But they shouted all the louder, 'Crucify him!'" (Matt. 27:22–23).

With hundreds of thousands of pilgrims in Jerusalem for the Passover, the last thing Pilate wanted was a Jewish uprising. So when he saw that "an uproar was starting he took water and washed his hands in front of the crowd. 'I am innocent of this man's blood,' he said. 'It is your responsibility!'" (Matt. 27:24). In words that would carry more than 2,000 years of consequences, the Jewish crowd said, "'Let his blood be on us and on our children!'" (Matt. 27:25). To silence and satisfy this angry mob, "Pilate released Barabbas to them. He had Jesus flogged, and handed him over to be crucified" (Mark 15:15).

The King Is Crucified

Now we will see the full extent of Satan's hatred and wrath, as he used cruel and merciless men to inflict pain on the Lord. Even before being crucified, Jesus was flogged by the Roman soldiers. This was not a regular whipping; this was extreme torture, so excruciating that many men died while being flogged. The implement used for flogging was a modified cat o' nine tails. At the end of the leather straps were pieces of bone, broken glass, or nails. With every lash of the soldier's whip, these sharp objects were embedded into Jesus' back. When the soldier pulled the whip away, strips of flesh were torn from His body. To add insult to injury, the Roman soldiers "twisted together a crown of thorns and put it on his head. They clothed him in a purple robe and went up to him again and again, saying, 'Hail, king of the Jews!' And they struck him in the face" (John 19:2–3).

Jesus, carrying His own cross along with two other condemned thieves, was then led to a place outside the city known as Golgotha, which means "the place of the skull." The soldiers offered the Lord "wine mixed with myrrh" (Mark 15:23). This was a cheap Roman vinegar wine mixed with a drug to dull the senses. Some think the soldiers did this as an act of mercy, to lessen the pain of the victim. I believe they did it because it was just easier to deal with drugged men. Whatever the case, after tasting it Jesus "refused to drink it" (Matt. 27:34). A thousand years earlier, King David had said, they "gave me vinegar for my thirst" (Ps. 69:21).

In fulfillment of another prophecy, the soldiers "took his clothes, dividing them into four shares, one for each of them, with the undergarment remaining. This garment was seamless, woven in one piece from top to bottom. 'Let's not tear it,' they said to one another. 'Let's decide by lot who will get it'" (John 19:23–24).

Again, Jesus' forefather King David had spoken prophetically of this.

"They divide my garments among them and cast lots for my clothing" (Ps. 22:18).

Then the soldiers, driving nails into His hands and feet, nailed Jesus to the cross and stood the cross upright. Suspended on the cross in this position, the Lord could look down and count the bones in His own ribcage. King David had also prophesied of this when he wrote, "They have pierced my hands and my feet. I can count all my bones" (Ps. 22:16–17).

Most crucifixion victims died of suffocation because hanging in this position, pressure was put on the man's chest, making it difficult to breathe. To take even one breath, Jesus would have had to push up with His legs, with nails in His feet. In doing so, His back, raw from flogging, would rub against the cross.

Then came the mocking from His own people, the children of Israel.

> Those who passed by hurled insults at him, shaking their heads and saying, "So! You who are going to destroy the temple and build it in three days, come down from the cross and save yourself!" In the same way the chief priests and the teachers of the law mocked him among themselves. "He saved others," they said, "but he can't save himself! Let this Christ, this King of Israel, come down now from the cross, that we may see and believe." (Mark 15:29–32)

In response to these insults, the Lord could have called down fire from Heaven and destroyed them all. Instead, He prayed, "'Father, forgive them, for they do not know what they are doing'" (Luke 23:34). By now, it will not surprise you to learn that King David had made mention of this mocking: "All who see me mock me; they hurl insults, shaking their heads" (Ps. 22:7). Then, from noon till three o'clock came the strange darkness: "From the sixth hour until the ninth hour darkness came over all the land" (Matt. 27:45). God had announced He would do this, about 750 years earlier, through the prophet Amos: "'In that day,' declares the Sovereign LORD, 'I will make the sun go down at noon and darken the earth in broad daylight'" (Amos 8:9). I believe this strange darkness was a sign that God was laying the sins of all mankind on His Son, as predicted by Isaiah the prophet, 600 years earlier: "We all, like sheep, have gone astray, each of us has turned to his own way; and the LORD has laid on him the iniquity of us all" (Isa. 53:6).

And then, somewhere around three o'clock, Jesus, with the exact same words that His forefather David had used in Psalm 22:1, shouted, "'Eloi, Eloi,' 'lama' 'sabachthani?'—which means, 'My God, my God, why have you forsaken me?'" (Matt. 27:46). Then He said, "'It is finished'" (John 19:30). Then, with the prophetic words of Psalm 31:5, He said, "'Father, into your hands I commit my spirit'" (Luke 23:46).

Then Jesus died.

But, dear friends, we must not suppose, even for a moment, that the suffering and death of Jesus came as a surprise to Him or His Heavenly Father. Oh no, Jesus was "the Lamb that was slain from the creation of the world" (Rev. 13:8). You might remember that on the very day that Adam and Eve fell into sin, God announced in Genesis 3:15 that the "offspring of the woman" would one day come and He would be "bruised" by Satan. And as we toured the Old Testament, did we not see countless pictures and prophecies of the coming Christ that foretold of His suffering? And as we have just seen, during the last three hours of His life alone, no less than ten Old Testament prophecies were fulfilled.

Before the world began, by His infinite knowledge and wisdom, God devised a plan that would use the evil of man to bring about good for man. With the suffering and death of Jesus, we have witnessed the completion of that eternal plan. Now we understand why Jesus, with His dying words, said, "*It is finished*."

Now let's get to the good part.

The King Conquers Death

At the instant of Jesus' death, something good for man immediately happened. "And when Jesus had cried out again in a loud voice, he gave up his spirit. At that moment the curtain of the temple was torn in two from top to bottom" (Matt. 27:50–51). Do you remember when the Tabernacle (later called the Temple) was built at Mount Sinai, Moses was instructed to hang a veil between the rooms called The Holy Place and The Most Holy Place? This veil was a barrier, preventing sinful men from coming into the presence of a Holy God.

I'm not usually so arrogant that I quote my own words, but just this once bear with me. Back in Lesson 6, when we were learning about the veil in the Tabernacle, I said,

> Wouldn't it be wonderful if someone could do something about this veil? Wouldn't it be fabulous if someone could come to God with a sacrifice so perfect, with blood so pure, that God Himself would tear open this veil and then actually invite human beings into His holy presence? Take comfort, dear friends. Stay with me on the tour. Someone is coming! One day, God Himself would tear this veil from top to bottom.

With the sacrificial death of Jesus, that day had come! The instant the Lord died on the cross, God Himself tore open this veil (from top to bottom). Now, whoever believes in Jesus will have their sins forgiven and their soul cleansed by His blood. Such a person, whose heart has been purified by faith, is now invited to come (boldly) into God's Holy presence.

But the tearing of the veil is just the beginning of good news. In the upper room on Thursday night, Jesus had told His disciples that they would soon experience two powerful emotions, extreme grief followed by extreme joy: "'I tell you the truth, you will weep and mourn while the world rejoices. You will grieve, but your grief will turn to joy'" (John 16:20). The grief, of course, came on Friday afternoon when Jesus died.

With Jesus' death, the disciples went into a state of despair and confusion. Not only had they lost the Lord, they themselves were lost and bewildered. They had come to believe that Jesus was the Christ, the Son of God. But they still also believed, wrongly, that the Christ could never die. Also, as John tells us, "They still did not understand from Scripture that Jesus had to rise from the dead" (John 20:9). So the grief that the Lord had predicted lasted from three o'clock Friday until Sunday morning.

But then, on Sunday morning, came the promised joy. At dawn on the first day of the week (Sunday), a small group of women, who were followers of Jesus, came to the tomb, bringing sweet spices to anoint Jesus' body for final burial. But His body was nowhere to be found! There had been

> a violent earthquake, for an angel of the Lord came down from heaven and, going to the tomb, rolled back the stone and sat on it. His appearance was like lightning, and his clothes were white as snow. ... The angel said to the women, "Do not be afraid, for I know that you are looking for Jesus, who was crucified. He is not here; he has risen, just as he said. Come and see the place where he lay." ... So the women hurried away from the tomb, afraid yet filled with joy, and ran to tell his disciples. (Matt. 28:2–3, 5–6, 8)

Mary Magdalene was the first person to actually see Jesus after His resurrection. On that first Easter Sunday, the risen Lord appeared five times to different disciples in different places. The fifth and final appearance that day was to His apostles who were hiding in the upper room.

> On the evening of that first day of the week, when the disciples were together, with the doors locked for fear of the Jews, Jesus came and stood among them and said, "Peace be with you!" After he said this, he showed them his hands and side. The disciples were overjoyed when they saw the Lord. (John 20:19–20)

But the joy that Jesus promised was not just for those first followers; it was for all mankind! To help us understand what Jesus has done for all of us, let me share an illustration. Many years ago, I watched a movie entitled *Lonely Are the Brave*. The story was about a cowboy and his younger brother. The younger brother had committed a crime and had been arrested, tried, convicted, and thrown into prison. To rescue his younger brother, the cowboy did something radical. He deliberately got himself arrested and thrown into the same prison. Unbeknownst to the guards, however, the cowboy had hidden a hacksaw blade in his boot. At night, when the guards weren't watching, the cowboy sawed through the bars to make a way of escape for him and his brother.

Likewise Jesus, like a loving older brother, saw that we all had gotten ourselves into serious trouble. Because of our crimes (sins) against God, we had all been cast into the prison of sin and death, with Satan as the warden and his demons as the guards. To rescue us, the Lord did something radical; He became one of us. Jesus allowed Himself to be arrested and thrown into prison with us. But His plan all along was to break out. By His death, burial, and resurrection, the Lord has made for us a way of escape that leads not only out of prison but into the presence of God. As He once said about Himself, "'I am the way and the truth and the life. No one comes to the Father except through me'" (John 14:6). In the words of an old hymn,

"Low in the Grave He Lay"

Death cannot keep his prey—
Jesus, my Savior;
He tore the bars away—
Jesus, my Lord.
Up from the grave he arose
With a mighty triumph o'er his foes.
He arose a victor from the dark domain,
And he lives forever with his saints to reign.
He arose! He arose! Hallelujah! Christ arose!

Words: Robert Lowry, 1826–1899; Music: Robert Lowry, 1826–1899

If you have a question about this lesson, or other questions about the Bible, please visit my website www.FredWoodwardBible.com. There you can obtain my contact information and we can communicate through email. I'll do my very best to answer your questions.

Lesson 21

The Birth and Consolidation of the Church

Acts 1–7

With the death, burial, and resurrection of His Son, God created a message that He wants the entire world to hear. Since this message is such wonderful news for man, it will be called the gospel of Jesus Christ. The word "gospel" comes from the Greek word EUANGELLION and literally means "good tidings," "a good message," or "good news."

The good news is this: although the entire human race has fallen from God because of sin, God Himself has solved our sin problem. As the Apostle Paul wrote, "God demonstrates his own love for us in this: While we were still sinners, Christ died for us" (Rom. 5:8). Now that Jesus had finished His work on the cross and had been raised from the dead, reconciliation with God became remarkably simple. Whoever hears this message and responds to it with sincere repentance and faith will be forgiven of sin, will be restored to God's favor, and will forever rejoice in God's fellowship. In Jesus' own words, "'For God so loved the world that he gave his one and only Son, that whoever believes in him shall not perish but have eternal life'" (John 3:16).

All four Gospels end with the resurrection of Christ. Where the Gospels end, the book of Acts begins. In this book, we will learn what happened after Jesus rose from the dead, and we'll observe the acts of the apostles during the forty-year period that followed His resurrection. As we will see, the gospel of Christ would first be proclaimed in

Jerusalem, but in only a few short years, this good news would be heard in all parts of the known world.

The Assignment from the Lord

It is believed that a physician named Luke, who wrote the Gospel of Luke, was also the author of the book of Acts. Luke begins his account in Chapter 1 by telling us that, after Jesus rose from the dead, He did not immediately ascend into Heaven. Instead, "he showed himself to these men [the apostles] and gave many convincing proofs that he was alive. He appeared to them over a period of forty days and spoke about the kingdom of God" (Acts 1:3). The illustration below shows the fifty-day period from the Feast of Passover (when Jesus was crucified) to the Feast of Pentecost.

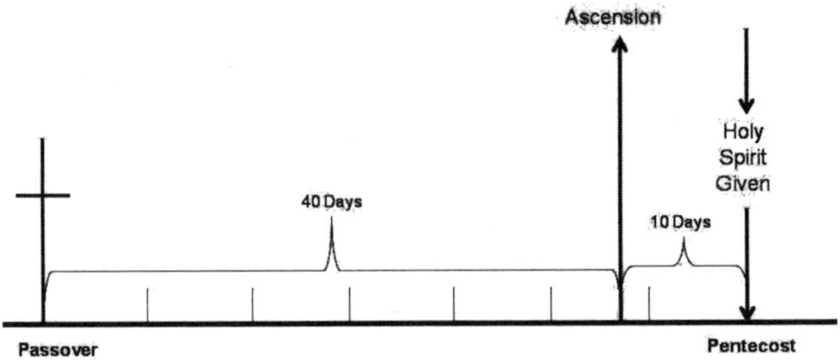

Luke tells us that for forty days after His resurrection, the Lord continued to appear to the apostles "and spoke about the kingdom of God." It was during this period that Jesus gave His disciples the following assignment. It has come to be known as "The Great Commission."

> "All authority in heaven and on earth has been given to me. Therefore go and make disciples of all nations, baptizing them in the name of the Father and of the Son and of the Holy Spirit, and teaching them to obey everything I have commanded you. And surely I am with you always, to the very end of the age." (Matt. 28:18–20)

The Lord speaks again of His Great Commission in Acts 1:8: "'But you will receive power when the Holy Spirit comes on you; and you will be my witnesses in Jerusalem, and in all Judea and Samaria, and to the ends of the earth.'"

Jesus' assignment for His followers, then, is to go into the entire world proclaiming His gospel and making disciples from every country, from every culture, and every color. His followers are to continue carrying out this Great Commission until He returns to Earth at the end of the age. But He also instructed them to remain in Jerusalem and "'wait for the gift my Father promised, which you have heard me speak about. For John baptized with water, but in a few days you will be baptized with the Holy Spirit'" (Acts 1:4–5). To carry out this holy commission, His followers would have to be empowered by the Holy Spirit.

The Ascension of the Lord

When the forty days were over,

> he was taken up before their very eyes, and a cloud hid him from their sight. They were looking intently up into the sky as he was going, when suddenly two men dressed in white stood beside them. "Men of Galilee," they said, "why do you stand here looking into the sky? This same Jesus, who has been taken from you into heaven, will come back in the same way you have seen him go into heaven." (Acts 1:9–11)

Thus ends "The First Coming" of Jesus Christ. With His work on Earth completed, the Lord ascended into heaven and was "exalted to the right hand of God" (Acts 2:33). He will sit in that position of authority, guiding the advancement of His kingdom until "this gospel of the kingdom will be preached in the whole world as a testimony to all nations, and then the end will come" (Matt. 24:14). And then, at the end of this age, what the angels proclaimed to the apostles will come to pass. *"This same Jesus, who has been taken from you into heaven, will come back in the same way you have seen him go into heaven."* This is the blessed hope of all Christians: "The Second Coming of Jesus Christ."

The Anointing of the Lord's Followers

As you may recall, when John the Baptist began his ministry, almost four years previously, he prophesied and said, "'After me will come one more powerful than I, the thongs of whose sandals I am not worthy to stoop down and untie. I baptize you with water, but he will baptize you with the Holy Spirit'" (Mark 1:7–8). John's prophecy was about to be fulfilled. Exactly ten days after Jesus ascended into Heaven came the Feast of Pentecost. And then it happened.

> When the day of Pentecost came, they were all together in one place. Suddenly a sound like the blowing of a violent wind came from heaven and filled the whole house where they were sitting. They saw what seemed to be tongues of fire that separated and came to rest on each of them. All of them were filled with the Holy Spirit and began to speak in other tongues as the Spirit enabled them. (Acts 2:1–4)

To confirm that this was indeed the Baptism of the Holy Spirit, God granted three observable signs:

1. "*a sound like the blowing of a violent wind*"
2. "*tongues of fire ... on each of them*" and
3. the disciples spoke "*in other tongues as the Spirit enabled them.*"

It was the speaking in foreign languages that drew a large crowd. Bear in mind that Jerusalem was once again filled with thousands of Jewish people who had traveled hundreds of miles to attend the Feast of Pentecost. These were Israelites (who might have been able to speak Hebrew), but they lived in foreign countries and normally spoke the languages of those countries. This explains why they were so bewildered when

> each one heard them [the disciples] speaking in his own language. Utterly amazed, they asked: "Are not all these men who are speaking Galileans? Then how is it that each of us hears them in his own native language? Parthians, Medes and Elamites; residents of Mesopotamia, Judea and Cappadocia, Pontus and Asia, Phrygia and Pamphylia, Egypt and the parts of Libya near Cyrene; visitors from Rome (both Jews and converts to Judaism); Cretans and Arabs—we hear them declaring the wonders of God in our own tongues!" Amazed and perplexed, they asked one another, "What does this mean?" (Acts 2:6–11)

To answer the question of the crowd, Peter stood up and said, "'Fellow Jews and all of you who live in Jerusalem, let me explain this to you; listen carefully to what I say'" (Acts 2:14). Peter went on to proclaim, for the first time, the gospel of Jesus Christ. In the power of the Holy Spirit, and using Old Testament prophecy and Psalms, he convinced this crowd that Jesus was indeed the long-awaited Christ: "'Therefore let all Israel be assured of this: God has made this Jesus, whom you crucified, both Lord and Christ'" (Acts 2:36).

The crowd responded to Peter's message with tender hearts and humility: "When the people heard this, they were cut to the heart and said to Peter and the other apostles, 'Brothers, what shall we do?'" (Acts 2:37). Peter replied, "'Repent and be baptized, every one of you, in the name of Jesus Christ for the forgiveness of your sins. And you will receive the gift of the Holy Spirit'" (Acts 2:38). Before this day was over, "those who accepted his message were baptized, and about three thousand were added to their number that day" (Acts 2:41).

Thus, on this historic day of Pentecost, more than 3,000 Jewish people repented of their sins, became believers in Jesus Christ, were baptized, and received the gift of the Holy Spirit. Bible scholars refer to this day as The Birth of the Church.

I can't resist the urge to remind you of a couple of things that we learned in the Old Testament. First of all, do you remember back in Genesis 11 when we observed what happened at the Tower of Babel? On that day, about 2300 BC, God introduced the confusion of languages in order to scatter evil men and slow down the acceleration of sin. But notice on the day of Pentecost, God did just the reverse. He enabled the disciples of Jesus to speak in other languages in order to signal the gathering of men under the lordship of Jesus Christ. This gathering continues to this day as the gospel of Christ is proclaimed around the world.

Second, let me remind you of what we've learned about the anointing. Up to this point in the Bible, we've seen individuals anointed with power when the Holy Spirit came upon them: Saul, David, Solomon, and finally Jesus at His baptism. But always there was just one anointed at any given time. Notice how the day of Pentecost has changed that. Now, because of the cleansing power of Christ, the Holy Spirit will come upon all who believe, thus making an army of anointed ones! This army, known as the church, will carry the light and life of Christ to a dark and dying world. Concerning His church, the Lord Jesus once said, "'the gates of Hades will not overcome it'" (Matt. 16:18).

The Adding of Thousands

Under the guidance of the apostles, the early church soon became a very unique spiritual community. "Everyone was filled with awe, and many wonders and miraculous signs were done by the apostles" (Acts 2:43). Many of the Jews who had come from foreign countries for Pentecost stayed in Jerusalem to be a part of this new family of God. Many wealthy Jerusalem Jews, who had received Christ, sold their excess possessions and property and donated the money to "anyone as he had need" (Acts 2:45). With their new love for God and for each other, they were an impressive and attractive group. "And the Lord added to their number daily those who were being saved" (Acts 2:47).

In Acts 3, Luke tells us of another attention-getting miracle. On their way to the Temple to pray, Peter and John encountered a beggar who had been lame from birth. The beggar looked up at them, expecting to receive money.

> Then Peter said, "Silver or gold I do not have, but what I have I give you. In the name of Jesus Christ of Nazareth, walk." Taking him by the right hand, he helped him up, and instantly the man's feet and ankles became strong. He jumped to his feet and began to walk. Then he went with them into the temple courts, walking and jumping, and praising God. When all the people saw him walking and praising God, they recognized him as the same man who used to sit begging at the temple gate called Beautiful, and they were filled with wonder and amazement at what had happened to him. (Acts 3:6–10)

Upon seeing this miracle, a large, curious crowd came running to Peter and John. Once again, Peter was given a golden opportunity to proclaim the gospel of Christ, which he immediately took advantage of. Filled with the Holy Spirit, Peter persuaded this crowd that Jesus is the long-awaited fulfillment of God's promise to Abraham: "'The God of Abraham, Isaac and Jacob, the God of our fathers, has glorified his servant Jesus. ... You killed the author of life, but God raised him from the dead'" (Acts 3:13, 15). "Many who heard the message believed, and the number of men grew to about five thousand" (Acts 4:4).

The Adversary Strikes Back

From the third chapter of Genesis and through our entire tour of the Bible, we have seen that every time God creates something new and good for mankind, Satan immediately sets out to destroy it. Through the death and resurrection of Christ, God has created a new medicine for man, the medicine of His Son, Jesus Christ. To distribute this new medicine, God has also established a new movement, the church. When the apostles, anointed with the Holy Spirit, proclaimed this good news in Jerusalem, right away thousands of Jewish people took the medicine by believing in Jesus. True to his evil nature, Satan would surely strike back. He would do everything in his power to silence this new message and stop the flow of this new medicine.

The devil's first attack came from the same group that had persecuted Jesus, the Sanhedrin, and it came in the form of intimidation.

> The priests and the captain of the temple guard and the Sadducees came up to Peter and John while they were speaking to the people. They were greatly disturbed because the apostles were teaching the people and proclaiming in Jesus the resurrection of the dead. They seized Peter and John, and because it was evening, they put them in jail until the next day. ... The next day the rulers, elders and teachers of the law met in Jerusalem. Annas the high priest was there, and so were Caiaphas, John, Alexander and the other men of the high priest's family. They had Peter and John brought before them and began to question them: "By what power or what name did you do this [healing of the lame man]?" (Acts 4:1–7)

Peter answered boldly that he and the other apostles were acting in "'the name of Jesus Christ of Nazareth, whom you crucified but whom God raised from the dead'" (Acts 4:10). The Sanhedrin, wanting to "'stop this thing from spreading any further among the people'" (Acts 4:17), let the apostles go with a warning and "commanded them not to speak or teach at all in the name of Jesus" (Acts 4:18). But Peter and John responded by saying, "'Judge for yourselves whether it is right in God's sight to obey you rather than God. For we cannot help speaking about what we have seen and heard'" (Acts 4:19–20).

Having failed in his attack from outside the church, Satan's next strike came from within the church. Using two church members, he tried to introduce contamination. "Now a man named Ananias, together with his wife Sapphira, also sold a piece of property. With his wife's full knowledge he kept back part of the money for himself, but brought the rest and put it at the apostles' feet" (Acts 5:1–2).

Let's remember that many Jerusalem Jews, who had converted to Christ, sold their excess lands and properties in order to help support and feed this growing crowd of believers. They would lay the money from these sales at the apostles' feet for proper distribution.

Ananias and his wife Sapphira were under no obligation to sell their land. And once it was sold they could have donated any portion of the sale—a lot, a little, or none—to the church. But they committed a grievous sin when they "*kept back part of the money*" and then, to make a show of their generosity in front of the church, pretended that they were donating the entire amount. This was hypocrisy.

To help us understand why this was such a serious threat to the church, let's consider what Jesus once said to His disciples: "'Be on your guard against the yeast of the Pharisees, which is hypocrisy'" (Luke 12:1). Yeast (sour dough) is in a high state of fermentation and spreads rapidly through the dough in which it is mixed. For this reason, yeast (or leaven) became a symbol in the Bible of sin and corruption. Satan was attempting to use Ananias and Sapphira to introduce this "yeast" of hypocrisy into the church. Had he been successful, this evil would have quickly spread through the community of faith, destroying the church from within. For their sin of hypocrisy, both Ananias and Sapphira died at the hand of the Lord. But this severity was not so much to punish the man and his wife; it was to protect the church from contamination.

Satan's next strike was an inquisition. Despite the warning from the Sanhedrin, the apostles continued to proclaim Christ, and "more and more men and women believed in the Lord" (Acts 5:14).

> Then the high priest and all his associates, who were members of the party of the Sadducees, were filled with jealousy. They arrested the apostles and put them in the public jail...they made them appear before the Sanhedrin to be questioned by the high priest. "We gave you strict orders not to teach in this name," he said. "Yet you have filled Jerusalem with your teaching and are determined to make us guilty of this man's blood." (Acts 5:17–18, 27–28)

When Peter and the other apostles responded, "'We must obey God rather than men'" (Acts 5:29), the members of the Sanhedrin "were furious and wanted to put them to death" (Acts 5:33). Ultimately, they decided not to kill them, but rather they "had them flogged. Then they ordered them not to speak in the name of Jesus, and let them go" (Acts 5:40). Please notice that Satan is increasing the intensity of his attacks. The first time the apostles were arrested by the Sanhedrin (Chapter 3), they were let go with a warning. This second time (Chapter 5), they were released after a flogging. But the apostles were undeterred. "Day after day, in the temple courts and from house to house, they never stopped teaching and proclaiming the good news that Jesus is the Christ" (Acts 5:42).

Not one to give up, the devil again focused his attention inside the church, hoping to cause a division. "In those days when the number of disciples was increasing, the Grecian Jews among them complained against the Hebraic Jews because their widows were being overlooked in the daily distribution of food" (Acts 6:1).

As mentioned earlier, after the day of Pentecost, many out-of-town Jews, after converting to Christianity, remained in Jerusalem. Because they came from Greek-speaking countries, they were called "the Grecian Jews." The "Hebraic Jews" were those who lived in and around Jerusalem. Up to now, with the love of Christ, these two groups had lived together in harmony. Satan saw an opportunity to drive a wedge between these two cultural groups by stirring up an issue of favoritism. Whether true or not, the Grecian Jews felt that their widows were being neglected. But the apostles were on to Satan's game and took action to prevent the polarization and division of the church. They wisely instructed the disciples to "'choose seven men from among you who are known to be full of the Spirit and wisdom. We will turn this responsibility over to them'" (Acts 6:3). After the congregation chose seven good men, "they presented these men to the apostles, who prayed and laid their hands on them" (Acts 6:6). These seven men took charge of the distribution of food, made sure that no one was neglected, and brought harmony and unity back to the church. Problem solved.

When all else had failed, the devil resorted to all-out persecution. Stephen, one of the seven, discovered that he was gifted to do more than just carry food. Full of faith and power, he "did great wonders and miraculous signs among the people" (Acts 6:8). As a result, he, too, was arrested and brought before the Sanhedrin. He was given a chance to defend himself, but he chose rather to be a witness for Christ. After they heard his words, the members of the Sanhedrin

> were furious and gnashed their teeth at him. But Stephen, full of the Holy Spirit, looked up to heaven and saw the glory of God, and Jesus standing at the right hand of God. "Look," he said, "I see heaven open and the Son of Man standing at the right hand of God." At this they covered their ears and, yelling at the top of their voices, they all rushed at him, dragged him out of the city and began to stone him. (Acts 7:54–58)

Dying for Jesus, Stephen became the first Christian martyr.

After the stoning of Stephen, the Sanhedrin became zealously determined to stamp out this new movement. "On that day a great persecution broke out against the church at Jerusalem, and all except the apostles were scattered throughout Judea and Samaria" (Acts 8:1). As a result of this severe persecution, thousands of Jewish Christians fled Jerusalem. This first blessed fellowship of believers was broken up, and God's family of faith was separated.

With the followers of Jesus leaving Jerusalem and fleeing for their lives, it would appear that Satan had won. Apparently he had been able to stop (by force) this new movement and silence the message they were carrying. But, dear friends, we have learned something else on our tour of the Bible. We have seen that God is able to take the evil of Satan and turn it into good. In our next lesson, we will watch the Lord turn the persecution of His early church into something very positive for all mankind.

For quite some time, our tour bus has been parked on the Jericho road, overlooking the holy city. Now it's time to get back onboard. We will follow the fleeing Christians and watch them carry out the Great Commission, as the Lord predicted, "'in all Judea and Samaria, and to the ends of the earth'" (Acts 1:8). Next stop...Samaria.

If you have a question about this lesson, or other questions about the Bible, please visit my website www.FredWoodwardBible.com. There you can obtain my contact information and we can communicate through email. I'll do my very best to answer your questions.

Lesson 22

The Transition and Expansion of the Church

Acts 8–28

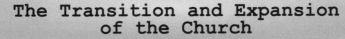

As you have probably noticed, I really enjoy showing you how a promise from God in the Old Testament is fulfilled in the New Testament. This time, the fulfilled promise that I want to show you is one that God made to Abraham, somewhere around 2000 BC. Among the many promises that He made to Abraham, God also said, "'and all peoples on earth will be blessed through you'" (Gen. 12:3). In other words, in addition to blessing Abraham and his descendants, the Jews, God also promised to bless the Gentile world through Abraham. The word "Gentile" comes from Greek ETHNOS and simply means "the nations." In the first seven chapters of Acts, we saw that the blessing of Jesus Christ, the son of Abraham, came first to the Jews in Jerusalem. In the remaining chapters of Acts, we will see this blessing come to "*all peoples on earth.*"

We finished our last lesson on a sad note. After the stoning of Stephen, "a great persecution broke out against the church at Jerusalem, and all except the apostles were scattered throughout Judea and Samaria" (Acts 8:1). This persecution was led by a zealous young Pharisee named Saul. Anxious to impress the Sanhedrin, "Saul began to destroy the church. Going from house to house, he dragged off men and women and put them in prison" (Acts 8:3).

But our wonderful Lord, remember, has the ability to take what Satan intends for evil and transform it into good. The devil's plan was to use persecution to stop the growth of the church and silence the gospel message. The exact opposite happened. God used the persecution to expand the church and spread the message! According to Luke, "those who had been scattered preached the word wherever they went" (Acts 8:4).

The Gospel Comes to Samaria

The first non-Jewish ethnic group to receive the gospel was the Samaritans.

> Philip went down to a city in Samaria and proclaimed the Christ there. When the crowds heard Philip and saw the miraculous signs he did, they all paid close attention to what he said. With shrieks, evil spirits came out of many, and many paralytics and cripples were healed. So there was great joy in that city. (Acts 8:5–8)

Philip, like Stephen, was one of the seven men chosen by the apostles to serve the church in Jerusalem. And, like Stephen, Philip discovered that in addition to serving, he also had a gift of speaking. When he went to Samaria and proclaimed Christ, the Samaritans eagerly believed. As we learned earlier, the Samaritans were a race of foreigners who had been imported from other countries mixed together with Jews of the Northern Kingdom. In short, they were not pure-blooded Jews.

This explains why the apostles Peter and John, after they heard that the Samaritans had believed, came down to Samaria and "placed their hands on them [the Samaritans], and they received the Holy Spirit" (Acts 8:17). Evidently, the presence and the approval of the apostles were necessary to confirm that God was opening a new ethnic door.

The Conversion of Saul

Earlier we learned that an ambitious young Pharisee named Saul was leading the charge of persecution against the church. This man was now about to have a life-changing experience.

> Meanwhile, Saul was still breathing out murderous threats against the Lord's disciples. He went to the high priest and asked him for letters to the synagogues in Damascus, so that if he found any there who belonged to the Way, whether men or women, he might take them as prisoners to Jerusalem. (Acts 9:1–2)

Not content persecuting the disciples in Israel, Saul obtained permission from the Sanhedrin to track them down in foreign countries as well. (Damascus is in Syria.) Many years later, Paul confessed that during this period of his life, he was "a violent man" (1 Tim. 1:13). The word "violent" comes from the Greek HUBRISTES, which means "violence carried out with insolence," or "anger mixed with arrogance." In other words, Saul not only hurt people, he enjoyed hurting people. If you need a visual image for this, just think of a Nazi SS officer, going from house to house, arresting "enemies of the state."

But something happened to Saul on his way to Damascus.

> As he neared Damascus on his journey, suddenly a light from heaven flashed around him. He fell to the ground and heard a voice say to him, "Saul, Saul, why do you persecute me?" "Who are you, Lord?" Saul asked. "I am Jesus, whom you are persecuting," he replied. "Now get up and go into the city, and you will be told what you must do." ... Saul got up from the ground, but when he opened his eyes he could see nothing. So they led him by the hand into Damascus. For three days he was blind, and did not eat or drink anything. (Acts 9:3–9)

Saul was completely bewildered by this personal appearance of Jesus. Up to this point, like all his Pharisee friends, he had refused to believe in the Lord, and even thought that this new movement was some form of heresy that must be stopped. But now, Saul had seen the risen Jesus with his own eyes and had heard His voice with his own ears. How could he go on refusing to believe in Him? After the three days of blindness, the Lord sent a disciple named Ananias to Saul.

> Placing his hands on Saul, he said, "Brother Saul, the Lord—Jesus, who appeared to you on the road as you were coming here—has sent me so that you may see again and be filled with the Holy Spirit." Immediately, something like scales fell from Saul's eyes, and he could see again. He got up and was baptized. (Acts 9:17–18)

Thus the chief prosecutor/persecutor of the church of Jesus became a believer in Jesus!

> At once he began to preach in the synagogues that Jesus is the Son of God. All those who heard him were astonished and asked, "Isn't he the man who raised havoc in Jerusalem among those who call on this name? And hasn't he come here to take them as prisoners to the chief priests?" (Acts 9:20–21)

We will hear much more about Saul. By and by his name would be changed to Paul. More than any other man, the Lord used him to proclaim the gospel and establish the church in the Gentile world. Before his life on Earth was over, he had written almost half of the books of the New Testament.

The Gentiles Receive the Holy Spirit

When the Lord was still on earth, He once said to Peter, "'I will give you the keys of the kingdom of Heaven'" (Matt. 16:19). As we have already seen, Peter used his "keys" on the day of Pentecost to open the door for the Jews to enter the kingdom of Heaven. We might call that Door #1. Peter again used his keys to allow the second ethnic group, the (half-Jew/half-Gentile) Samaritans, into the kingdom back in Acts 8. That would be Door #2. One more door would have to be opened so that "*all peoples on earth*" could hear the gospel. In order to watch Peter use his keys to open Door #3, the door to the Gentiles, we must get on the bus, leave Samaria, and travel about twenty-five miles to the seaport city of Caesarea.

> At Caesarea there was a man named Cornelius, a centurion in what was known as the Italian Regiment. He and all his family were devout and God-fearing; he gave generously to those in need and prayed to God regularly. One day at about three in the afternoon he had a vision. He distinctly saw an angel of God, who came to him and said, "Cornelius!" Cornelius stared at him in fear. "What is it, Lord?" he asked. The angel answered, "Your prayers and gifts to the poor have come up as a memorial offering before God. Now send men to Joppa to bring back a man named Simon who is called Peter. He is staying with Simon the tanner, whose house is by the sea." (Acts 10:1–6)

From the above passage, we learn several important things about this man, Cornelius. First of all, he was a Gentile. There was not one ounce of Jewish blood in his body. Second, he was a centurion, which means he was a Roman soldier in charge of one hundred other Roman soldiers. He was also "*devout and God-fearing*," meaning that he had a genuine hunger for God and a desire to please God. He conscientiously obeyed everything he had learned about God while being stationed in Israel. But he had not yet been given the opportunity to hear and respond to the gospel of Christ. That was about to change. The angel instructed Cornelius to send men to Joppa, a town about thirty miles away, and bring back a man named Peter.

While Cornelius's messengers were making their way to Joppa, Peter also had a vision. The next day, about noon,

> Peter went up on the roof to pray. He became hungry and wanted something to eat, and while the meal was being prepared, he fell into a trance. He saw heaven opened

> and something like a large sheet being let down to earth by its four corners. It contained all kinds of four-footed animals, as well as reptiles of the earth and birds of the air. Then a voice told him, "Get up, Peter. Kill and eat." "Surely not, Lord!" Peter replied. "I have never eaten anything impure or unclean." The voice spoke to him a second time, "Do not call anything impure that God has made clean." This happened three times, and immediately the sheet was taken back to heaven. (Acts 10:9–16)

Obviously, with these visions, the Lord was orchestrating a meeting between Cornelius and Peter. But what was the meaning of Peter's vision in which a large sheet came down from Heaven containing several different kinds of unclean (according to the Law of Moses) animals?

To understand this, we must bear in mind that despite the clear assignment from the Lord to "'go and make disciples of all nations'" (Matt. 28:19), the early Jewish believers were slow to accept the fact that Gentiles could be saved. For centuries, the Jews had been instructed to avoid Gentiles because they were "unclean." Some Jewish rabbis even taught that God created the Gentiles to be fuel for hell! No doubt Peter himself was caught up in this type of thinking, which explains why Peter's thinking needed to be corrected. This vision was not really about the cleansing of unclean animals. It was about the Lord's desire to cleanse the Gentiles from their sin, and Peter needed to accept God's will on this matter.

"While Peter was still thinking about the vision, the Spirit said to him, 'Simon, three men are looking for you. So get up and go downstairs. Do not hesitate to go with them, for I have sent them'" (Acts 10:19–20). With the combination of the vision and the voice of the Lord, Peter (against his natural inclinations) went with the messengers back to Caesarea.

When Peter finally arrived at Cornelius's house, he found that Cornelius "had called together his relatives and close friends" (Acts 10:24). Seeing this crowd before him, Peter knew what he had to do. Like so many times before (only with Jewish audiences), he proclaimed the gospel of Jesus Christ.

> While Peter was still speaking these words, the Holy Spirit came on all who heard the message. The circumcised [Jewish] believers who had come with Peter were astonished that the gift of the Holy Spirit had been poured out even on the Gentiles. For they heard them speaking in tongues and praising God. Then Peter said, "Can anyone keep these people from being baptized with water? They have received the Holy Spirit just as we have." So he ordered that they be baptized in the name of Jesus Christ. (Acts 10:44–48)

When Peter saw these Gentiles speaking in foreign languages, just as he had done on the day of Pentecost, he realized that this was truly the work of God and no man should resist it. If the Lord had accepted these Gentiles, who was he to reject them?

Thus the third and final ethnic door had been opened, the door allowing Gentiles to enter into the kingdom of God by faith in Jesus Christ. From this point on, there would be no need for the Apostle Peter to be present to confirm the baptism of the Spirit. Going forward, and to this day, whoever repents of sin and receives Jesus Christ will receive the gift of the Holy Spirit.

The First Missionaries Are Sent Out

Shortly after the conversion of Cornelius, God again used the persecution that began in Jerusalem to further the cause of Christ. To follow the expansion of the church, we need to board our bus, leave Caesarea, and travel north to Antioch of Syria. Antioch was a city of about 500,000 people, located some 300 miles north of Jerusalem.

> Now those who had been scattered by the persecution in connection with Stephen traveled as far as Phoenicia, Cyprus and Antioch, telling the message only to Jews. Some of them, however, men from Cyprus and Cyrene, went to Antioch and began to speak to Greeks also, telling them the good news about the Lord Jesus. The Lord's

hand was with them, and a great number of people believed and turned to the Lord. (Acts 11:19–21)

As the above passage indicates, when the gospel came to Antioch, "*a great number of people believed and turned to the Lord*," and a new church was established. When the apostles in Jerusalem heard of this, they sent a Jewish believer named Barnabas to Antioch to teach and train these new disciples. Barnabas, seeing how much work needed to be done, "went to Tarsus to look for Saul, and when he found him, he brought him to Antioch. So for a whole year Barnabas and Saul met with the church and taught great numbers of people" (Acts 11:25–26).

Concerning this new church in Antioch, allow me to share several details. First of all, it has been nearly twelve years since the church in Jerusalem was born on the day of Pentecost. Second, this church was made up of both Jewish and Gentile believers in Christ. Third, it was here that the "disciples were called Christians first at Antioch" (Acts 11:26). Fourth, Saul, whose name at this point was changed to Paul, reenters our story. Finally, as we will now see, this church in Antioch would become Paul's home base for three missionary journeys. We'll leave our bus parked in Antioch in order to follow Paul on these journeys over land and sea.

Paul's First Missionary Journey: Acts 13:1 to 14:28

While Saul (Paul), Barnabas, and other teachers "were worshiping the Lord and fasting, the Holy Spirit said, 'Set apart for me Barnabas and Saul for the work to which I have called them.' So after they had fasted and prayed, they placed their hands on them and sent them off" (Acts 13:2–3).

Thus begins the first missionary journey into the Gentile world. As the following map indicates, Paul and Barnabas made their way across the island of Cyprus, then to the mainland of Asia Minor (present-day Turkey), where they visited the cities of Perga, Antioch (of Pisidia), Iconium, Lystra, and Derbe. Everywhere they went, they proclaimed the gospel, led people to Christ, and established small groups of believers into churches. Then they retraced their steps and sailed back to their home church in Antioch of Syria.

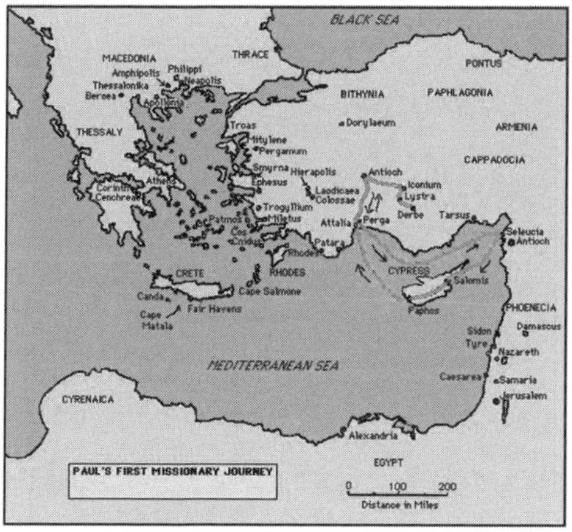

www.biblemapper.com

Paul's Second Missionary Journey: Acts 15:36-18:22

Looking at the following map, on Paul's second missionary journey, he traveled over land to revisit the cities where disciples had been made on the first journey. But then he was led by the Holy Spirit to carry the gospel much farther west. After crossing the Aegean Sea, Paul and his team made their way through Macedonia and Greece, where they preached the gospel and made converts. New churches were established at Philippi, Thessalonica, and Corinth. After a brief stop at Ephesus, they again sailed to Caesarea and then back home to Antioch.

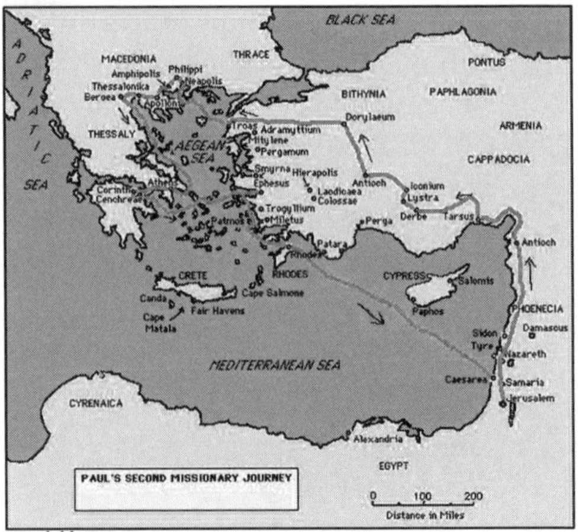

www.biblemapper.com

Paul's Third Missionary Journey: Acts 18:23-20:38

As the map below indicates, on Paul's third missionary journey, he headed directly for Ephesus, a magnificent city with a population of about 225,000. Paul remained here for over two years, preaching the gospel and teaching new converts. Vast numbers of people became Christians and new churches were established for hundreds of miles around Ephesus. After revisiting the disciples in Macedonia and Greece, Paul sailed for Israel, hoping to be in Jerusalem for the Feast of Pentecost.

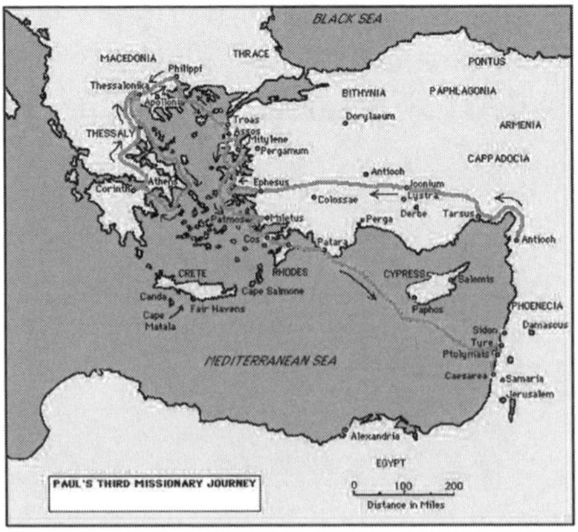

www.biblemapper.com

The Relentless Resistance of Satan

We must not suppose, however, that Satan just sat silently by as Paul carried the gospel to all parts of the Gentile world. No indeed! In one of his inspired letters, Paul gives us a brief testimony of the trials and tribulations he faced on his journeys.

> Five times I received from the Jews the forty lashes minus one. Three times I was beaten with rods, once I was stoned, three times I was shipwrecked, I spent a night and a day in the open sea, and I have been constantly on the move. I have been in danger from rivers, in danger from bandits, in danger from my own countrymen, in danger from Gentiles; in danger in the city, in danger in the country, in danger at sea; and in danger from false brothers. I have labored and toiled and have often gone without sleep; I have known hunger and thirst and have often gone without food; I have been cold and naked. (2 Cor. 11:24–27)

Paul Goes to Rome...Shackled!

In the final chapters of the book of Acts, Luke tells us that while Paul was attending the Feast of Pentecost in Jerusalem, "some Jews from the province of Asia saw Paul at the temple. They stirred up the whole crowd and seized him, shouting, 'Men of Israel, help us! This is the man who teaches all men everywhere against our people and our law and this place'" (Acts 21:27–28).

Just as this angry mob was about to tear Paul to pieces,

> news reached the commander of the Roman troops that the whole city of Jerusalem was in an uproar. He at once took some officers and soldiers and ran down to the crowd. When the rioters saw the commander and his soldiers, they stopped beating Paul. The commander came up and arrested him and ordered him to be bound

with two chains. (Acts 21:31–33)

Since his Jewish father had somehow become a Roman citizen, Paul was born with the unique status of dual citizenship. He was not only a Jew, he was also a Roman citizen. This proved to be very much to Paul's advantage. When the Roman governor, Festus, asked him if he was willing to be tried in Jerusalem, Paul answered, "'I appeal to Caesar!' After Festus had conferred with his council, he declared: 'You have appealed to Caesar. To Caesar you will go!'" (Acts 25:11–12).

Paul was then "handed over to a centurion named Julius" (Acts 27:1) who personally escorted him on the long journey to Rome. Paul had always wanted to go to Rome to proclaim the gospel. He probably never imagined that he would go there under arrest, accompanied by a Roman soldier. The map below shows the route that was taken.

www.biblemapper.com

The book of Acts ends with Paul still under "house arrest," awaiting trial in Rome. Just in case we might think that Satan had finally won, Luke tells us: "For two whole years Paul stayed there in his own rented house and welcomed all who came to see him. Boldly and without hindrance he preached the kingdom of God and taught about the Lord Jesus Christ" (Acts 28:30-31). It was during this period that Paul wrote a letter to the church at Philippi. In it he said,

> Now I want you to know, brothers, that what has happened to me has really served to advance the gospel. As a result, it has become clear throughout the whole palace guard and to everyone else that I am in chains for Christ. Because of my chains, most of the brothers in the Lord have been encouraged to speak the word of God more courageously and fearlessly. (Phil. 1:12–14)

Oh, Mr. Satan, will you never learn? The God of Jesus Christ can always take your evil and transform it into good!

The Bible does not tell us exactly what happened to Paul after this incarceration in Rome. From what we can glean from his letters, it is thought that he was acquitted and released but then a few years later was rearrested and taken back to Rome. It is believed that as a result of his second arrest and trial, he was executed by beheading somewhere around the year 67 AD.

The Letters That Became Inspired Scripture

As you know, the book of Acts is not the last book of the Bible. There are still twenty-two more books in the New Testament that come after the book of Acts. These books are letters, written by men like Paul and others with apostolic authority. Most of them were written before 70 AD, and all of them were written before the close of the first century. They are all inspired by the Holy Spirit and therefore very important. They contain priceless information about Christ, insights for living the Christian life, and instructions for the local church. But while they are important for theology, they do not add significantly to our understanding of New Testament history. For this reason, we are going to pass over these books and head straight for the book of Revelation. I strongly encourage you to study these letters at some later date.

Believe it or not, dear friends, we are almost finished with our tour of the Bible. We have just one more stop to make and many things yet to see...on the island of Patmos.

If you have a question about this lesson, or other questions about the Bible, please visit my website www.FredWoodwardBible.com. There you can obtain my contact information and we can communicate through email. I'll do my very best to answer your questions.

Lesson 23

Things to Expect as We Approach the End

Revelation

In our tour of the New Testament, we have seen that in less than one hundred years, God accomplished things that changed the course of human history and mankind's eternal destiny. Through a miraculous virgin birth, He brought His Son, Jesus the Messiah, into the world. At thirty years old, Jesus began His public ministry. By age thirty-three, He had finished His mission on Earth by dying for the sins of all mankind. With His death, burial, and resurrection, God created a message of salvation to be proclaimed to all people everywhere. Ten days after Jesus' ascension into Heaven, the Holy Spirit came upon the Lord's followers establishing a movement, the church, which would carry the Gospel of Christ to the world. And even before the end of the first century AD, to preserve all this truth for future generations, God had it all carefully recorded on sacred manuscripts, the twenty-seven inspired books of the New Testament.

Despite Satan's relentless resistance, the life-giving message of Christ has been proclaimed throughout the world for nearly 2,000 years. Because Christians have always been anxious to share their faith, countless souls from every country, culture, and color have been reconciled to God by hearing and heeding the gospel. It is estimated that currently every minute about 120 people from around the world come to believe in Jesus Christ.

The fact that Christianity has survived for so long is a testimony to the power and faithfulness of God. For twenty centuries, the Lord has protected and preserved His church through tribulations, persecutions, reformations, and imperfections. And we can be sure that God will protect and preserve His message and His people who carry it until the end of time.

This brings us to the subject of this final lesson: the end of time. What's in store for the human race? What does the future look like? How does the unfolding story of the Bible end? To answer these questions, we will turn our attention to the last book of the Bible, the book of Revelation.

Somewhere around 95 AD, to stop him from proclaiming Christ, John, the last living apostle of the original twelve, was exiled from the mainland of Asia Minor (present-day Turkey) and sent to the nearby island of Patmos. It was on this island that the risen, glorified Lord Jesus appeared to John. And it was here that he received from Jesus "the revelation of Jesus Christ, which God gave him to show his servants what must soon take place" (Rev. 1:1). This information in Revelation concerning the future originated with God the Father, who gave it to His Son Jesus, who in turn gave it to John so that John could accurately record it and save it for us.

In John's words,

> I, John, your brother and companion in the suffering and kingdom and patient endurance that are ours in Jesus, was on the island of Patmos because of the word of God and the testimony of Jesus. On the Lord's Day I was in the Spirit, and I heard behind me a loud voice like a trumpet. ... His head and hair were white like wool, as white as snow, and his eyes were like blazing fire. His feet were like bronze glowing in a furnace, and his voice was like the sound of rushing waters. ... His face was like the sun shining in all its brilliance. When I saw him, I fell at his feet as though dead. Then he placed his right hand on me and said: "Do not be afraid. I am the First and the Last. I am the Living One; I was dead, and behold I am

> alive for ever and ever! And I hold the keys of death and Hades. Write, therefore, what you have seen, what is now and what will take place later." (Rev. 1:9–10, 14–15, 16–19)

We need to understand that the book of Revelation is not the only place in the Bible that speaks of the end of the world. Truths about the end times are found throughout the Old and New Testaments. Jesus often spoke of the future of mankind, as did His apostles. So, as we work our way through the book of Revelation, we'll also consider prophecies from other passages of the Bible. In the process, I hope to point out to you several things to expect as we approach the end.

The Wickedness of Man

John begins the book of Revelation by declaring, "Look, he is coming with the clouds, and every eye will see him, even those who pierced him; and all the peoples of the earth will mourn because of him" (Rev. 1:7). We might assume that when Jesus returns to Earth, the world will welcome Him with open arms. But John's declaration that "*all the peoples of the earth will mourn because of him*" clearly indicates that instead of being happy at the second coming of Christ, most of the world will grieve. There can be only one reason for this: by the time we get to that point in history, the bulk of the human race will have rejected the gospel of Christ and will have fallen into a state of great wickedness.

When speaking to the disciples about His second coming, Jesus taught the same truth: "'As it was in the days of Noah, so it will be at the coming of the Son of Man'" (Matt. 24:37). Back in Genesis 6, we saw what the world was like in the days of Noah just before the Flood: "The LORD saw how great man's wickedness on the earth had become, and that every inclination of the thoughts of his heart was only evil all the time" (Gen. 6:5). That pre-Flood world had become so wicked that

> the LORD was grieved that he had made man on the earth, and his heart was filled with pain. So the LORD said, "I will wipe mankind, whom I have created, from the face of the earth—men and animals, and creatures

> that move along the ground, and birds of the air—for I am grieved that I have made them." (Gen. 6:6–7)

So, according to Jesus, when He returns to Earth, the entire world (for the second time) will have reached a state of wickedness that is beyond repair and ripe for judgment.

The Apostle Paul also speaks of this future worldwide wickedness.

> But mark this: There will be terrible times in the last days. People will be lovers of themselves, lovers of money, boastful, proud, abusive, disobedient to their parents, ungrateful, unholy, without love, unforgiving, slanderous, without self-control, brutal, not lovers of the good, treacherous, rash, conceited, lovers of pleasure rather than lovers of God. (2 Tim. 3:1–4)

The Wrath of Man

From the beginning of the Bible, we have seen that when men become wicked, they also become full of wrath. And in what direction do unrighteous men vent their anger? Toward righteous men. The first time we saw this was in Genesis 4 with Cain and Abel. Cain was angry with Abel because his brother's righteous life of faith, like a light, exposed Cain's sinfulness, which made Cain uncomfortable. Cain's solution to this discomfort was to snuff out the light, which he accomplished by murdering his brother!

As it was in the beginning, so it will be as we approach the end, only on a much larger scale. In the last days, the world will be filled with multitudes of unrepentant "Cains," who will hate and persecute a relatively small number of righteous "Abels." In short, as the end draws near, persecution of believers will increase in frequency and intensity.

In the book of Revelation, John often makes mention of the terrible persecution that believers will face in the latter days. He shares with us what he was allowed to see in the future.

> I saw under the altar the souls of those who had been slain because of the word of God and the testimony they had maintained. They called out in a loud voice, "How long, Sovereign Lord, holy and true, until you judge the inhabitants of the earth and avenge our blood?" Then each of them was given a white robe, and they were told to wait a little longer, until the number of their fellow servants and brothers who were to be killed as they had been was completed. (Rev. 6:9–11)

What John saw is entirely consistent with what Jesus had said to His disciples concerning the end of the world. "'You will be betrayed even by parents, brothers, relatives and friends, and they will put some of you to death. All men will hate you because of me'" (Luke 21:16–17). As I write these words, Christians are being actively persecuted in many countries around the world. It is estimated that over 160,000 believers will be martyred this year. This persecution will intensify and the number of martyrs will increase as we approach the end.

The Time of Woe

Also, as we have repeatedly seen on our tour, falling away from God never ends well. Wickedness always leads to a time of woe. The sorrows that follow sin have a predictable sequence. Hoping that man will repent, God removes some of His blessing and allows man to experience the earthly consequences of sin. But eventually, if men refuse to repent and choose rather to persist in wickedness, God will bring condemnation. In short, falling away from God leads to wickedness. Wickedness is followed by a time of woe, which hopefully results in repentance. But when men refuse to repent, the time will come for God's wrath.

Unfortunately, according to John in the book of Revelation, this is what we must expect as we approach the end of the world. There is coming a time of great tribulation on Earth. There will be wars, famines, earthquakes, plagues, cosmic disturbances, diseases, devastation, and, like never before in history, death. We would assume that all this misery will surely bring the human race to repentance, but we would be wrong. John shares with us something that he saw in the future that surprised him.

> The rest of mankind that were not killed by these plagues still did not repent of the work of their hands; they did not stop worshiping demons, and idols of gold, silver, bronze, stone and wood—idols that cannot see or hear or walk. Nor did they repent of their murders, their magic arts, their sexual immorality or their thefts. (Rev. 9:20–21)

"They were seared by the intense heat and they cursed the name of God, who had control over these plagues, but they refused to repent and glorify him. ... Men gnawed their tongues in agony and cursed the God of heaven because of their pains and their sores, but they refused to repent of what they had done" (Rev. 16:9, 10–11).

The Lord Jesus also spoke of this coming time of great tribulation: "'There will be signs in the sun, moon and stars. On the earth, nations will be in anguish and perplexity at the roaring and tossing of the sea. Men will faint from terror, apprehensive of what is coming on the world, for the heavenly bodies will be shaken'" (Luke 21:25–26). "For then there will be great distress, unequaled from the beginning of the world until now—and never to be equaled again. If those days had not been cut short, no one would survive, but for the sake of the elect those days will be shortened" (Matt. 24:21–22).

We are thankful the Lord said that "*those days will be shortened.*" If not, "*no one would survive.*" From statements that John makes in Revelation Chapters 11–13 and prophecies from the Old Testament book of Daniel, many Bible scholars believe this period of woe will last seven years. "During those days men will seek death, but will not find it; they will long to die, but death will elude them" (Rev. 9:6).

The Rise of the Wicked One and His One-World Government

During this time of great tribulation, the people of the world will be looking for a cure for all the chaos, confusion, and suffering on Earth, but they will not look to God. Satan will give them what they seek. He will raise up a "messiah" who promises to end all the misery, a substitute savior, a counterfeit Christ. You might have heard of him as "the Antichrist." The Apostle John calls this person "the beast."

In Revelation 13, John tells us about the beast.

> The dragon [Satan] gave the beast his power and his throne and great authority. One of the heads of the beast seemed to have had a fatal wound, but the fatal wound had been healed. The whole world was astonished and followed the beast. Men worshiped the dragon because he had given authority to the beast, and they also worshiped the beast and asked, "Who is like the beast? Who can make war against him?" The beast was given a mouth to utter proud words and blasphemies and to exercise his authority for forty-two months. He opened his mouth to blaspheme God, and to slander his name and his dwelling place and those who live in heaven. He was given power to make war against the saints and to conquer them. And he was given authority over every tribe, people, language and nation. All inhabitants of the earth will worship the beast—all whose names have not been written in the book of life belonging to the Lamb that was slain from the creation of the world. ... He also forced everyone, small and great, rich and poor, free and slave, to receive a mark on his right hand or on his forehead, so that no one could buy or sell unless he had the mark, which is the name of the beast or the number of his name. (Rev. 13:2–8, 16–17)

From the above passage, I've made a list of the characteristics of the Antichrist.

1. He will derive his power from Satan.

2. He will recover from some type of fatal wound (a pseudo-resurrection).
3. He will be worshipped and obeyed by the entire world.
4. He will speak blasphemous words against God.
5. He will persecute (to death) those who believe in Jesus.
6. He will have complete control over "*every tribe, people, language and nation.*"
7. He will force "*everyone*" on Earth "*to receive a mark on his right hand or on his forehead.*" Those who refuse this mark will be considered troublemakers to the new world order and will not be allowed to buy anything (food, clothing, shelter, cars, etc.) or sell anything.

The Faithful Witnesses to the Word of God

But despite the intense persecution of Satan and his subordinate, the Antichrist, there will be men and women who remain faithful to Jesus Christ even during these awful times. Many will lose their lives rather than deny their faith. John saw that "they overcame him [the devil] by the blood of the Lamb and by the word of their testimony; they did not love their lives so much as to shrink from death" (Rev. 12:11).

In Acts 7, we watched as Stephen became the first believer to die for the name of Jesus Christ. As he was being persecuted by the Sanhedrin, "Stephen, full of the Holy Spirit, looked up to heaven and saw the glory of God, and Jesus standing at the right hand of God. 'Look,' he said, 'I see heaven open and the Son of Man standing at the right hand of God'" (Acts 7:55–56). Because Stephen took his stand for Jesus, the Lord stood up for him and gave him the grace to die courageously. Likewise, during these perilous last days, the Lord will stand with many of His people as they remain faithful unto death. Our Lord promises: "'Be faithful, even to the point of death, and I will give you the crown of life'" (Rev. 2:10).

The time will come, however, when, because of the hardness of men's hearts, the harvest of souls will be over. According to Jesus, when the world reaches this point, the end will be very near. "And this gospel of the kingdom will be preached in the whole world as a testimony to all nations, and then the end will come" (Matt. 24:14).

The Wrath of God

During these years of great tribulation, the Antichrist will continue to grow in popularity and power. When he gains complete control of the world, there will even be a very brief period of world peace. But this pseudo-peace will just be the calm before the storm of God's wrath. According to Paul, "While people are saying, 'Peace and safety,' destruction will come on them suddenly, as labor pains on a pregnant woman, and they will not escape" (1 Thess. 5:3).

The Antichrist himself will commit an atrocious act that will arouse the terrible wrath of God. In teaching about the end times, Jesus, citing from the Old Testament prophet Daniel, calls this act the abomination that causes desolation: "'So when you see standing in the holy place 'the abomination that causes desolation,' spoken of through the prophet Daniel—let the reader understand—then let those who are in Judea flee to the mountains'" (Matt. 24:15–16). An abomination is an atrocity, a disgrace, an obscenity, an outrage, or a monstrosity. Likewise, the Apostle Paul refers to this heinous act of the Antichrist: "He will oppose and will exalt himself over everything that is called God or is worshiped, so that he sets himself up in God's temple, proclaiming himself to be God" (2 Thess. 2:4).

Thus Daniel, Jesus, Paul, and John are all in agreement on this point. When the Antichrist reaches the peak of his power and pride, he will declare himself to be God! This is really nothing new. Throughout history, many deranged, demented men have claimed to be God, but very few people believed them. However, when the Antichrist makes this claim, the whole world will believe him! When we come to that point in history, human beings will be so spiritually and morally corrupt that they will readily believe the lie that man can become God. The prevailing attitude will be, "What further need do we have of God, since we can become God?" Do you remember the first lie that Satan told Adam and Eve concerning the forbidden fruit? "'You will not surely die,'" the serpent said to the woman. "'For God knows that when you eat of it your eyes will be opened, and you will be like God'" (Gen. 3:4–5).

This abominable act of the Antichrist, and the world's acceptance of it, will demonstrate that mankind has become incurably evil, and it will arouse the final wrath of God. According to John, "I saw in heaven another great and marvelous sign: seven angels with the seven last plagues—last, because with them God's wrath is completed" (Rev. 15:1). Again John says, "Then I heard a loud voice from the temple saying to the seven angels, 'Go, pour out the seven bowls of God's wrath on the earth'" (Rev. 16:1).

The White Horse

The terrible time of tribulation will at last come to an end with the second coming of the Lord.

> I saw heaven standing open and there before me was a white horse, whose rider is called Faithful and True. With justice he judges and makes war. His eyes are like blazing fire, and on his head are many crowns. ... He is dressed in a robe dipped in blood, and his name is the Word of God. The armies of heaven were following him, riding on white horses and dressed in fine linen, white and clean. Out of his mouth comes a sharp sword with which to strike down the nations. ... He treads the winepress of the fury of the wrath of God Almighty. On his robe and on his thigh he has this name written: KING OF KINGS AND LORD OF LORDS. ... Then I saw the beast and the kings of the earth and their armies gathered together to make war against the rider on the horse and his army. But the beast was captured, and with him the false prophet. ... The two of them were thrown alive into the fiery lake of burning sulfur. The rest of them were killed with the sword that came out of the mouth of the rider on the horse, and all the birds gorged themselves on

their flesh. (Rev. 19:11–12, 13–15, 15–16, 19–20, 20–21)

Thus John shares with us his vision of the glorious return to Earth of Jesus Christ. What John saw is in total harmony with what Jesus said about His second coming: "'For as lightning that comes from the east is visible even in the west, so will be the coming of the Son of Man'" (Matt. 24:27).

The Lord's first coming to Earth was in humility. His second coming will be in glory. His first coming was a mission of mercy. He gave His life to save mankind from God's wrath. His second coming will be to execute God's wrath on a wicked and unrepentant world. At His first coming, He rode a gentle donkey colt into Jerusalem. When He comes again, He'll be riding a white war horse. Following Him will be the armies of Heaven, also on white horses. Jesus will lead the armies of Heaven against the armies of the Antichrist in a battle called "The Battle of Armageddon." Jesus will of course win this battle, and finally, after several thousand years of Satan's ruthless rule over mankind, the devil's dark kingdom will be destroyed. At that point, all of the kingdoms of this world will "'become the kingdom of our Lord and of his Christ, and he will reign for ever and ever'" (Rev. 11:15).

At this point please join me as we shout "Hallelujah!"

The Warning Against "Date Setting"

It's only normal for us to want to know exactly when these things will take place. When will Jesus return to Earth and this world come to an end? On more than one occasion, Jesus' disciples asked Him this very question. In Matthew 24:3 for example, "'Tell us,'" they said, "'when will this happen, and what will be the sign of your coming and of the end of the age?'" His answer was, "'No one knows about that day or hour, not even the angels in heaven, nor the Son, but only the Father'" (Matt. 24:36). They asked the Lord a similar question right after His resurrection: "'Lord, are you at this time going to restore the kingdom to Israel?'" (Acts 1:6). His answer was, "'It is not for you to know the times or dates the Father has set by his own authority'" (Acts 1:7).

So, according to the Lord, only God knows exactly when the world will end. We will have to humbly accept the Lord's statement that "*it is not for you to know.*" I would caution you, dear friends, from following anyone who claims to know the exact dates of these future events. Down through the centuries, many false prophets (Jim Jones, David Koresh, etc.) have made such claims. And those who followed them have always ended up humiliated, discouraged, and, in some cases, dead. To prepare us, God has given us in His word general signs to look for. But we will never know the exact time of these events until they happen. Until then, let us heed the Lord's warning, "'therefore keep watch, because you do not know the day or the hour'" (Matt. 25:13).

The Welcome of Believers into Heaven

In Revelation Chapter 20, John reveals that after the second coming of Christ, there will be two resurrections, the resurrection of the righteous and the resurrection of the unrighteous. The resurrection of the righteous will be only for those who have been saved by faith. This will include people from the beginning of time to the end of the world who have returned to God by genuine repentance and faith in His word. These will be resurrected from the grave to stand before Jesus at what is called "The Judgment Seat of Christ" (2 Cor. 5:10).

It is extremely important that we understand that the judgment seat of Christ will not be to determine if these people will be allowed into Heaven. That question was settled on Earth when, like Abraham, they "believed the LORD" (Gen. 15:6), and God, because of their faith, declared them to be righteous. At the judgment seat of Christ, there will be no condemnation (Jesus took care of that), only commendation for faithful service. There will be no punishment (Jesus also took care of that), only varying degrees of praise for a life well lived. Believers will hear the wonderful words of our Lord, "'Well done, good and faithful servant! You have been faithful with a few things; I will put you in charge of many things. Come and share your master's happiness!'" (Matt. 25:21).

The Wretchedness of Unbelievers

Please don't ask me to sugarcoat this next section. I cannot do that and still be faithful to God's word. The second resurrection is called the resurrection of the unrighteous and will be only for those who are lost because of unbelief. This will include people from the beginning of time to the end of the world who, though given an entire lifetime to consider it, refused to repent of sin and return to God by faith. These will be resurrected from the grave to stand before God at what will be called "The Great White Throne Judgment." According to John,

> Then I saw a great white throne and him who was seated on it. Earth and sky fled from his presence, and there was no place for them. And I saw the dead, great and small, standing before the throne, and books were opened. Another book was opened, which is the book of life. The dead were judged according to what they had done as recorded in the books. The sea gave up the dead that were in it, and death and Hades gave up the dead that were in them, and each person was judged according to what he had done. Then death and Hades were thrown into the lake of fire. The lake of fire is the second death. If anyone's name was not found written in the book of life, he was thrown into the lake of fire. (Rev. 20:11–15)

Please notice that the Great White Throne, which will be for unbelievers, is in every way different than the Judgment Seat of Christ for believers. Those brought to the Great White Throne, in abject fear, will try to flee "from his presence," but there will be no place to hide. Four times John refers to these souls as "the dead," because on Earth they had refused to come to Jesus to receive the gift of eternal life. This judgment will not be to determine if they will be allowed to enter Heaven. That question was settled on Earth when they chose to reject Christ. At this judgment, there will be no commendation; there will be only condemnation. Here there will be no praise, only varying degrees of punishment for a life ill lived. The last words that unbelievers will hear from the Lord will be: "'Depart from me, you who are cursed, into the eternal fire prepared for the devil and his angels'" (Matt. 25:41).

Dear friends, God does not want "anyone to perish, but everyone to come to repentance" (2 Pet. 3:9). He has done everything (divinely) possible to enable all mankind to enter Heaven. He sent His Son to Earth to die for our sins. For two thousand years, He has sent out an open invitation (the gospel) to the world, the Holy Spirit pleading with every person on Earth to repent and return to God by faith in Jesus. But when people reject God's gracious invitation, they are choosing their own destiny—eternal separation from God.

The World to Come

In the last two chapters of the Bible, John describes for us what he calls the "*new heaven and the new earth*."

> Then I saw a new heaven and a new earth, for the first heaven and the first earth had passed away, and there was no longer any sea. I saw the Holy City, the new Jerusalem, coming down out of heaven from God, prepared as a bride beautifully dressed for her husband. And I heard a loud voice from the throne saying, "Now the dwelling of God is with men, and he will live with them. They will be his people, and God himself will be with them and be their God. He will wipe every tear from their eyes. There will be no more death or mourning or crying or pain, for the old order of things has passed away." He who was seated on the throne said, "I am making everything new!" (Rev. 21:1–5)

No doubt this was the place that Jesus was referring to when He said, "'In my Father's house are many rooms; if it were not so, I would have told you. I am going there to prepare a place for you'" (John 14:2).

Please notice that God's world to come is, in many ways, similar to the first world He created. It will be a world without sin. Therefore it will also be a world without sickness, suffering, sorrow, sighing, or crying. Most important, God and mankind will again dwell together forever in holiness, harmony, love, peace, and joy.

But there will be an important difference between the world that God made in Genesis Chapters 1 and 2 and the one He will make in Revelation Chapters 21 and 22. In the first world that God created, He made it clear that He wanted to dwell with mankind. Each day, God came to walk with Adam and Eve "in the garden in the cool of the day" (Gen. 3:8). But in the world to come, those who are in Heaven will have shown, by receiving His Son, that they also want to dwell forever with God. In short, God already loves us, but He wants us to choose to love Him in return. We have one lifetime on Earth to make this choice.

At this point, dear friend, may I urge you to make this choice for your own life. God created you to bless you and be good to you. He wants to dwell with you forever. He already loves you. Please choose to love Him in return. The Bible ends with one last invitation from God to man: "'The Spirit and the bride say, "Come!"...Whoever is thirsty, let him come; and whoever wishes, let him take the free gift of the water of life'" (Rev. 22:17). Please respond to God's invitation. Please return to God by receiving His Son, Jesus Christ.

If you have a question about this lesson, or other questions about the Bible, please visit my website www.FredWoodwardBible.com. There you can obtain my contact information and we can communicate through email. I'll do my very best to answer your questions.

Conclusion

Just One More Bus Ride Back to Where We Started

Now that we have seen what the Apostle John saw on the island of Patmos, our tour of the Bible will come to an end. We'll leave this tiny island and make our way back to Antioch of Syria where we parked the bus. From there, we have about a ten-hour bus ride back to where we began our tour, the area in present-day Iraq thought to be the location of the original Garden of Eden. Thank you for allowing me to be your tour guide. It has been my honor and privilege.

Please allow me to share my hopes. While our tour has come to an end, I hope that your love for the Bible is just beginning. I hope that you will remember the many sights that we've seen as we traveled through the scriptures. I hope and pray that what you have learned about God's word will lay a foundation of understanding in your heart that you can build upon throughout the rest of your life. I hope you've enjoyed our time together as much as I have. I hope you consider it time well spent.

And finally, dear friends, I hope to see you again. Perhaps we'll meet someday in this world. More important, I hope to see you in the world to come, the eternal kingdom of God and His Son, Jesus Christ.

Books of the Bible(NIV)

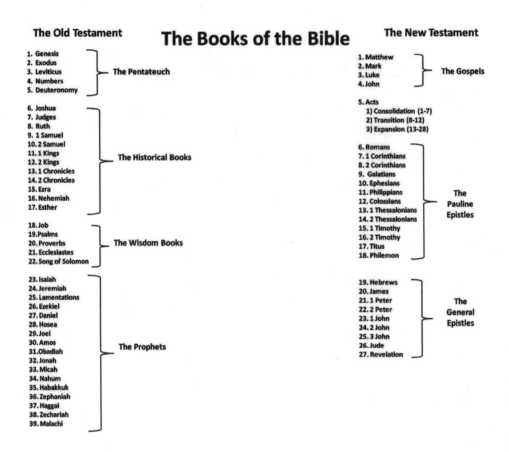

The Books of the Bible

The Old Testament

The Pentateuch

1. Genesis
2. Exodus
3. Leviticus
4. Numbers
5. Deuteronomy

The Historical Books

6. Joshua
7. Judges
8. Ruth
9. 1 Samuel
10. 2 Samuel
11. 1 Kings
12. 2 Kings
13. 1 Chronicles
14. 2 Chronicles
15. Ezra
16. Nehemiah
17. Esther

The Wisdom Books

18. Job
19. Psalms
20. Proverbs
21. Ecclesiastes
22. Song of Solomon

The Prophets

23. Isaiah
24. Jeremiah
25. Lamentations
26. Ezekiel
27. Daniel
28. Hosea
29. Joel
30. Amos
31. Obadiah
32. Jonah
33. Micah
34. Nahum
35. Habakkuk
36. Zephaniah
37. Haggai
38. Zechariah
39. Malachi

The New Testament

The Gospels

1. Matthew
2. Mark
3. Luke
4. John

5. Acts
   1) Consolidation (1-7)
   2) Transition (8-12)
   3) Expansion (13-28)

The Pauline Epistles

6. Romans
7. 1 Corinthians
8. 2 Corinthians
9. Galatians
10. Ephesians
11. Philippians
12. Colossians
13. 1 Thessalonians
14. 2 Thessalonians
15. 1 Timothy
16. 2 Timothy
17. Titus
18. Philemon

The General Epistles

19. Hebrews
20. James
21. 1 Peter
22. 2 Peter
23. 1 John
24. 2 John
25. 3 John
26. Jude
27. Revelation

COMING SOON!

In addition to the book, I have also created a series of videos that will soon be available on my website at FredWoodwardBible.com. For every lesson in the book, there is a corresponding video lesson. In the video series, there are charts, maps, diagrams, and pictures, and much more information than I had time and space for in the book. For the best learning experience, I would encourage you to read the book and watch the videos.

Fred Woodward is an ordained minister who has been teaching and preaching the Bible for nearly forty years. For many of those years, he served the Lord as the pastor of various churches. Currently, his ministry is in the workplace, serving as a chaplain with Corporate Chaplains of America. Fred obtained his theological training first at Fort Wayne Bible College, Fort Wayne, Indiana, where he acquired a Bachelor of Arts in Pastoral Ministries. Later he obtained a Master of Arts in Ministry from Moody Bible Seminary, Chicago, Illinois.

More Praise for *Let Me Be Your Guide...*

"I would like to say that this book is a must read for all who are interested in what the Bible is all about. It is written in such a way that is easy to read and understand. The truth of the scripture comes alive and you will feel like you are experiencing God in these lessons."
~Loraine Jones, Retired First Vice President, Banking

"I had only a fragmented and incomplete knowledge of the Bible until I read Chaplain Woodward's concise and highly readable book *Let Me Be Your Guide*. He took all the partially understood and disjointed stories from the Bible I was familiar with and put them into a coherent and chronological order. His book allowed me to make sense of the Bible as a whole and showed me the overall story in an easily understandable and summarized format. I found Chaplain Woodward's book a joy to read and the perfect book to clarify the Bible for those of us with an incomplete or partial understanding of it. It was so fascinating that I read it in a few days."
~Christopher Sobczak, Machinist

"It's an easy to understand and a fun way to learn about the Bible. You will get a better knowledge of the Bible and may actually learn a thing or two as well." ~Aaron Fabera, High School Student

"If the Bible has always baffled you, I recommend this book. It's written by a man who loves the Lord and His word, and he wants to share his knowledge of God's word so that all can have a better understanding and grow in faith." ~Patty Althaus, Certified Travel Specialist

"This is an easy read that shows God's mercy, grace, and sacrifice. It relates our current continual failures to the Old Testament and reminds us of God's New Testament which gives us Eternal Life. When you study the Bible for years, this book really brings it all together as a reminder of God's grace and love for us, His Children." ~Michael Shore, Supply Chain Manager

"Mr. Woodward has done an admirable job of summarizing the history of the Old and New Testaments in a simple but informative way. He has a gift of saying in a few words what the authors of the Bible have said with many. However, he lingers at important places in the history to the profit of all who will read his book. He has used catching illustrations of biblical truths. I predict that all who read it will receive benefit from it for their own lives and ministries." ~David Salstrom, former Missionary/Teacher in the Philippines

"I believe this book will assist in clarifying the Bible for both the practicing Christian and the seeker. It gives a clear understanding of the contents of the Bible. I will recommend the book to many of my friends and family, and I plan to hand out copies where appropriate." ~Richard Shore, Sr, CEO, Automation and Modular Components, Inc.

"Have you always wondered what the Bible is all about? Have you always planned to read it sometime? This book will give you an outstanding overview and help you understand how it all fits together. A great help for anyone." ~Stephen Bindon, President, Trijicon, Inc.

"This book is your boarding pass to a tour of the Bible. Once on the bus, your journey can lead to the discovery of God's provision for your final destination."
~Dr. Richard L. Cockman, Managing Chaplain